WICKED DEEDS

JAMES O'KANE

MURDER IN AMERICA

WICKED DEEDS

ta

Transaction Publishers
New Brunswick (U.S.A.) and London (U.K.)

Library of Congress Catalog Number: 2005050592
ISBN: 0-7658-0289-9
Printed in the United States of America

Library of Congress Cataloging-in-Publication Data

O'Kane, James M.
  Wicked deeds : murder in America / James O'Kane.
      p. cm.
  Includes bibliographical references and index.
  ISBN 0-7658-0289-9 (alk. paper)
    1. Murder—United States. 2. Manslaughter—United States. I. Title.

HV6529.O53 2005
364.152'3'0973—dc22   2005050592

Dedicated To

My Wife Marge

My Children and their Spouses
J.B. and Julie
Dan
Pat and Charity
Joe and Michele
Mary Rose

My Grandchildren
Mary Alina
Caitlin
Christine
J.P.
Michael
Tiernan

Now Abel was a keeper of the flocks and Cain a tiller of the soil. In the course of time Cain brought to the Lord an offering of the fruit of the ground. Abel also brought some of the firstlings of his flock with their fat portions. The Lord was pleased with Abel and his offerings; but for Cain and his offering he had no regard. Cain was very angry and downcast. The Lord said to Cain, "Why are you angry and why are you downcast? If you do well, will you not be accepted; but if you do not do well, will not sin crouch at the door! Its desire is for you, but you must master it."

Cain said to his brother Abel, "Let us go out into the field." Now when they were in the field, Cain turned against his brother Abel and slew him. Then the Lord said to Cain, "Where. is your brother Abel?" He answered, "I do not know. Am I my brother's keeper?" And the Lord said, "What have you done? The voice of your brother's blood cries to me from the ground. And now cursed are you in the soil which has opened its mouth to receive your brother's blood from your hand. When you till the soil, it shall not give its fruit to you; a fugitive and a wanderer shall you be on the earth." Cain said to the Lord, "My punishment is too great to bear. You are driving me today from the soil; and from your face I will be hidden. And I shall be a fugitive and a wanderer on the earth, and whoever finds me will kill me." But the Lord said to him, "Not so! Whoever kills Cain shall be punished sevenfold." Then the Lord gave Cain a token so that no one finding him should kill him. And Cain went out from the presence of the Lord in the land of Nod, to the east of Eden.

Genesis 4:2–16

Contents

Acknowledgements

Wicked Deeds could not have been written without the assistance of dozens of people who aided me in every step of its conceptualization and writing.

Foremost thanks goes to my wonderful wife Marge, and my children – J.B., Dan, Pat, Joe and Mary Rose; all listened to, discussed, and argued with me about various aspects of murder in general, and specific cases in particular. Though probably baffled by my interest in such a macabre topic, each encouraged me at every step in the book's composition.

Various police officers provided me with valuable insights into the homicide scenarios. Foremost among these are the detectives from New York Police Department's Brooklyn North Homicide Task Force, particularly Detective Paul Weidenbaum (deceased), and Detective Dave Carbone both of whom became not only great sources of information, but close friends as the years went by. Both provided to me their immense accumulated knowledge drawn from the hundreds of murders they had investigated in their NYPD careers. Extremely helpful also were my brother-in-law, Tom Moran, Palm Beach, Florida, Police Department, Bob Creighton, a close friend of thirty years and former Commissioner of Police for Suffolk County, New York, and current Chief Investigator for the D.A.'s office of that county, and Jim Trahon, a good friend and neighbor, now with the Boston office of the FBI. All have been great observers of the human condition and the reality of homicide, which they discussed with me on many enlightening occasions.

Numerous other law enforcement personnel also assisted my efforts in locating specific interesting cases, some of which were quite bizarre. Included here are the following: Sheriff Robert Foerster, Richmond County, Illinois; Detective Anthony Yoakum, Upland, California

ix

Police Department; Detective Chris Kearns, Allegheny County, Pennsylvania, Homicide Division; Detective Charles Brown, Sparta, Michigan, Police Department; Detective A.E. Black, Tampa, Florida, Homicide Division; Robert Anderson, Prosecutor, Loudan County, Virginia; and John Zakowski, District Attorney, Brown County, Wisconsin.

My good friend, Dr. Ron Suarez, Chief Medical Examiner, Morris County, New Jersey provided me with an in-depth look at the homicide act itself as he recounted to my Drew University criminology classes the actual process of death by homicide. Phyllis Schultze, Chief Librarian of the Rutgers University School of Criminal Justice, went out of her way to provide the resources of her disposal that helped me enormously in researching homicide. So also did three of my former students: Andy Baron, a former Assistant Prosecutor, Middlesex County, New Jersey; Lou Fasulo, former Supervising Attorney for the Legal Aid Society, New York City; and Laura Hook, Prosecutor Sex Crimes-Domestic Violence unit of the Union County, New Jersey, Prosecutor's office. All not only helped me in myriad ways but also made me so thankful that I chose a teaching career at Drew University where I had the privilege of knowing them as students and learning from them.

Special thanks should be extended to Drew University for providing release time and research funds that helped me considerably in completing this project. I am deeply grateful to the following colleagues at Drew who aided me in countless ways: Vice President Paolo Cucchi; Professors Phil Jensen, Roxanne Friedenfels, Merrill Skaggs and Paul Wice. Also to be thanked are not only my student assistants who aided me in my research – Liz Mullarkey, Vic Macam, Molly Schulman, Katherine Girard, Mike Grohowski, Alexis Ramirez-Arnold, Rob Davelis, Liz Vail, Sarah Sampson, and Anne Dorrance, and other Drew staff who helped me formulate my ideas – Neil Clark, Lydia Feldman and Scott Wood. Two former Drew colleagues, Jeff Cromarty and Mike Meagher, assisted me in formulating the conceptual framework of the book and aided me in the initial writing of it. So also did Buzz and Kris McLaughlin, close friends who politely prodded me to complete it in a timely fashion, supporting me at every step with their kind encouragement and actual enthusiasm about the work in progress. I am also deeply indebted to Bob Lynch, a Professor of Humanities, New Jersey Institute of Technology, a life-long friend who did a magnificent job in helping edit the manuscript. His objective comments and corrections provided me with a wealth of ideas about the structure and composition of the manuscript. So also did Professor Jim Mills, Drew University, who proved invaluable in helping with the layout of the work. Jim Gray, Dan and Mary O'Kane, Helen and Bob Grubbs, Linda and Greg Pasternak, Peter Signiorelli, John Caporaso, Steve Huvane, John Guegan, Mark Young, Harvey and Leslie Weinberg deserve special thanks for their advice and encouragement; each provided me with interesting cases, timely data, and frequent insights into the act of homicide.

To each of these people I am forever indebted.

Case Sources

The accounts of homicides cited in this work come from many sources in the mass media. Foremost among these is the Clari New Service to which my employer, Drew University, subscribes. Clarinet.com transmits news stories from numerous news organizations such as the Associated Press, Reuters, and United Press International. The murder, and crime subgroups have been invaluable in locating murders throughout the United States since they present actual press accounts for each crime in a short, well-documented manner.

All of the cases cited in the book have been rewritten and summarized from the Clari News source, as well as the other media sources and attribution has been made to those journalists who composed the original story where indicated. All of the cases cited have been annotated from the original press account.

Equally valuable were the actual news stories from dozens of American daily newspapers that described murders in their locales. I have attempted to draw from a cross section of geographical areas of the country, searching papers such as the *Los Angeles Times*, the *Chicago Tribune*, the *Miami Herald*, the *Philadelphia Inquirer*, the *New York Daily News*, the *Boston Globe*, the *Richmond Times-Dispatch*, the *New York Times*, the *Milwaukee Journal Sentinel*, the *Topeka Capital-Journal*, the *Baltimore Sun*, the *Savannah Morning News*, the *Newark Star Ledger*, the *Washington Post*, and the *Salt Lake Tribune*, for accounts of homicides and their aftermath.

Follow ups to the cases were attempted by using search engines such as Google.com and Crimelibrary.com to find the results of court proceedings in order to discover what happened to those charged with the initial crimes. In addition, access to the websites of many of the Departments of Correction throughout the United States yielded invaluable information as to the prison sentences and parole stipulations of those found guilty.

Finally, conversations with police and prosecutors who investigated many of the cases cited gave me an excellent resource from which to expand upon the circumstances of each murder. Without exceptions, these homicide detectives and district attorneys willingly assisted me in my inquiries, often adding substantially to the details found in media accounts of the crimes they investigated and prosecuted.

One final note – the cases contained in the book are not a random sample of murders that occurred in the United States. Instead, they represent a selection of cases that illustrate and exemplify the specific topic discussed. In fact, most of the cases are somewhat unusual, for oftentimes it is the unusual, bizarre and relatively uncommon murders that make the headlines. The more typical everyday murders, though tragic and disturbing, rarely receive more than a few lines in a newspaper, if even that. A killing of one crack addict by another in New York or Los Angeles or Washington isn't major news; such a killing rarely makes the evening news, and if it appears in a newspaper, it often is in the crime file section, routinely reported, but rarely followed-up in subsequent editions. Thus the street prostitute, the gang banger, the small-time drug user, etc often die violently in oblivion, accounted for only in the daily statistics of police agencies. Hence this book is not a sociological research analysis that incorporates the typical research design, complete with a scientific sample selection, and empirical evaluation of data presented. Rather, it is a sociological overview of what sociologists know about murder and its components, literally a primer on murder in America, complete with actual cases that highlight the categories and patterns depicted.

Introduction

The scene remains fixed indelibly in my mind; fifty-four years later I still vividly recall the corpse, its legs protruding beyond the counter of the shoe repair shop in Brooklyn's Bedford-Stuyvesant neighborhood. Police estimated that the shop owner had been murdered twenty-four hours earlier, stabbed twice in the chest in an apparent robbery attempt. We called him Otto. I can't recall his last name.

I was only ten years old at the time of his death, and I have only vague recollections of Otto – he spoke with a German accent; he was middle-aged, balding, dark in complexion, heavy set, but not fat; he lived alone in the back of his dingy store and apparently had neither family nor friends. A cantankerous man, he was feared by the children in the neighborhood. Today people would call him a loner.

The news of Otto's murder spread quickly along Ralph Avenue, Halsey Street, Hancock Street, and Patchen Avenue. Upon hearing the shocking news, my sisters and I, along with our friends, raced to the shoe repair shop that was being guarded by a uniformed police officer from the New York City Police Department's 81st Precinct. His task was to guard and preserve the crime scene. A towering Irishman, he would let none of us near the store. "Now you wouldn't be wanting to see a poor man like that lying dead on the floor, would you?" he said. Eventually he relented and let each of us peek in the front door window.

All I could see were Otto's outstretched legs, for the rest of his corpse was concealed by the counter. I did not dwell long on the sight since it was upsetting. Some of my friends claimed they saw lots of blood, but I hadn't seen any. Perhaps it was too dark to get a more accurate view. Perhaps a psychological defense mechanisms sanitized the crime scene for my own benefit.

A few days later police arrested a sixteen-year-old gang member and charged him with Otto's murder. I don't recall what happened to this suspect nor did I ever learn his motive, though a consensus of the neighborhood agreed that it was a botched robbery, that Otto had resisted and died in the struggle. For weeks after the murder, I feared walking past Otto's shop and did so only at a fast pace. Eventually I ventured a peek into the long-abandoned store, remembering Otto's legs poking from behind the counter. In my mind's eye, I could now see the blood that had earlier eluded my gaze, and I envisaged Otto's fierce struggle with his killer. Otto's tragic death clearly shocked me. It was my first conscious realization of the violence that one human being can do to another.

Sudden death occurred with alarming frequency in our neighborhood. I recall the removal of the body of an elderly woman who had died alone in her apartment, undiscovered for two weeks; the police, wearing gas masks, retrieved her body and Fr. Francis McCabe, the local parish priest, emerged visibly ashen after administering the last rites to her. Another elderly woman on our street died of gas poisoning, an apparent suicide. She frequently left the unlit gas stove on, with her apartment door slightly ajar. Typically a neighbor who arrived home from work would smell the gas, rush in, save the woman; on that summer's day however, he didn't arrive as usual. I wonder if her death was accidental or deliberate, her behavior a cry for help or a true suicide. Dogs and cats killed by trolleys, cars, horses dying from loads pulled in wagons, men and women dropping dead on the street, wakes typically taking place in the homes of the deceased – all attested to the "normality" of death and its relative frequency.

In a few short years, many other murders occurred in the neighborhood, which continued to amaze me. Most were related to the feuds among the violent teenage gangs of Brooklyn's Bedford-Stuyvesant – the Chaplins, the Stompers, and the El Quintos – during the long, hot summers of 1955, 1956 and 1957. Other homicides involved more typical scenarios—family violence, robberies, drunken assaults, and petty quarrels.

Decades later, the brutality that permeates segments of American society still amazes me. Homicide is still a matter of routine in our society, and many readers probably have a murder similar to Otto's engraved in their memory. Rare indeed is the person who has not been touched in some way by the ultimate crime. We become voyeurs of the murderous act that simultaneously repels and fascinates us.

This fascination affects each person in a different way. One is mesmerized by the fictional "whodunit" with all of its improbable characters and quirks of fact and fate. A second enjoys the true detective genre of crime reporting with its emphasis on the sensational and macabre aspects of the act. A third type probes the psychopathic minds of serial and mass murderers, searching for the ultimate meaning of evil embodied in their killings. Still another finds compelling and incomprehensible murders within the family, the one place where each of us is meant to feel safe and secure. Whatever its source or form, our fascination spills over into our conversations with family and friends as we discuss our disbelief of the latest murder highlighted by the media.

We are presented daily with the grim realities of homicide in a never-ending portrait of carnage, massacre, and depravity. Nightly television news numbs our senses with scenes of human destruction. Newspapers present us personal, in-depth details of the lives of victims, survivors, and assailants. Tabloid magazines and news shows accentuate, in grotesque fashion, the more bizarre cases of this human drama.

In a nation that averages approximately forty-five murders a day, 16,500 per year, only the truly sensational killings come to our attention: child murders, serial murders, celebrity murders, multiple victim murders, murders occurring in safe communities, murders involving middle-class victims and assailants, sexual murders, and murders involving peculiar weapons or circumstances. Relatively rare, these types of crimes make the news because they are qualitatively different from the vast majority of killings, which are rarely deemed newsworthy.

The majority of killings, which typically involve lower-income victims and assailants, are ignored for the most part. Predictable and expected, these homicides elicit little public attention. They are ordinary events of minimal concern to those who reside beyond the immediate locale of the murder. If these killings make the TV news, they are on nights when little else is happening. If they are reported in the press, they appear on page 18 with only a brief paragraph presenting a meager synopsis of the event. Regular obituary columns command more space than do these homicides. These killings usually involve drug-related violence, inner-city spouse killings, robbery murders of poor victims, teenage gang murders, bar and after-hour social club killings, and prostitute and homosexual murders. Though viewed as tragic and sad by the general public, these homicides are seen as typical behaviors of "them," not "us." Consequently, this violence does not evoke the concern and furor so commonly associated with killings that occur in middle-income areas.

As a result, the media present a distorted view of homicide in America by highlighting the rare and downplaying the ordinary. But what are the alternatives? If each of forty-five plus were to be presented by typical nightly news programs, there would be no time to air other noteworthy news, sports, weather, film, reviews, Hollywood gossip, human interest stories and commercials. The public's fascination with murder would quickly turn to boredom. Perhaps the media know more about us than we would like to admit. Perhaps the sensational and notorious cases distract us from recognizing the grim reality of American homicide—that apparently 16,500 people are murdered every year.

Fascination with homicide is one thing; explaining it in a coherent fashion is an entirely different matter. Criminologists try to move beyond the fascination, probing deeper and further, seeking to uncover its patterns and the regularities that link it to normal, non-criminal behavior. For decades, social scientists have alerted us to these recognizable patterns of social behavior – how we act with others; what roles we play in our interactions with family, friends, superiors, subordinates, and strangers; where we live; what we eat and drink; how we worship, vote, and work; whom we love and hate; when we are born, marry, retire, and die; what our social class is; what values we espouse; how we treat others different from ourselves.

The list is simply endless because society abounds with rituals and patterns of behavior that link us to each other. If this were not true, if all behavior were totally random, chaos would ensue, and there would be nothing for sociologists and criminologists to study, for such inquiry implies that there is an underlying order and comprehensible pattern to people's behaviors. Murder is no different. The act of homicide has a regularized pattern of behavior within it. The assailant and the victim do not operate in a social vacuum, even if they are totally unaware of how their patterned behavior relates to the larger social order. They are part of a larger picture, one wherein their behavior and motives fit rather predictably with other similar, though seemingly isolated, murderous acts. For example, the following item appeared in a northern New Jersey daily newspaper giving us a glimpse of an "ordinary" murder:

> An argument between an Irvington couple escalated into murder last Friday when forty-three-year-old Elizah Hankerson was stabbed once in the chest with a kitchen knife by his wife, police said yesterday.
>
> Irvington Police Director Samuel Williams said Maryann Hankerson, also 43, was being held on homicide, aggravated assault, and various weapons charges. She is expected to be arraigned tomorrow.
>
> Detective Edward Aimutis Jr., who is investigating the incident, said police were called to the Hankerson's third floor apartment on Ellis Avenue shortly after 11 P.M. Friday by Mrs. Hankerson. Her husband was found inside the apartment with a single stab wound to the chest and was taken to University Hospital in Newark where he was pronounced dead.
>
> Aimutis said the couple, who had no children, had a history of domestic problems. "We've been there several times on family disturbances complaints," he noted. "This time it was a verbal argument that elevated into a physical confrontation."
>
> The weapon was an ordinary kitchen knife, which was recovered by police. The matter continues to be investigated by Irvington police and the Essex County Prosecutor's Office.[1]

Undoubtedly, the couple in this tragedy remained ignorant of the clearly recognizable pattern illustrated in the murder. Family members and neighbors of the victim and the killer, and the killer herself, probably viewed this killing as a unique, shocking, and inexplicable event. Presumably the victim and assailant both acted out of rage, unaware that the ensuing homicide would practically mimic the pattern of contemporary murders observed ad nauseam by homicide detectives and academic criminologists. The day of the week (Friday), the hour of day (11 P.M.), the assailant and the weapon (female with a kitchen knife), the motive (argument), the background of the motive (previous ongoing family disputes), and the relationship between killer and victim (wife and husband) all combine to produce a "typical" murder.

Study after study replicates the same basic pattern. Murders occur most frequently between individuals who know each other and on the weekends between 8 P.M. and midnight. When women kill, they frequently kill their mate, and do so with a kitchen knife in an apartment or a house. The murderous act itself is a climax to earlier, longstanding violence or abuse. Little is strange or unusual about Mr. Hankerson's death. Few police officers, social workers, or criminologists would be shocked by it. In a strangely perverse way, Mr. Hankerson was a homicide waiting to happen, though presumably neither he nor his wife understood or recognized the unfolding pattern.

The patterns and relative predictability of murder remove the act from the realm of the inexplicable and the incomprehensible. Murder is rarely a random deed committed by some crazed individual for no reason. We may not know or understand or agree with the reason, but there is usually a motive that, to the killer at least, is logical and rational. What may appear to the public as a senseless, cold-blooded act is actually a highly purposeful, logical action from the killer's perspective:

"God told me to execute my children to send them to a better place."

"The old lady was crippled, on welfare and a real pain to everyone in the building, so why are you cops hassling me for doing everyone a favor by killing her?"

"He disrespected me by trying to stare me down on the subway—no one does that to me."

"She sneered at me when she refused to go out with me."

"I only wanted to scare him with the gun when I was robbing him, but he tried to punch me in the face."

"He insulted me by not paying the $10 he owed me."

"Even though she claimed she loved me, I know she was fooling around with other guys."

"At the party, he laughed at the dress I was wearing in front of all my friends."

Though it may seem irrational from our point of view, what the killer perceives eventually organizes and explains the resultant homicide. For the killer it was the only logical course of action at the time. Hence, few killers show any true remorse or sorrow for their deeds. From their perspective, why should they? They did what had to be done. As every crime buff knows, there is always a motive in homicide. It is the motive and the circumstances surrounding the murder that create the patterns that encompass the majority of killings. In some murders, the motive and the circumstances produce crimes that are highly planned and carefully executed. These are the first-degree murders so commonly written about in the Agatha Christie novels, but in reality these murders are quite rare. Most murders fall into the second-degree category. They are rarely planned or premeditated and they often seem to occur in the heat of passion. Yet they also follow an observable pattern. For example, Otto's death was almost predictable. Evidently he resisted the robbery attempt that probably "spooked" his assailant. We know that robbery victims who resist their attackers are forty-nine times more likely to be killed than those who do not resist.[2] Elizah Hankerson's death was equally patterned because of the circumstances of the case and the availability of a lethal weapon.

Let us now attempt to probe these patterns and regularities in order to present a reasonable account of how, when, where, and why people kill each other. In doing so, a heavy emphasis must be placed on sociological analyses using those variables commonly employed to help explain various forms of social behavior. Brief accounts of actual homicides will be included to "put some flesh on the skeleton" and fill in the dull, academic explanation of murder. Very little in the forthcoming chapters will be surprising to those criminologists actively engaged in ongoing empirical research into homicide, for this book is not a presentation of new research. Rather, this book is an attempt to summarize what we know about murder in the United States and present a plausible explanation of it. In this sense, the work is a primer that introduces the reader to the fascinating realm of homicide. Its goal is to make intelligible that which seems chaotic, to render predictable what seems unpredictable, tumultuous and disorganized, to make sense out of the seemingly senseless.

Notes

1. Woman Held . . . , 1992, p.14.
2. Zimring, 1986, 18–19.

1

Is It Murder?

At first glance the definition of murder used by the Federal Bureau of Investigation in its Uniform Crime Reports appears simple and straightforward. The FBI defines murder as the willful (non-negligent) killing of one human being by another.[1] Excluded from the statistics on murder are those deaths caused by suicide, negligence, accident, or those judged to be justifiable homicides. In homicide things are not as simple as they first appear. The following case examples illustrate how difficult it is to classify some deaths as actual murders even when initially there seems to be little doubt as to what has occurred.

So also are legal abortions and deaths associated with acts of domestic terrorism. Raging debates between pro-life and pro-choice advocates over the taking of innocent human life and the definition of human life continue with a ferocity scarcely matched in any other area of public life. Somewhat more muted are those debates that revolve around the incidents of domestic terrorism witnessed in the past few years. How should homicide specialists categorize those tragic events? Should the victims of the bombing of the World Trade Center in 1992 and the Murrah Federal Building in Oklahoma City in 1995 be classified as murder victims, or war casualties? Should the victims of September 11, 2001, be categorized in the same fashion? Should the 2,800 victims of the 9–11 World Trade Center disaster be recorded as 2,800 separate victims, or listed as one collective entity in the statistics of federal, state, and city data? Are they similar or dissimilar to the typical murders involving innocent victims that occur daily? Obviously each death is a loss of precious life, and surviving family and friends probably could not care less how the deaths are classified, whether they be victims of murder, war, or terrorism. For them, their loved ones are gone, their lives suddenly and violently snatched from them.

Even when the actual definition of murder used by the FBI and other law enforcement agencies– the willful killing of one human being by another– is applied, problems of interpretation occur with what can be considered "ordinary" killings.

CASE 1

In the mid—1970s, officers of New York City's Forty-First Precinct ("Fort Apache") encountered a gruesome scene in a South Bronx street. In the gutter lay a body, apparently that of a 300-pound, nude, decapitated African American male covered with wounds—a sight that nauseated the police at the scene. When a medical examiner arrived, he carefully examined the body and calmly announced to the officers that this was not a homicide. To the amazement of all he said that the body in the street was not that of a human being but rather that of a skinned gorilla!

A new mystery now unfolded: how did the body of a skinned gorilla arrive in the middle of the South Bronx? Police quickly solved the mystery, for the gorilla's body had fallen from a truck delivering it to a meat-packing plant a block away. The plant produced hot dogs and apparently used dead animals obtained from zoos as primary ingredients. This revelation understandably upset the police officers, some of whom had been eating this specific brand of hot dog for many years before the incident. Needless to say, they changed their dietary preferences after that strange encounter. This bizarre non-homicide was not an isolated event; six months later a skinned bear appeared at the same location!

What first had appeared to be an obvious murder turned out to be something quite different. Since the "corpse" was non-human, the case cannot be considered a homicide. It falls instead into the lap of other agencies such as the health department, the ASPCA, and the city's food inspectors.

CASE 2

New York City police were called to an apartment where they discovered the body of an attractive twenty-seven-year-old female.

Her throat had been slashed and she had three stab wounds in her chest. She had been found in her sister's fiancé's apartment where she had sought refuge from her boyfriend with whom she frequently quarreled. Certainly an open-and-shut case of homicide, no?

Lieutenant Commander Vernon Geberth, an internationally recognized NYPD homicide investigator, carefully examined the woman's throat. He found hesitation marks that often occur in suicide attempts wherein the victim makes a few superficial cuts, presumably to see how it feels before proceeding further with the suicide act. Frequently the victim hesitates. Even if these slashes are numerous, they tend to be superficial and non-lethal. In the classic throat-slashing homicide, the wounds are generally few in number, deep, and vicious in nature. Geberth ruled the death a suicide, noting that the woman's hand prints appeared on the knife discovered at the scene, that she left a note behind indicating that she was depressed, and that the apartment, locked from the inside, showed no signs of a struggle. Furthermore, the victim had a history of drug and alcohol abuse and had attempted suicide once before. He reconstructed what had happened; the woman started to cut her throat, "chickened out," and then stabbed herself three times in the chest.

What initially appeared to be a classic lover's quarrel murder surprised everyone. The importance of a correct determination of the cause and manner of death is underscored in this case, for had Geberth not made a thorough examination of the body and the circumstances in which the event took place, more than likely, the case would have been ruled a homicide, with potentially disastrous consequences for the parties involved (the woman's boyfriend, her sister, her sister's fiancé, etc).

CASE 3

In the early 1990s West Texas had been experiencing a prolonged heat wave when police arrived at the scene of the apparent crime. There they found a body of a man hanging in his home. Near his body there were small drops of blood on the wall and on the ceiling. The body had been there at least three days and had started to decompose rapidly. It appeared to the officers at the scene that the victim had been severely beaten before being hanged, since blood splatter and its distribution often appear on walls and ceilings after a victim has been stabbed, slashed, or hit numerous times with-a blunt object. Curiously there were no droplets of blood on a light bulb that had been left on during and after the incident.

Was this a homicide or a suicide? Police were not sure. It is unusual to find a corpse that has apparently been severely assaulted and then hanged. Typically, it's one or the other, not both. Photographs and other evidence of the victim and the scene were submitted to Linda Harrison, an expert with the FBI's DNA Analysis Unit who concluded that the blood droplets on the ceiling and wall came from flies that had been feeding on the decomposing corpse, tracking the droplets on these surfaces as they touched them as well as excreting the digested blood and depositing it there. The Texas heat wave speeded the process of the man's decomposition making it appear that he had been severely beaten when in fact he had not. Harrison noted that no blood excretions appeared on the lighted bulb because flies did not touch it because it was too hot. What initially had appeared to be homicide was more likely a "straight" suicide exacerbated by hot weather, flies, and rapid body decomposition.

CASE 4

Police in Miami, Florida, discovered the victim, a thirty-one-year-old white female slouched on the kitchen floor of her apartment in a pool of blood. Next to her partially nude body the officers found broken soda bottles, a mop and broom with blood on them, and garbage from the nearby trash container. Police believed her to be a rape-homicide victim.

However, pathologists at the Dade County Medical Examiner's Office autopsied the corpse and noted that the woman weighed approximately eighty pounds. Her thin, anorexic appearance contrasted sharply with her large, distended stomach, which was completely out of proportion to the rest of her body. When the examiner inspected the contents of her stomach he found the remains of two quarts of milk, three boxes of crackers, and five pounds of hot dogs (or approximately forty franks, assuming eight franks per pound).

The medical examiner concluded that the victim died of asphyxia since the enormous weight and distended volume of the stomach pressed upon and elevated her diaphragm, eventually compressing her lungs and preventing her breathing. Her bulimic condition with its binge eating-vomiting sequence created the underlying circumstances of her death. What at first appeared to be a sexual murder turned out to be a death due to polyphagia or massive overeating. The blood surrounding the victim resulted from a deep cut in her thigh, probably caused by her thrashing and falling on the soda bottles as she gasped for air. The strewn garbage likewise resulted from knocking over the trash canister as she slowly asphyxiated. As further confirmation of a death by natural causes rather than homicide, police found large amounts of vitamins, laxatives, appetite control medications, sleeping pills, and baking soda in the kitchen.

Case 5

Field representatives of the local gas company had attempted unsuccessfully to enter the basement of the Queens, New York, home of Chinese immigrants to read the gas meter. After a year of futile attempts, they obtained a court order to do so. On entering the basement they witnessed a truly startling sight—a fully clothed, headless, skeletonized corpse sitting upright in a chair. The skull lay under the chair. Police officials quickly determined that the remains were that of the homeowner, a sixty-nine-year-old male. His wife appeared surprised at the discovery, claiming that her husband had disappeared months earlier and that she had no idea of his whereabouts.

Police at first suspected that an assailant murdered and decapitated the victim, a reasonable assumption particularly since his wife had never reported him missing to police. Again things were not quite what they first seemed to be.

After a complete investigation, homicide was ruled out as the cause of death. The victim had been depressed and an empty bottle of antidepressant medication was found near his skeleton. The man died in his chair—whether by natural causes or suicide was not determined—and his body quickly decomposed in the overheated basement. Apparently the head fell from the body in the decomposition process.

Did his wife know about his death? If she did know, why did she conceal it? The mystery remains for psychiatrists or social workers to ponder rather than police or criminologists, for evidently, no crime was committed on her part.

Each of these somewhat bizarre cases (involving hot dogs, gorillas, flies, decapitations, etc.) underscores the importance of the complete application of murder's legal definition—the willful (non-negligent) killing of one human being by another. Every phrase in this definition is crucial to the determination of criminal homicide. None of the strange examples cited could be classified as murders since either the "victims" were non-human, or the manner of their deaths was either accidental or self-inflicted. Each case emphasizes the importance of establishing precisely what happened in the death scenario as well as legally ascertaining whether or not the death can be ruled a criminal homicide. Then there are those deaths that at first appear to be either accidental deaths or suicides but upon further investigation are classified as murders. Often the murderer cleverly arranges the corpse and the circumstances to hide the crime, frequently fooling police as to the true nature of the death, the real nature of which is discovered only after a thorough autopsy conducted by a competent medical examiner.

Case 6

At first appearance, it looked liked a typical suicide by hanging. The victim, a sixty-one-year-old male, suffered from chronic alcoholism and received a disability pension because of his muscular dystrophy condition. He lived in his own home and rented rooms to five boarders, all of them alcoholics.

Police found his body hanging by a nylon rope, suspended from a bookcase that had fallen forward, resting on a weight lifting bench. There were no signs of a struggle, no mirrors in the room, and no evidence of pornographic material, thus ruling out accidental autoerotic death by sexual asphyxia. No suicide note was discovered. The autopsy revealed a different picture quite inconsistent with suicidal hanging. The victim's body exhibited numerous fresh bruises; his face was swollen; the stem of his brain evidenced microscopic bleeding; and severe swelling in another part of his brain suggested that he had received a severe blow to his head that would have rendered him unconscious. Furthermore, there were no scratch or claw marks around the rope, further supporting the idea that he had been alive, but unconscious immediately before his hanging. The autopsy report concluded that this was a homicidal hanging, not a suicidal hanging, an exceptionally rare form of murder. When it does occur, the victims are generally intoxicated, under the influence of narcotics, weak from illness, unconscious, or too young to offer any real resistance to the person hanging them.

The subsequent police investigation revealed that the victim had been terrorized by one of his alcoholic tenants for quite some time. The day before his death, the victim informed his subsequent murderer that he would have to move out of the house, the event that probably triggered the fatal encounter. All five tenants eventually admitted to beating the victim when they were drunk, but none would admit to the hanging. Eventually, all but one of them established that they were not in the house at the time of the killing that the medical examiner determined to have been between 3 P.M. and 9 P.M. of that fateful day. The one remaining boarder had no such alibi and subsequently received a twelve-year sentence for manslaughter; his fellow tenants received sentences of a half to two and a half years for assault.

CASE 7

In August 1973, Alma Blaikie, sixty-four, was found dead in the basement of her Waltham, Massachusetts, home with a .38 caliber gunshot wound to the back of her head. Her son James Blaikie, twenty-seven, discovered her body as well as a suicide note that read "I can't stand how I am anymore." Police ruled her death a suicide and her son inherited $33,000. A year later James Blaikie's business associate, Edwin Bacon, forty-four, was found dead in his office with a suicide note that read "I can't stand it anymore." An autopsy indicated that he died of cyanide poisoning. To the surprise of Bacon's family, his $50,000 insurance policy listed Blaikie as the only beneficiary.

The Bacon family became suspicious and an investigation commenced. The FBI confirmed that Bacon's signature had been forged on the insurance document. As police investigated Blaikie's finances they discovered that he was deeply in debt ($100,000) and had borrowed $12,000 from Caesar Dealt, a friend of his wife's. After meeting with Blaikie to discuss the loan's repayment, Dealt disappeared. Shortly after, Blaikie and his wife moved to Arizona where he was arrested for armed robbery and subsequently charged with forgery in the Bacon case. His life became more complicated when the new owner of his former Massachusetts house noticed a depression in the concrete basement floor. When authorities excavated the site, they found Dealt's mummified remains in a plastic bag. He had been shot in the back of the head with a .38 caliber bullet, the same caliber used in Blaikie's mother's death.

Claiming self-defense in Dealt's murder, Blaikie was tried in 1976 and convicted of first-degree murder, receiving a life sentence with no possibility of parole. Further court proceedings found that Blaikie had murdered Bacon. The reinvestigation of his mother's death found no new evidence that would warrant the changing of that death from a suicide to a homicide.

Case 8

At first glance the death of Lawrence Ocrant, fifty-two, appeared to be a death by suicide. The successful Greenwood Village, Colorado, stockbroker was found dead in his bed by his wife Sueann with his left arm stretched across the bed and his right hand clutching a handgun underneath his chin. He had been shot through the head. The police chief, Darryl Gates (no relation to the former Los Angeles Chief Darryl Gates), came to the scene and told another officer that it was a homicide. Two hours later he called it a suicide. Gates also helped clean up the scene and kept the coroner out of the luxurious home for twenty minutes. Subsequently, Ocrant's body was cremated with the bullet still inside it— destroying a crucial piece of forensic evidence.

Ocrant's two children by his first wife, Nancy Ocrant, never believed his death to be a suicide. For years they tried to have the case reopened as a homicide. Ocrant had left Nancy, his wife of twenty years, for his secretary Sueann, whom he showered with gifts of jewelry and a $600,000 home. In time Sueann told friends that she wanted a divorce from him, accusing him of being physically abusive.

The resolution to the case came about when his children discovered an old photo of Ocrant sleeping in the same position as his body was found— his left arm stretched across the bed and his right fist tucked under his chin. How, they asked, could someone who just shot himself look as if he was sleeping peacefully? How could he tuck a gun under his chin after shooting himself in the head? Experts told the children that it would have been almost impossible for Ocrant to have killed himself.

The investigation was eventually reopened and the case was ruled a homicide. No arrests were ever made in the incident. Police Chief

Gates was forced to resign and Sueann inherited $1 million in assets and life insurance. She eventually squandered her newfound wealth and filed for bankruptcy.

In March 1998, a federal grand jury heard almost two weeks of testimony in which Greenwood Village police admitted that there was no murder investigation and that crucial evidence had been destroyed. The grand jury found that Ocrant did not commit suicide and that police had covered up the entire matter. The Ocrant children were awarded $2.3 million in damages.

Each of these cases further illustrates the necessity of determining the exact circumstances of the death so as to enable authorities to properly label the act as a homicide, suicide, or accidental death. The three cases clearly demonstrate that the assailants tried "to get away with murder" by masking their deeds as either suicides or accidents. Were it not for determined investigators, they may easily have done so.

Then there are situations that are unclear as to what actually happened, when those accused of murder argue that the death was accidental and police and prosecutors argue that the death was criminal. Typically this occurs in those deaths when there are no witnesses other than the person accused whose version of the event is disputed by police. It remains to a trial jury to decide whose version—the accused, or the police—should be believed, thus determining either the innocence or the guilt of the person charged in the death.

CASE 9

At first it appeared that Sandra Orellana, twenty-seven, died on November 13, 1996, as a result of an accidental fall from the balcony of her Los Angeles suburb hotel room. She had accompanied her boss Robert Salazar, thirty-three, on a business trip to California. Salazar told police that he and the victim had been drinking and making love on the balcony of her room and that she accidentally slipped to her death. Salazar did not report the fall but went back to his room and slept until taken into custody by police who found articles of his clothing in Orellana's room. Two months later the Los Angeles County Coroner's office said that her death was consistent with being pushed from the balcony rather than falling from it. Police attempted to duplicate the fall by dropping a mannequin from the same balcony and found that the place where Orellana landed was inconsistent with an accidental fall. Also, the abrasions on her body ruled out her jumping to her death. Furthermore, because of her height she would have required assistance to climb over the balcony's railing. The police and Coroner's office thus ruled out both suicide and accident as the possible causes of her death and labeled it an "assisted drop" and therefore a homicide. At the trial, a jury found Salazar not guilty, indicating that there was insufficient evidence to prove that he murdered Orellana.

Finally there are rare situations that almost defy either a rational analysis or coherent explanation, and that legally bear no relationship to criminal homicide. A case in point is the execution of an animal for a crime against a human being.

Perhaps the best-known case entailed the execution of Mary, a circus elephant, in Erwin, Tennessee, in 1916. During the circus performance, Mary ran amok, killing three people. The vengeful populace subsequently charged Mary with murder, found her guilty, and condemned the elephant to a public hanging. On September 13, 1916, before a throng of 5,000 spectators, the animal was hoisted on a cable suspended from a railroad crane. On the first attempt the cable snapped; the second attempt was successful.[2]

To point out the legal absurdity of trying and condemning an elephant incapable of reasoning (and consequently "willful" behavior) would probably have been unappreciated by the gleeful crowd of pathetic spectators.

Notes

1. *Crime in the United States*, 1993, p.13.
2. Sefakis, 1982, p.24.

2

Types of Homicide

Just as it is not always simple to classify a suspicious death as a murder, it is also difficult for many of the public to distinguish between homicide, murder, and manslaughter. To the average American, homicide and murder are synonymous terms and the media usually treats them as such; manslaughter generally confuses most people not only because of the archaic nature of its name, but also because people are not quite sure about what type of death it refers to. Yet these terms have precise meanings in the field of criminal justice and are not as interchangeable as they may appear.

Homicide: Non-Criminal or Criminal?

For starters, homicide—the willful killing of one human being by another—is not necessarily a crime. Depending on the circumstances in which the killing took place and the characteristics of the person who killed another, the act can be categorized as either non-criminal homicide or criminal homicide; if it is non-criminal it is not a murder, since murder legally applies only in criminal situations. Let us briefly delineate the main categories:

Non-Criminal Homicide

Non-criminal homicide implies that the loss of life was not due to a criminal act on the part of the "killer." Generally it is divided into two main types: justifiable homicide and excusable homicide.

Justifiable homicide occurs in those situations where the "killer's" actions are legal. For example, the state executioner who administers a lethal injection to a prisoner condemned to death does so without criminal intent. He willfully kills another person, but his actions are not criminal since he is carrying out the legal mandate of the state by virtue of the obligations of his office. Similarly, a police officer who kills an armed felon who points a gun at the officer is not guilty of a crime. He fulfills his legal mandated role of protecting the public by stopping the criminal, literally arresting the felon's criminal intent and actions. Yet another example of justifiable homicide occurs when an individual kills another in self-defense in an unprovoked confrontation where the killer, believing himself to be in imminent danger of death, had no other reasonable means of eluding his attacker.

Case 10

Edward Schaeffer, forty-one, upset about his upcoming divorce, broke into his wife's home in Phoenix, Arizona, on March 13, 1996. Schaeffer took his wife and their two children hostage and threatened to kill them. Fortunately, they quickly escaped the home, leaving Schaeffer to confront the police. He barricaded himself in the house and threatened to kill himself and any officers who attempted to apprehend him. The police tried various means, including tear gas, to dislodge Schaeffer but nothing worked. Finally, after a six-hour siege, police entered the home. When they confronted Schaeffer, they hit him with a "bean bag" shot calculated to knock him off balance, but it also failed. At that point Schaeffer pointed a handgun at two of the officers who then shot him dead. The case was ruled justifiable homicide since the police officers were neither irresponsible nor negligent in their actions, and their duty to protect themselves and others necessitated their action against Schaeffer.

Case 11

On October 3, 1999, David Barber, twenty-five, was pulled over by Police Officer James Demarco in the parking lot of a Patchogue, New York, shopping center. Barber received a summons for driving without a license and insurance and was also cited for making a turn without signaling. Officer Demarco informed him that he was no longer allowed to drive his car. Barber took the ticket, went into a local pharmacy, and then attempted to drive away after exiting the store. Demarco pulled Barber over again to arrest him but he suddenly put his car into reverse, dragging Demarco forty feet as he clung to the vehicle's side door. The officer opened fire and shot Barber three times as the car sped across the parking lot and crashed into a wall, pinning the officer. Barber died three hours later in a local hospital where Demarco was treated for shoulder and rib injuries. A preliminary investigation exonerated the officer.

CASE 12

In June 1997, Sabato Raio, twenty-seven, argued heatedly with three men outside a Portland, Maine, bar at which he was the bartender. Hours later the three men, Kevin Pinette, twenty-two, Nick Patenaude, twenty-three, and Dana Matthews, twenty-four, appeared at Raio's home to continue their disagreement. According to Raio, all three had a reputation for violence and he feared for his life. When one of the trio reached for what Raio thought was a weapon, he pulled out his .22 caliber handgun and shot each of his adversaries in the head, killing them. In his own court testimony, Raio claimed that he acted in self-defense since he was sure the trio were going to kill him. The jury agreed and in December 1995 acquitted Raio of all charges after two days of deliberations, indicating that he had indeed acted in self-defense.

Each of these examples illustrate the non-criminal type of homicide in which fatal but legal acts have been performed by a "killer" but without either criminal intent or consequences on his part.[1]

Excusable homicide occurs when a killing results from accidents or misfortunes stemming from legal actions or when the killer is found to be legally insane and thus not held responsible for the crime. An example of the first type could include a mother who prepares a dinner for her child who dies from an allergic reaction to its contents. While her willful action of preparing and serving the meal caused the child's death, the mother did not will the death of the child. The death is an accident, a tragic misfortune beyond the scope of criminality. Similarly, a driver who swerves on the road to avoid hitting an animal in his path is not guilty of murder if his passenger is killed as the car hits a tree on the side of the road. His legal actions created the scenario wherein a person died, but the death is accidental and hence excusable in the eyes of the law. Likewise, in the case of insanity, individuals who are found to be insane or mentally incompetent and unable to distinguish right from wrong cannot be tried, sentenced or executed since they are not legally responsible for their actions, nor are they capable of understanding police and court proceedings or assisting rationally in their own defense. A man who kills a stranger seated next to him on a bus because "voices in my head from God told me to kill him" and no other motive can be found would probably be judged legally insane at the time of the act and not subject to criminal prosecution. The act may be reprehensible but the actor may not be legally responsible for it. What constitutes legal insanity or legal mental retardation is of course controversial and subject to the different and often contradictory evaluations set forth by various state legislatures.

In each of the following cases the actors have taken another's life but did so in either a justified manner or in an excusable fashion. The resultant deaths are not due to criminal acts or criminal intent, thus they are beyond the scope of criminology.

CASE 13

Mark Bechard, thirty-seven, had suffered for many years from manic depression and schizophrenia, illnesses that often became uncontrollable when he used alcohol or refused to take his medication. He had been institutionalized briefly in 1994 and 1995. Earlier in his life he had played trumpet professionally in a Maine jazz combo; in recent years he drifted in and out of psychiatric care facilities and worked sporadically in his parent's tire store and garage.

On the night of January 27, 1996, Bechard smashed his way into the convent of the Servants of the Blessed Sacrament in Waterville, Maine—a place well known to him since he frequently attended mass there. He believed that the Catholic Church was about to revoke his Baptism. Voices of the "One" and the "Votese" told him to get the nuns to save the "Pixie." The convent housed nine poor elderly nuns who depended on the support of the people of Waterville to survive. He attacked four nuns, killing two, assaulting them with a knife, a statue of the Virgin Mary, and the walking cane of one of the victims. The killing shocked the nation and police described the rampages as one of the worst crimes in the history of the state. When apprehended at the scene of the slayings Bechard offered no motive, but did inquire about the condition of the nuns and told police he was sorry for his actions. In his jail cell he smashed his head and face against the wall and tried to gouge his eye with his toe. In October 1996, Bechard was found not guilty of murder by reason of insanity.

CASE 14

Denver, Colorado, police responded to a call from the Cherry Oaks apartment complex to a possible domestic violence disturbance in December 1996. There they found Lewis Rose, eighty-five, lying on the floor. He told police and paramedics that he had been hit on the head with a telephone receiver and that his wife Ruth, seventy-nine, had been the assailant. He also stated that she frequently verbally and physically assaulted him. She told police that her husband tried to assault her. She then attacked the investigating authorities, attempting to bite one officer and scratching a paramedic. Lewis Rose suffered a broken neck and a fractured pelvis from the fall following the attack and he died a month later from complications. Family members claimed that they had never witnessed any violence from the couple, who had been married for fifty-six years. Subsequent investigation concluded that Ruth Lewis suffered from dementia and was frequently disoriented, a diagnosis confirmed by the physicians treating her. The district attorney's office declined to prosecute the suspect since it felt that there was no reasonable chance of attaining a conviction.

CASE 15

Elise and John Ledvina married in 1986 and lived a seemingly normal life until 1991 when the first symptoms of Elise's mental illness surfaced. The couple and their two sons, John Edward, nine and Joe, eight lived in Milwaukee, Wisconsin. In treatment, Elise's symptoms appeared controlled. When not in treatment, she often refused her medications and her schizo-affective psychotic behavior left her delusional and out of control. By 1994, her husband filed for divorce and moved his sons to his parents home. In 1995, Elise's condition improved and the family reunited. Yet on August 26, 1997, her delusions that her sons would be better off in Heaven with God exploded into lethal violence. That evening she entered the boy's bedroom and assaulted John Edward with a baseball bat as he sat in bed reading. He died from several blows to his head. She also struck Joe who suffered a fractured skull, but he survived. Her husband, hearing the screams, ran into the bedroom, and prevented further violence. At a court hearing, the judge concluded that Elise suffered from a debilitating mental disorder and declared her legally insane, confining her to the Winnebaga Mental Health Institute near Oshkosh, Wisconsin. For years later, in 2002, psychiatrists argued that her disease was under control and that she should be released conditionally to a group home. In May 2002, a judge denied this request, stating that she was too dangerous to be released.

Criminal Homicide

Criminal homicide implies that a criminal act has taken place and the resultant loss of life thus falls within the jurisdiction of the criminal justice system. The categories of criminal homicide and the legal definitions of each type vary from state to state. What follows constitutes a generalized explanation of the most common types of criminal homicide; a more exhaustive explanation can be found in reviewing individual states' penal codes.

Criminologists generally divide criminal homicide into three categories: murder in the first degree; murder in the second degree; and manslaughter, either voluntary or involuntary. Some states sub-divide these categories into other types. New York State, for example, has categories for criminally negligent homicide, vehicular manslaughter in the first and second degree, intentional murder, felony murder, etc.

How does one decide into what category an unlawful killing falls? What differentiates a manslaughter conviction from a first-degree murder conviction? In this determination, two factors play a crucial role: premeditation and malice aforethought. Premeditation means that the killer has thought out the murderous act before it occurs. He has literally pre-meditated his crime by planning its execution in some manner. This can be done in a sophisticated way (as readers of Sherlock Holmes would know), or in a simple manner as in the case of a robber who decides beforehand to eliminate any witnesses to the robbery by executing them at the crime site. Courts have decided that the amount of time in planning and "meditating" the killing must be appreciable.

This appreciable time can be a considerable period, or as the North Carolina Supreme Court stated, it can occur "in the twinkle of an eye."

Malice aforethought (another of those archaic legal terms!) simply implies the intent to kill at the time of the act. In essence, the term means that the killer's specific intent was to cause the death of the victim. Thus we can assume that if an armed robber shoots a convenience store owner in the head during a robbery, his intent was malicious and he was prepared to kill his victim, evidenced by his possession of a gun.

Degree of Murder—Murder One. The legislative statutes of each state determine the degree of murder. Generally, murder in the first degree (Murder One), means that both premeditation and malice aforethought are present. The killer has thought out his act in a willful, deliberate manner before committing the murder. Murder in the first degree also includes those murders committed during the course of serious and dangerous felonies such as rape, kidnapping, arson, and robbery, and are commonly referred to as felony murders. A rapist who kills his victim in the course of rape would be prosecuted under a charge of murder in the first degree. Similarly, so would an arsonist who deliberately sets a dwelling on fire in which a firefighter is subsequently killed. The premeditation and malice aforethought, though not direct, are implied and many courts have allowed the charge of first-degree murder against such assailants.

CASE 16

In Prince George's County in Maryland, in September 1995, Alex Clermont, twenty-three, and three companions followed John McMullen, twenty-eight, a Persian Gulf War veteran, and a female companion who were traveling in his BMW convertible. When McMullen reached his residence in Maryland City, Clermont and his associates accosted the couple, robbed McMullen of $18, and proceeded to carjack his BMW. McMullen was put in the trunk of the BMW and his companion left unharmed. Some time later the BMW was found in a park in Beltsville, Maryland, by park police who had been summoned to investigate a car with a bullet hole in its trunk. They found McMullen dead in the trunk. Clermont, the accused gunman in the slaying, and his accomplices were traced by calls made from the murdered man's cellular phone and from attempts to use his ATM card. The men were arrested four days after the crime. In the subsequent investigation, Police determined that Clermont had shot McMullen as the other three (Harold Mootoo, Shanon Boner, and Rawle White) looked on. Since this was a classic first-degree murder scenario, Prince George's County Prosecutors decided to seek the death penalty against Clermont, and life without parole for the other defendants. A jury sentenced Clermont to death; one of the other robbers testified against Clermont for a reduced sentence; the others received a life sentence.

CASE 17

On February 15, 1997, Kenneth Mosley, thirty-eight, entered Bank One in Garland, Texas, and proceeded to rob it. Bank officials alerted Garland police who quickly arrived at the scene. One officer, Michael Moore, thirty-two, approached the robber from behind, grabbed one of his arms, and struggled with him. Mosley then pulled out a gun and repeatedly shot the officer above his bulletproof vest, killing him. Mosley, who was wounded in the scuffle, was apprehended by police as he attempted to flee the bank. At the time of the killing, he was wanted for another armed robbery in Mesquite, Texas. Officer Moore left behind a wife and three young children. Police officials announced that they would file capital murder charges with the Dallas District Attorney's Office. Mosely received a death sentence following his conviction.

CASE 18

Auden Campbell, thirty, a successful computer engineer and Heather Domenie, thirty-three, a schoolteacher planned to marry. Yet Campbell had been having a three-month affair with another woman, Magalie Le Long, twenty-three. On July 25, 2002, Campbell strangled his fiancée Domenie in their Wake County, North Carolina home. Prosecutors claimed that Campbell murdered his future bride so that he could be with Le Long, and also collect the $750,000 life insurance policy that Domenie had on her life. At the trial, Campbell's defense lawyers agreed that he had strangled Domenie, but said that he did so because he had been provoked, that his fiancée slapped him twice in her rage in discovering his affair with Le Long. His actions were impulsive and not premeditated. They asked the jury to find him guilty of voluntary manslaughter. Prosecutors argued that there had been no struggle, that Campbell strangled her from behind, that the only scratch marks found were on her neck as she tried to remove the towel used to strangle her. No marks or scratches were found on Campbell. Prosecutors argued that he murdered Domenie in a planned manner, in a cool state of mind with the intention of getting the insurance money and living with Le Long. Futhermore, Campbell had earlier lied to police, claiming that his fiancée had strangled herself. The jury found Campbell guilty of first-degree murder and sentenced him to life in prison. Ironically, the life insurance application that Domenie had submitted for the $750,000 policy had been denied by the insurance company. Whether or not it had been a precipitating factor in Campbell's mind is known only to Campbell.

Degree of Murder—Murder Two

Murder in the second degree (Murder Two) refers to those cases where only malice aforethought exists, with no evidence of any real premeditation on the part of the killer. In most states all murders not classified as first-degree murders become second-degree murders. This category includes intentional murders, depraved indifference murders, and non-dangerous felony murders.

Intentional murders refer to those homicides where the culprit intended to kill the victim but had not previously planned or contemplated the act. Thus a woman who kills her lover because he is leaving her for another woman, a man who kills an acquaintance in an argument over money, and a driver who shoots and kills another driver in a dispute over a parking space all constitute intentional murder.

Depraved indifference murder is sometimes referred to as reckless homicide and means that the killer recklessly engaged in behavior that showed depraved indifference to the lives of other human beings. The killer's behavior is a gross deviation from normal social behavior. His actions must be inherently dangerous and represent a very high risk to the lives of others. Thus a motorist who purposely drives his car on the wrong side of the road while speeding and kills a pedestrian would be guilty of a depraved indifference murder, as would be a burglar who lights a paper torch to illuminate a basement in an occupied home he is burglarizing and knowingly leaves it there, eventually causing a fire that asphyxiates the home's occupants. In both instances the driver and the burglar displayed wanton, depraved indifference for the lives of others.

Murders committed during felonies which in themselves are not inherently dangerous are also classified as second-degree murders. Thus a pickpocket who becomes involved in a struggle with his intended victim and kills the victim in the ensuing struggle would be charged with second-degree murder. The felony of larceny-theft, which encompasses pickpocketing, is not an inherently dangerous, life-threatening type of crime. Consequently the resultant murder would not be judged as a first-degree homicide.

CASE 19

In October 1994, attendants at a Pasadena, California, gas station observed Peter Burza, forty-two, place something covered by a sheet in the dumpster on their property. Curious about the contents, they checked the bin and saw a toe protruding from under the sheet. They called the police who went to Burza's home to question him. As they approached his house, they smelled burning flesh and saw smoke rising from the home's chimney. Upon investigation they learned that Burza, a landlord, had shot Craig Kensinger, his tenant. He dismembered the body and tried to burn some of its parts to conceal the murder. Burza had repeatedly warned his tenant not to bring drugs into the house and upon discovering Kensinger doing so, Burza murdered him. Following his 1996 trial, Burza was sentenced to nineteen years-to-life in prison for a second-degree murder conviction because it could find no real evidence of premeditation. The gruesome aspects of the case—the dismemberment of the body and the burning of parts of it—occurred after the homicide and did not relate to the murderous act itself, however heinous and upsetting they may be to the public.

CASE 20

A court in Bentenville, Arkansas, sentenced Ricky Crisp, twenty-four, to fourteen years in prison for second-degree murder for letting his daughter, Vicky, sixteen months old, and her cousin, Sidney Pippen, die in his unventilated car. On April 25, 1998, Crisp and a friend,

Justin Griffith, twenty-eight, high on drugs and alcohol, left the two infants strapped to their car seats for almost eight hours as they searched for mushrooms and arrowheads in the Bentenville area. Investigators indicated that the temperature inside the car reached at least 130 degrees. Young Vicky was in such pain that she actually pulled out her own hair. Griffith pleaded guilty of manslaughter.

CASE 21

Robert Corday, forty-nine, lived with his wife, Mary, and stepdaughter, Kristen Leech, thirteen, in a house situated on the site of an abandoned missile silo in Lyon County, Kansas. Local teenagers frequently partied at the site, trespassing on the Corday property. On February 16, 2000, Corday and his stepdaughter chased two male teens from the driveway of their home and confronted them after noting their car's license plates. The two teens argued with Robert Corday and allegedly indicated "there will be trouble if you turn our plates into the sheriff's department." The driver, Jeff Huey, later testified that Corday stated if they returned to his property, there would be "dead bodies in the driveway," a statement Corday denied making. Later that evening, a car with ten teenage males approached the Corday property and again Corday and Leech chased it away. Soon after, two cars with approximately ten teenagers backed into the driveway with their occupants cursing and threatening Corday. Leech testified that she then heard gunshots directed at her stepfather. Corday, armed with a high-power riffle, fired what he claimed was a warning shot, killing Scott Brown seventeen, and wounding two of his classmates, Jeremy Bowman and Brent Simonis. At his trial Corday said he acted in self-defense but the jury convicted him of second-degree murder. Corday received a nine-year sentence, the minimum term allowed under Kansas sentencing guidelines.

Manslaughter

Manslaughter is the unlawful killing of another without malice in the commission of an unlawful act.[2] Manslaughter may be either voluntary or involuntary, but in either type there is no prior deliberation or premeditation on the part of the assailant, nor is there any rational intent to kill the victim.

(1) *Voluntary Manslaughter.* Voluntary manslaughter occurs in a killing that takes place in the "heat of passion." The circumstances surrounding the killing generally mitigate but do not justify the killing. The killer must be so provoked that any other reasonable person in his or her shoes would lose control and act similarly.[3] A typical case would occur when a spouse encounters his or her mate in the act of adultery and kills either one or both adulterers "in hot blood." Another would be an individual who, after a heated argument, is attacked by a patron in a bar and kills the attacker in the ensuing struggle. The killing took place under circumstances that rule out classic self-defense since the killer had other options, such as leaving the scene before a fight began. Hence, this is not a classic justifiable homicide.

CASE 22

In February 1996, an Arlington, Virginia, jury convicted Marlon Taylor, thirty, of voluntary manslaughter in the stabbing death of his father Charles, fifty, father and son had a poor relationship and violence between them was common. Earlier, in 1994, Charles had stabbed his son during an argument and was subsequently arrested. Marlon then moved to Ohio for hand surgery and in June 1994 returned to Arlington to retrieve his belongings from the apartment the two had shared. On that occasion another heated argument took place, with Charles accusing his son of taking his car to Ohio without his permission. In that encounter, the son claimed that his father attacked him with a knife and that he killed him in self-defense. Other relatives testified that the father often resorted to violence; he always carried a knife and was quick to use it against those who upset him. Years earlier, Charles had been convicted of manslaughter in the killing of a Washington D.C. man.

After stabbing his father, Marlon decapitated him and dumped the headless body in Maryland where it was discovered two years later in 1996. He also forged his father's signature on the title of the car and claimed he feared telling police about the incident because they might not believe him. Prosecutors argued that the killing was not a classic case of self-defense, that the real motive was the son's greed since he forged the signature on the car's title, decapitated his father, and maintained his silence about the killing for two years. He only admitted to the event when police traced him after identifying the father's fingerprints from his corpse. His first trial resulted in mistrial since the jury could not reach a verdict. During the second trial he was convicted of voluntary manslaughter and received an eight-and-a-half year jail term.

Case 23

On May 28, 1998, a hundred-plus teenagers attended a "sweet sixteen" birthday party in the upscale Encino section of Los Angeles, California. Alcohol and drugs allegedly were used by some at the celebration. One drunken male teenager began to destroy furniture in a drug sale dispute. Friends of the hostess wanted to fight him but she said no, not in her house. As the party broke up, friends of the hostess, and friends of the disruptive teenager confronted each other. In the ensuing fight, Abtin Tangestanifar, seventeen, an uninvited guest and friend of the disruptive adolescent was stabbed fatally eleven times. Charged in the homicide were Ari Tomasian and Peter Makjdomian, both seventeen. In April 2000, Tomasian received a fifteen-years-to-life sentence for second-degree murder. Makjdomian pleaded guilty to voluntary manslaughter receiving an eleven-year prison sentence. The killing shocked the close-knit Armenian community to which the victim, assailants, and most of the guests belonged.

Case 24

John Blain Williams, thirty-eight, received a twenty-year prison sentence—the maximum under Georgia law—for the voluntary manslaughter of his companion, Robert Lewis Jr., twenty-six. Williams, a former assistant principal, and Lewis, a special education teacher at the Bartlett Middle School in Savannah, Georgia had been in a relationship but Williams moved out of their apartment two weeks before their fatal encounter on August 22, 2001, at Allen's Georgetown Crossing apartment. Williams admitted that he strangled Lewis but his defense attorney argued that it was in self-defense, claiming that Lewis had attacked him with a knife, cutting his neck. Prosecutors argued that Williams had no real concern or remorse for his actions, that he went on line after Lewis had died, and only called an ambulance after friends had arrived at the apartment. The jury convicted Williams of voluntary manslaughter rather than felony murder.

2) *Involuntary Manslaughter.* Involuntary manslaughter occurs when one person unintentionally and without malice kills another while engaging in behavior that consciously disregards a unjustifiable risk to the other person, endangering his or her life. The reckless conduct of manslaughter is different from second-degree murder recklessness; the former is not inherently dangerous to the lives of others; the reckless behavior of the latter is inherently dangerous and, in the terminology of the New York State Penal Law entails, "unmitigated wickedness, extreme inhumanity . . . exhibiting high degree of wantonness."[4] Typical examples of involuntary manslaughter would include: a motorist who consciously disregards traffic laws and operates the vehicle in a careless manner and in so doing kills a pedestrian; a parent who leaves young children unattended in an apartment who subsequently die in a fire. Both the motorist and the parent are guilty of involuntary manslaughter since both were negligent in their legal responsibility to either drive or supervise children properly.

CASE 25

In March 1996, a fourteen-year-old Lynnfield, Massachusetts, boy shot and killed his two-and-half-year-old half-brother. Following the shooting, the boy called police to report what had happened. The Essex County District Attorney's office charged the youth with involuntary manslaughter, noting that he had been high on drugs and alcohol. Stating that the older boy had no intention of hurting, let alone killing the two year old, the D.A.'s office nevertheless identified his behavior as "reckless and wanton" and crossed from the realm of personal tragedy towards reckless disregard for human life.

CASE 26

A crowd had gathered on the pier of the Casino Bar and Restaurant on Kelley's Island, Ohio, to view the judging of a bikini contest on June 24, 1995. To everyone's horror, a speeding, airborne, thirty-seven-foot powerboat landed on the dock; miraculously no one was hurt. However, the boat *Top Gun* had just rammed another craft and ran over it, killing one of its occupants—Scott Brabander, twenty-four, a graduate engineering student who was enjoying a relaxing day with family members on Lake Erie.

The *Top Gun* was driven by Ollie Mastronardi, a wealthy Canadian who witnesses claimed had been drinking all day. Erie County police charged Mastronardi with aggravated vehicular homicide and involuntary manslaughter and prosecutors at the trial argued that his drinking behavior had recklessly caused the death of Brabander. Mastronardi's defense claimed that the accident occurred because of mechanical failure, that the throttle of the *Top Gun* had jammed and could not be moved. The jury thought otherwise and found Mastronardi guilty of involuntary manslaughter. He received a five-to-ten year sentence and was paroled in 2002.

CASE 27

In October 1998, David Connell, twenty-nine, was shooting his Colt .45 handgun at a tin can in a friend's backyard in the Buckingham County, Virginia. At the same time, John Sollecito, forty-nine, was driving his car on a nearby road while talking with his wife and a friend. Suddenly his side window shattered and he slumped forward. Connell's bullet had missed the tin can target, ricocheted off a log, hit the car's rear view mirror and struck Sollecito in the eye, killing him instantly. Connell was convicted of involuntary manslaughter at a trial in March 1999 and received a five year suspended sentence.

Some jurisdictions have added a subcategory to involuntary manslaughter which allows for the grossly reckless or negligent killing of another yet with little or no substantial risk to the offender.

CASE 28

In October 2000, Paul Wayment, thirty-seven, and his son Gage, two, drove to the mountains near Coalville, Utah. Leaving Gage asleep in his pickup truck, the father entered the woods where he scouted for deer. When he returned thirty to sixty minutes later, he found the boy missing. Five days later, searchers found Gage's frozen body under a covering of snow. The father, totally distraught over the death of his son, initially fought the charge of criminally negligent homicide but in July 2001, pled guilty to the charge and received a thirty-day prison term. Upon leaving the courthouse, Wayment drove to the area where his son had been found and shot himself in the head with a blast from his shotgun. Relatives found his body a day after the shooting.

Notes

1. Black, 1968, p. 867.
2. Black, 1968, p.1116.
3. Fink, 1982, p.252.
4. People v. Northrup, 1981, 83 A.D. 2d 737, 442 N.Y. S 2d 658.

3

The Demography of Murder

On countless occasions those who view local TV news see disturbing reports: a husband who has killed his wife, a robber who fatally wounded a storeowner, or a patron who was shot dead by a friend in a local bar. Often the reporter interviews nearby residents and bystanders who excitedly voice their shock over the incident. In so many words, they respond that "things like this never happen in this neighborhood," that the parties involved "were such nice people," that they "can't believe what has happened," and so on.

Such images convey the notion that murder is more or less a random, unpredictable event governed by invidious forces such as luck, chance, or destiny. Though many people realize that homicides occur most often in lower-income minority areas, they are still fearful of what they perceive as the randomness of the act. They feel that everyone has an equal chance of becoming a homicide statistic, that one never knows "when the bullet has your name on it," that anyone can become a hapless victim of a crazed murderer.

Such fears are simply unrealistic. Long ago sociologists confirmed that social behavior is highly patterned and that few events or behaviors are truly random. Murder is no different, for it is very rarely a chance event. Consider the hypothetical case of a five-year-old girl shot dead in a drive-by shooting as she plays in front of her home in a gang-infested section of East Los Angeles or in the East New York section of Brooklyn. To most, this appears to be a truly random killing: no one intended to kill her. She was in the wrong place at the wrong time as her killer sought the actual target, but shot her by mistake.

On closer examination her murder is not as haphazard and unpredictable as it first appears, given the cultural and socio-economic makeup of her neighborhood with its high incidence of lethal violence, its patterned response of retaliatory gang shootings, and the proclivity of the area's residents to settle their disputes violently. The little girl's family and friends are probably unaware of these social factors that, at any rate, provide neither comfort nor solace to them in this tragedy. Yet from a statistical and criminological perspective, the little girl fits a pattern, one that clearly recognizes the number of innocent bystanders killed in such incidents in any of our major cities. They are murders waiting to happen.

Nor is her murder senseless. It is, in fact quite rational from the killer's perspective. While he may not have wanted to kill her, she simply got in the way of his true target—members of an opposing gang who had "disrespected" either him or his gang, an insult that had to be avenged to show the world that one's honor and reputation cannot be insulted or berated. "The five-year-old victim shouldn't have been there to begin with and her death is her own fault"—so reasons the killer in his logical manner, a manner that the public can scarcely believe or fathom. What appears to be senseless and bizarre to most people is often considered quite rational from the gang members' perspectives as they battle each other for status, territory, revenge, and so on.

Even a cursory glance at homicide data will illustrate the crime's non-random patterned regularity not only in the United States, but in other nations as well. Year after year similar profiles of murderers and victims emerge. The overall number and rate of homicides does vary from one year to the next but within these data similar characteristics of perpetrators and victims prevail. These patterns explain how and why most murders are solved, for homicide detectives are, in reality, good sociologists (a disturbing comparison to many of my sociologist colleagues and my police friends!). Similar to sociologists, they look for the social and behavioral circumstances in individual murders and mentally compare these to other killings they have investigated or studied. How is this murder similar or different from the thousands of murders in the collective murder "data bank" of homicide investigators? Was the victim male or female? Was the victim killed indoors or outdoors? If indoors, was the victim killed in the kitchen or in the bedroom? If outdoors, was the victim murdered near a bar or tavern?

Was the victim shot or stabbed once or multiple times? Was the victim clothed or naked? Was there a forced entry into the premises? Were its contents undisturbed or ransacked? Did the victim use alcohol, drugs, or have a history of mental illness? Were there multiple assailants? Victims? Were there other witnesses to the homicide? Did the assailant and victim know each other? Were they in the same family? Was the victim white or black? How old was he or she? Was money or jewelry in the deceased's possession when the murder took place? Did the victim have any known connection to organized crime, prostitution, deviant sexual behavior or drug selling? Was he or she associated with violent gangs in the area?

The answers to these questions provide detectives with the data to fit the crime to a pattern of behavior that serves to answer the questions of what happened, how it happened, why it happened, and when it happened. It doesn't take much to solve the murder of a male found lying dead on the kitchen floor with a thirteen-inch butcher knife protruding from his chest, next to a table filled with empty beer cans and wine bottles, with a sobbing female nearby telling police that the victim made her do it because of his abusive, drunken behavior. An open and shut case.

But what are these categories or patterns that detectives implicitly and sociologists explicitly use in defining the logical pattern of homicide? They are mainly those demographic variables that help explain all other non-criminal patterns of behavior (i.e., age, gender, race/ethnicity, socio-economic status, etc). Let us examine these and other demographic characteristics that help complete the jigsaw puzzle of homicide.

Similarly other patterns of lethal assault suggest who killed whom, and why. Bodies that have been stabbed or shot multiple times—far beyond what was sufficient to kill the victim (overkill)—suggest that the victim and assailant knew each other, possibly as spouses or lovers. Such violence is often noted in homosexual and intimate partner murder. Bodies fully clothed, with wallets full of cash, and placed in trunks of cars parked in public areas (i.e., as airports, shopping malls, etc.) suggest organized crime assassinations. Bodies found along public highways suggest that the killer wants police to find them, suggesting either serial killers, or domestic murders where the killer wants the victim discovered so as to ensure a proper burial. Bodies sexually dismembered and/or eviscerated suggest serial killers who are sexual sociopaths. Bodies fully clothed, washed, and well presented in the victim's home suggest spouse/lover murder since the killer doesn't want his victim's modesty compromised. Bodies found outdoors, in streets, fully clothed, with wallets/pocketbooks/jewelry/watches missing suggest robbery homicides. The list could go on, yet all of these are only suggestions as to what happened in the fatal encounter between killer and victim. Yet it is these clues that indicate patterns that police and medical examiners have seen before, leading them to tentative hypotheses as to what happened and why it happened. Again, it is the killer's acting out of a pattern of which he or she may be totally unaware which leads to the crime's solution.

Age

A cursory glance at homicide data for the United States in any given year clearly illustrates the importance of the ages of both victims and assailants in the murder scenario. The data for 2003 are typical: victims and their murderers are often young adults: 55 percent of victims and 44 percent of known assailants were between the ages of seventeen and thirty-four; 9 percent of the victims and 5 percent of known killers are under age eighteen.[1] When analyzing overall age patterns of victims and killers, victims tend to be "older" than their assailants, a finding largely explained by the fact that elderly victims are often killed by much younger assailants while the converse is not true: there are few senior citizen killers preying upon young victims. In general though, killers and their victims are approximately similar in age.

CASE 29

Steven Pfiel, eighteen, had a history of violence. In the Chicago suburb of Palos Park in July 1993 he was charged with first-degree murder in the death of Hillary Norskog, thirteen. She had been stabbed thirteen times and Pfiel, then seventeen, had been seen with her at a picnic area shortly before her murder. His trial in that case had been delayed at the request of Pfiel's defense attorney who needed more time to prepare his case in the assessment of the DNA evidence. Believing their son innocent, Pfiel's parents posted $100,000 bail and moved Steven and the rest of the family to another Chicago suburb, Crete Township, to avoid the anger and harassment of their neighbors. Subsequently, in March 1995, police arrested Pfiel for the murder of his brother Roger, nineteen, and the rape of his sister. The brother had been murdered with multiple stab wounds and blows to the head. Steven Pfiel confessed to both his brother's murder and his sister's rape. He received a life without parole sentence.

CASE 30

Francis Doyle, eighty, and Margarite Bacher, seventy-seven, had been life-long friends. After she had been widowed, Doyle frequently assisted her with chores around her home. In 1998, Bacher met Lawrence Kubik, also seventy-seven, at a high school reunion and the two started dating each other and were married after what police termed a whirlwind romance. Doyle could not accept this and immediately began stalking the couple. On February 4, 1999, Doyle entered the couple's home in Johnson County, Kansas, an affluent suburb of Kansas City and bludgeoned Kubik and his wife; Kubik died from the beating and his wife was severely injured. Doyle then called 911 and told police he had discovered the beaten couple and was trying to assist them. When police arrived, they discovered Doyle hiding behind a chair, still clutching the bloody weapon—a baseball bat. Convicted of first-degree murder in August 1999, Doyle was the oldest man ever tried for murder in Johnson County. He received a life sentence plus four years.

CASE 31

In May 1995, Matthew Galindo, fourteen, had a confrontation with Derrick Gracia, sixteen, in Mesa, Arizona. During the confrontation, Galindo shot Garcia. The victim was unarmed and threw up his hands; Galindo's friends begged him not to shoot Garcia. After his arrest, Galindo's trial took place in Marisopa County, Arizona Court. He was the youngest defendant ever tried there. On his fifteenth birthday in February 1996 he pleaded guilty to manslaughter and is facing seven to twenty-one years in prison.

CASE 32

In 1994 in Scottsdale, Arizona, Alfredo Tinajero-Morales, twenty-eight, crashed his pickup truck into a car driven by David Lucas, twenty-six, fatally injuring him. Tinajero-Morales, drunk at the time of the crash, claimed that he was merely a passenger in the truck, not the driver. In January 1996, after being convicted of manslaughter, aggravated assault and leaving the scene of the accident, Tinajero-Morales received a seventeen-year prison sentence.

CASE 33

On January 13, 1996, Francis McSherry, eighteen, Jerrell Holland, eighteen, and an unidentified sixteen-year-old boy were in a foul mood. They were seeking revenge on a man who had tried to abduct a girlfriend of one of them in Van Nuys, California. They encountered Nubar Chilian, fifty-seven, a retired produce dealer who raised parakeets and bees, and killed him in a case of mistaken identity as he walked his dog. Six days earlier Chilian's wife of thirty years had died from breast cancer. The shocked Chilian family was left to deal with two deaths in the same week. Holland pled guilty to the killing, receiving a two-year prison sentence; McSherry was found guilty in a jury trial and sentenced to twenty-five years-to-life in prison.

Gender

Murder is predominantly a male crime, with a vast majority of male murderers and a clear majority of male victims. National statistics for 2003 indicate that 90 percent of those arrested for murder were males while 78 percent of the victims were males. Clearly, females are "underrepresented" in the ranks of homicide participation even though public opinion surveys indicate that females are more concerned than males about becoming victims of crime.[2]

An examination of the 2003 *Uniform Crime Reports* data indicates that 90 percent of the women slain were killed by men. Hence, females killing other females is uncommon, less than 10 percent of all females murdered. Of the total number of females murdered in 2003, 32 percent were killed by their husbands or boyfriends whereas less than 3 percent of the murdered men in America were slain by their wives or girlfriends. Female killers differ from male killers: the female murderers' victims were either their husbands or boyfriends in almost one-third of their killings whereas male murderers' victims were either their wives or girlfriends in less than 10 percent of their killings.[3] Clearly, even though their murder rate is low, women show a greater tendency to kill their mates than do men, probably as a reaction to domestic abuse and violence within the family/romantic setting—a pattern that will be analyzed in greater detail in chapter 7.

Finally, the homicide pattern of female killers often involves the murder of other family members, either their own children or their parents, as well as the murder of female acquaintances. Typical examples include teenage mothers who kill a child at birth, mothers who murder their children in an act of rage, teenage girls who murder their parents for reasons varying from mental illness to differences in life style, and women who kill female acquaintances with whom they have quarreled.

Case 34

In March 1995, Nathalean Bolton, nineteen, was charged with murder and child abuse in the death of her eighteen-month-old daughter, Lanay Shquil Phipps, and the injury to her other children, Laquia Shenee Phipps, two, and Aaron Simm, three. When she appeared before a Sacramento, California, court she showed no emotion as the prosecutor detailed how she had plunged all three children into a bathtub filled with scalding water. She told police that she was having trouble handling the children. Lanay died of her burns and the other two children survived, though they suffered extensive burns. A fourteen-year-old who was present during the event was also charged with homicide and turned over to the juvenile court. She received a fourteen-year prison sentence for the crimes.

Case 35

In May 1995, a Fort Worth, Texas, jury convicted Dorothy Robards, nineteen, of the murder of her father, Steven Robards, thirty-eight. The murder took place two years before she was charged and had the earmarks of a perfect crime. She had poisoned her father by putting barium acetate (twenty times the lethal dose) in his takeout Mexican dinner. She smuggled the poison out of her high school chemistry lab. Apparently Dorothy had pangs of conscience over the homicide that were exacerbated by her college study of Shakespeare's *Hamlet*. Taking the stand in her own defense, she said that she was sorry for what she had done and that she had not meant to kill her father. She claimed that she wished only to make him ill so that she could go and live with her mother and stepfather, who subsequently supported her throughout the trial. Steven Robards' family was not as sympathetic or supportive of Dorothy, nor was the jury who sentenced her to twenty-eight years in prison.

CASE 36

In March 1996, Gale Zylstra, forty-four, was arrested by Phoenix, Arizona, police on suspicion of the first-degree murder of her roommate, a woman also in her forties. Acting on a complaint of foul odors from a freezer left for safekeeping by Zylstra at a friend's home, police discovered the unidentified roommate's partially thawed body in the freezer. Witnesses stated that the roommate had vanished mysteriously five years earlier and Zylstra told them that the woman had run off with a truck driver, leaving behind her eleven-year-old son. The body in the freezer fit the description of the missing roommate. Zylstra received a twenty-year prison sentence.

CASE 37

The Think Life Day Care Center in Fort Lauderdale, Florida, had been founded by Georgia Foster with $4,000 she won in the state's lottery. She dedicated the center to her son who had died of AIDS. Yet, on February 18, 1998, the intentions of the founder of the center were ignored when one of its volunteer workers, Odette Green, fatally stabbed Angela Brock with a kitchen knife. Brock's son Cedric told his mother that Green had pulled his ear and ordered him to sit down. After the two women pushed each other and exchanged blows in the daycare playground, Green left to get a knife from the center's lunchroom. She returned to murder Brock in front of the children. She died at the scene. A jury found her guilty of second degree murder, sentencing her to twenty years in prison.

CASE 38

Police found the body of Nada Lazarevic, sixty-seven, dumped in Kern County, California in 2001 after she had disappeared from her Antelope Valley residence. Arrested and charged with murder were her daughter Vanessa Walker, forty-four, and the daughter's husband Ken Walker, forty. Prosecutors in the case argued that the daughter and son-in-law had amassed almost $50,000 in debts, which had been charged to the murder victim. In a confrontation over the debt, the Walkers murdered Lazarevic and discarded her remains on a remote, rural road. A roadside can collector discovered the body. On July 7, 2003, separate Los Angeles Country juries convicted the husband and wife killers of second-degree murder. Ken Walker received a fifteen-years-to-life sentence. The judge sentenced Vanessa Walker to a thirty-five-years-to-life prison term primarily because she had been convicted of voluntary manslaughter in the shooting death of her first husband in 1989.

Male murderers comprise the vast bulk of killers in the United States, as they do in virtually every nation reporting its homicides. They are statistically over-represented both as victims and assailants. Men kill other men and they generally do so in non-family situations. In 2003, 89 percent of male murder victims were killed by other males; these killings are mainly murders of acquaintances, friends, or strangers, not family members, which is quite different from the female pattern. Much of this book details the manner and circumstances surrounding these male/male killings and a few examples of homicides occurring in the nation during the week of March 15–22, 1998, will help illustrate this regular pattern.

CASE 39

Philadelphia police described the murder of Anthony Turra, sixty-one, as a mob hit. Turra, wheelchair-bound and terminally ill, died of gunshot wounds inflicted by a masked gunman as he left his home on March 19, 1998. Turra was on his way to testify in federal court in a case in which he was accused of plotting to murder Joseph "Skinny Joey" Merlino, a reputed leader in the Philadelphia mob. Prosecutors in the case said that Turra and his son Louis, thirty-three, tried to muscle in on Skinny Joey's gambling operations by eliminating him, but the plot fell apart when the hit man reported the plan to the FBI. Turra's former associates, including his brother Rocco, fifty-eight, testified against him. His son Louis, the mastermind of the plot, committed suicide two months earlier in a New York prison. Police indicated that Turra was shot in the eye and the jaw, the same method allegedly used by his son three years ago in the murder of a restaurant owner whom he mistakenly suspected of informing to federal authorities.

CASE 40

In February, 2000, a relatively minor traffic accident in the Dorchester section of Boston quickly escalated into the murder of Kareem Holmes, twenty-three. Following the incident, Anthony Rivera, twenty-four, and Jesus Rodriquez, twenty-six, pursued Holmes in a car chase that ended at Logan Airport. When the two men confronted Holmes, a struggle ensued; Rivera stabbed Holmes fatally outside one of the airline terminals. Following the homicide, Rodriquez rammed Holmes' car and fled the scene with Rivera. On June 24, 2003, Rivera was convicted of second-degree murder in Holmes' death and Rodriquez convicted on an accessory to murder charge. Rivera received a life sentence while Rodriquez's sentence was two to three years in prison for providing assistance to Rivera.

CASE 41

Ramesh Swamynathan, twenty-seven, and Romarao Chittiprolu had been neighbors in the same apartment building in Park City, Illinois. In September 2002, they engaged in a heated argument over a lost job. Swamynathan held Chittiprolu responsible for his losing the job, and as the dispute escalated, he stabbed Chittiprolu fifty-seven times with a potato peeler knife. Both men had worked for the same employer. Originally charged with first-degree murder, Swamynathan was declared mentally unfit to stand trial. However, in July 2003, a new mental evaluation declared that he was mentally fit to stand trial. In May 2004, he received a twenty-year prison sentence.

Race

One of the more striking observations of homicide in America is the frequency of intra-racial murder. Individuals invariably kill people of their same race; in 2003, 92 percent of blacks were murdered by other blacks; 85 percent of whites were killed by other whites. Thus, even though the general public often believes that most murders are committed by one racial group against another, the facts indicate otherwise in approximately 80–90 percent of all homicides. The probabilities are very high that the assailant and victim will be of the same race, or perhaps even from the same ethnic group.

This pattern evolves mainly because most Americans live near, work with, socialize with, worship with, play with, and marry people like themselves. In spite of the fact that the United States is a multi-cultural/racial/ethnic nation, the patterns of socialization among its inhabitants are remarkably homogeneous; few people rarely interact on a meaningful basis with others from different backgrounds than themselves. Hence inter-ethnic and interracial sociability would be uncommon in places such as Chicago's Southside or New York's Spanish Harlem.

Yet one peculiar finding consistently appears in homicide data. Any overview of homicide in the United States would not be complete without an investigation into the very high rate of homicide among African Americans. Year after year, black Americans are disproportionately represented both among murder victims and murder assailants.[4] In 2003, blacks accounted for approximately 49 percent of all murder victims, and 51 percent of all those arrested for homicide, even though blacks comprise less than 13 percent of the American population. The homicide rate among black males is even more startling; in 1998, the rate per 100,000 population for black males was 42, as opposed to 9 for black females, 6 for white males, and 2 for white females.[5] In 1997 the FBI reported in its Uniform Crime Reports for 1999 that the lifetime probability of a black male being murdered was 1 in 40, as opposed to 1 in 709 for white females.[6] What accounts for such a high rate? Does race explain this data?

Robert Sampson presents the best current explanation of this phenomenon. He argues that black inner-city males have high unemployment rates, far higher than white males. This leads to family disorganization and disruption: single-parent households with no stable breadwinner to socialize young males who consequently have high rates of violence, far higher than black lower-income males raised in stable families. The same is true of white lower-income families that are disrupted by single-parenting. Hence race does not explain the high rate of black male violence, but family disruption does.[7] Edem Avakame confirmed Sampson's findings in a 1997 study of black homicides in Chicago between 1965–1994, indicating that the key variable in the relationship between race and homicide is the differential distribution of blacks in social disorganized communities.[8] Thus we may conclude that race alone explains nothing about homicide; low socio-economic status, combined with familial disorganization/disruption explains far more.

CASE 42 (WHITE/WHITE)

Ronald and Kathy Gauley, both thirty-four, had separated in 1993 when Kathy moved in with Edward Hand, thirty-three, in Bartow, Florida. In June 1994 she became disenchanted with Hand and threatened to return to her husband. A few months later, all three met in a tavern known as The Twilight Zone following her father's funeral. After drinking and arguing they were evicted from the tavern and drove to Hand's trailer in Bartow, a small town near Lakeland.

In the trailer they continued arguing: Kathy Gauley started packing her clothes and told Hand that she was leaving him to return to her husband. Hand became quite upset, pulled out a gun, and threatened to commit suicide if she left him. Finally he placed the gun under his chin and fired; the-bullet passed through his chin and mouth, ricocheted off his teeth, exited through his right cheek, crossed the room, and hit Ronald Gauley in the head, killing him instantly. Hand survived his suicide attempt and was eventually charged with manslaughter, kidnapping, and assault. It took police four months to uncover what actually took place. Following his trial in 1996 Hand was acquitted of the charges.

CASE 43 (WHITE/WHITE)

In Orlando, Florida, on October 12, 1996, two couples in separate cars got into an argument over one car tailgating the other on a busy

Orlando highway. When the cars pulled to the side of the highway to settle the dispute, Joseph Holden, twenty-five, struck the passenger of the first car with what witnesses claimed was a baseball bat. Georgetta Eaves, forty-four, a food service worker at Disney-MGM Studios died of her injuries three days later and Holden, an Orlando maintenance worker who had no prior criminal record, was charged with second-degree murder. Police had not been able to locate the murder weapon. Holden, found guilty of the charge, received a ten-year prison sentence.

CASE 44 (WHITE/WHITE)

William Sodders, twenty-one, had been fascinated by the film *Natural Born Killers* and later admitted to Suffolk County New York police that he admired the killers in the film. On January 3, 1997, he obtained a 9mm pistol and asked his friend Eric Calvin, nineteen, to drive him to the Centereach, Long Island, high school track where he wanted to try out the weapon. There he encountered James Halverson, a New York City firefighter who frequently jogged at the track. Sodders fatally shot Halverson. Halverson was found three hours later by his wife who was pregnant with twins; she had become concerned when he had not returned home from his run. No robbery took place, and police indicated that Sodders killed out of curiosity. He wanted to feel what it would be like to kill someone. Sodders was caught when his father alerted police that he suspected his son was the killer and feared that his son would kill again. Sodders was charged with second-degree murder and his friend was charged with criminal facilitation and hindering prosecution. Sodders received a twenty-five-year-to-life sentence.

CASE 45 (BLACK/BLACK)

Charles Banks, fifty-eight, ran a popular barbershop in Southeast Washington, D.C. On April 19, 1996, he argued with Michael Woody, twenty-one, who became incensed when he lost a quarter in the store's pay phone. To calm things down another barber gave Woody $1 and asked him to leave, which Woody did. However, he returned a few minutes later and shot Banks in the head after pistol-whipping him. Three customers in the shop identified Woody as the murderer. Banks' popularity in the neighborhood helped police enormously in solving his murder, since many people in the local area offered tips about the incident and the assailant. Banks left behind his wife of thity-one years and two adult sons. Woody claimed that he did not murder the barber and that he didn't even know where the barbershop was located. The jury convicted him of first-degree murder. The judge sentenced Woody to fifty-two years-to-life for the slaying.

<h2 style="text-align:center">CASE 46 (BLACK/BLACK)</h2>

On November 3, 1993, Ta Juana Davidson, three, died at Arizona's Casa Grande Hospital. The girl had more than 100 bruises, a broken shoulder blade, whip marks over her entire body, and a cracked skull. Doctors indicated that these injuries were consistent with a fall from a ten-story window. A pediatric pathologist said her injuries were "equivalent to torture" and that her death was one of the "most horrific cases of child abuse." Her foster parents, Cleveland Palmer, forty-seven, and Joquitta Palmer, thirty-one, were arrested for her murder. Facing a death sentence if convicted of the original charges of first-degree murder and child abuse, the couple pleaded no contest to charges of second-degree murder and guilty to attempted child abuse at their trial in December 1995. They had beaten Ta Juana with tree limbs, and the couple's relatives who testified against them stated that the Palmers had brutalized not only Ta Juana, but their eight-year-old son Brandon as well. The couple received a sentence of seventeen years in jail with no possibility of early release.

<h2 style="text-align:center">CASE 47 (BLACK/BLACK)</h2>

Arega Abraha, thirty-six, was well-known in the Decatur, Georgia, area. A professional long-distance runner, Abraha had won dozens of races including the Atlanta Marathon. All this came to an end on January 14, 1997, when he shot his cousin, Aster Haile, twenty-eight, because she backed out of an arranged marriage to an older white man. Abraha had brought Haile to America from Ethiopia and had helped her financially. He shot her in his car with a .25 caliber semi-automatic and dumped her body on the service road of a Georgia highway. Blood samples discovered in his car matched Haile's blood. He was convicted of murder and sentenced to life in prison.

CASE 48 (LATINO/LATINO)

Halloween 1994 proved to be deadly for Pedro Ramos, a tall, skinny, seventy-pound, twelve-year-old. As he passed an intersection in the Bushwick section of Brooklyn, New York, he found himself in the middle of a friendly pre-Halloween egg fight between a dozen children. One of the eggs accidentally hit an unidentified Hispanic man, approximately thirty years old, in the head. He and his companion, Roberto Delgado, twenty, had just emerged from a local bar and appeared to be drunk. Enraged at being struck by an egg, the assailant grabbed Pedro and stabbed him in the groin. Mortally wounded, Pedro cried for help as Delgado kicked and punched him, only stopping when two adults apprehended him and held him until police arrived. Pedro died in surgery early the following morning. Delgado was found guilty of first-degree manslaughter and received a five-to-fifteen-year prison term.

CASE 49 (LATINO/LATINO)

In a case similar to the murder of Charles Banks reported earlier, Horacio Agosta, twenty-nine, was murdered in Brooklyn in December 1994. His murderer, Manuel Waisome, thirty-six, came into the video store owned by Agosta's father and became enraged when he lost a quarter in the store's pay phone. He demanded his money from Agosta, who refused to give it to him. As the argument between them escalated, Waisome pulled out a gun and allegedly shot Agosta three times, killing him. The assailant then fled the scene in his car but was apprehended by police and charged with murder. A jury convicted Waisome of second-degree murder; he received a twenty-five-years-to-life sentence.

CASE 50 (LATINO/LATINO)

On January 26, 1996, Martin Mendoza, thirty-three, of Carson City, Nevada, decided to confront his wife, Rocio Cervantes, who had left him three weeks earlier and moved to Landers, California, with her four children. When he arrived at her new home Cervantes was putting the children and a niece in her car to take them to school. After a heated exchange Cervantes ran into the house to call the police. At this point Mendoza pulled out a gun and stated that the children were not going to school and that he would kill them if the police were called, but the call had already been made. Without warning, Mendoza pulled his stepdaughter, Sandra Resendiz, thirteen, from the car and held a gun to her head. When the police arrived he shot her at point-blank range, killing her. He then fired into the car killing Erik Resendiz (Cervantes' son by another father), eleven, and Wendy Cervantes (Cervantes' niece), eleven, and wounded his own son Martin Mendoza, seven. He then fired at two police officers who subsequently returned fire, wounding Mendoza and eventually arresting him. Everyone involved with Mendoza was shocked by his murderous rampage and stunned that he could be capable of such violence. Mendoza was convicted of first-degree murder of his two stepchildren and a niece and the jury recommended his execution.

CASE 51 (ASIAN/ASIAN)

Insults, assaults, and murders rarely go unavenged in the world of Los Angeles' ethnic gangs. In December 1993, May Leach, a member of the "Asian Boyz" gang was murdered in El Monte by an unknown assailant from the rival "Wah Ching" gang. A few months later, four members of the "Asian Boyz"—Ung Bang, nineteen; Don Sam Hac, twenty-one; Vi Quoc Chau, nineteen; and Cuong Chan Phan, twenty-one, retaliated. According to police accounts the assailants drove to a graduation party in San Marino on June 5, 1994, and sprayed the rival gang's party-site with gunfire, killing Dennis Buan, eighteen, and David Hang, fifteen. The weapon used was an AK–47 assault rifle. In court testimony, Leach's girlfriend "Tami" Tran stated that she had accompanied the assailants and carried a baseball bat with her since she couldn't find a gun. In 1997, Hac and Bang received life sentences, without parole; Chau received a fifty-two-year sentence, and Phan a thirty-two-year sentence.

CASE 52 (ASIAN/ASIAN)

Jennifer Tran, a sixteen-year-old high school student in Alhambra, California, had frequent learning problems throughout her high school career. She missed classes often and had been described by teachers as a very likeable girl who had numerous learning difficulties.

At 2:20 A.M. on May 15, 1996, her life quickly ended in a Vietnamese version of the card game known as Hearts. Jenny played the game with a fifteen-year-old boy whom police described as very bright and talented. The aim of the game was to expose the loser to a round of Russian Roulette. Apparently the boy, in front of four other teens, had rigged the cards so that Jenny would lose a series of hands. After winning the game, the boy held a.38 caliber handgun to her head, spun the chamber with one bullet in it, and fired the gun, killing Jenny instantly. What appeared at first to be a suicide was quickly ruled a homicide when detectives found gunpowder residue on the boy's hands. A detective investigating the incident stated, "The suspect in this [case] was obviously terribly talented and the victim deplorably inept." The killer's only concern at a subsequent court hearing a month after the incident was that he be granted visitation rights with a woman he claimed was his common law wife. The judge denied his request.

CASE 53 (ASIAN/ASIAN)

Pui Kei Wong and his wife Nga Seong Wong, forty-one, who immigrated from Hong Kong in the 1970s, settled in Hollywood, Florida, and set up a Chinese restaurant in North Miami. In August 1997, police had been called to their home to break up a disturbance between the couple. During the incident the husband punched his wife in the face in front of police who were attempting to break up the disturbance. Five months later the attacks continued. On the night of January 19, 1998, the husband became enraged over his wife's gambling habit and allegedly hacked her to death with a hatchet in front of their fifteen-year-old son and thirteen-year-old daughter. The attack continued even as the police arrived at the Wong home, ceasing only when officers threatened to shoot the husband unless he put down the hatchet. At that point he offered no resistance and was arrested and charged with homicide. Wong received a fifteen-year prison sentence after he was convicted of second-degree murder.

CASE 54 (AMERICAN INDIAN/AMERICAN INDIAN)

Kirk Billie, thirty-two, a Florida Miccosukee Indian, accused of drowning his sons Kurt, five, and Keith, three, was convicted of second-degree murder in February 2001. At his trial, he denied any knowledge that his sons were asleep in the backseat of his girlfriend's SUV, indicating that the boys' mother, Sheila Tiger, had told him that they were asleep at her mother's house. The prosecutorial team argued that Billie had been drinking all day on June 27, 1997, and became incensed when Tiger refused to bring the boys to see him. Billie, in retaliation, drove the vehicle into a canal. The 500-member Miccosukee tribe forgave Billie for the incident and sought unsuccessfully to prevent the state of Florida from trying the case, claiming that Florida had no jurisdiction, dismissing what tribal leader Billy Cypress termed "white man's justice." Billie received a life sentence for the crimes.

Case 55 (American Indian/American Indian)

Stanley Secatero, twenty-five, was apprehended by Navajo police on a remote reservation in Canoncito, New Mexico, after murdering his grandmother, uncle, and two aunts in July 1998. Apparently he was upset because he believed that they had turned his brother Wesley, thirty-three, in to authorities in order to collect a $1,000 reward. Wesley had been wanted on a charge of aggravated assault in Albuquerque. After shooting each victim with a .22 caliber rifle, Secatero fled to a rocky ridge where he eluded police for fifteen hours. When surrounded, he stood sobbing on the ridge and surrendered peacefully. Secatero was sentenced to life in prison.

Case 56 (Alaskan Native/Alaskan Native)

In April 1998, Alaskan police received an emergency call from Emmonak, a Yupik Eskimo village reporting that nine-year-old Patrick Bird had committed suicide with a 20-gauge shotgun. Upon investigation state troopers determined that Bird's death was in fact a homicide and arrested a fourteen-year-old boy from the same village of Emmonak. They discovered that he had been at the Bird home the night of the incident. Whether the shooting was intentional or accidental had not been determined by police at the time of the shooting.

Even though most murders are intra-racial, what accounts for the significant number that are interracial? Again, the normal patterns of social interactions help explain these killings, since interracial homicide usually entails murders between individuals who do not know each other and who do not typically interact socially. These are termed *stranger homicides*, killings where the assailant and the victim did not know each other before the lethal encounter. Typical examples include robbery homicides, and unforeseen encounters between individuals in public places—a Black robber kills a Latino bodega owner; a White driver kills a black pedestrian in a hit-and-run incident; an Asian gang member kills a black child in a drive-by shooting; a white motorist shoots a black driver in a case of road rage; a Latino drug dealer kills an arresting white police officer. Few, if any, of these encounters occurred among relatives or friends or even acquaintances, so-called *friendly homicides*. Instead, they often involve robbery of complete strangers or entail killings wherein the killer and the victim "were in the wrong place at the wrong time."

CASE 57 (WHITE/BLACK)

Joseph Paul Franklin, forty-seven, an admitted white supremacist and serial killer, terrorized the nation between 1977 and 1980. He admitted that he hated blacks and Jews and did not believe that either group was truly human. He shot and wounded Vernon Jordan, who was head of the Urban League at the time, and shot and paralyzed Larry Flint, the publisher of *Hustler* magazine, whom he accused of portraying interracial couples. Among the twenty-one black and Jewish victims of the shootings were cousins Darrell Lane, fourteen, and Dante Evans, thirteen, who were both Black and had been gunned down in Cincinnati, Ohio, in 1980. He also admitted to killing Arthur Smothers and Kathleen Mikula, an interracial couple with plans to marry in Johnstown, Pennsylvania. Franklin has been sentenced to several life sentences for his murders in different states and is awaiting execution for a 1997 Missouri killing.

CASE 58 (LATINO/BLACK/WHITE)

Jamie Knight, twenty-one, worked as a trainee at Friendly's Restaurant in Richmond, Virginia. On January 30, 1997, Knight, who was white, encountered Anthony Gomez, seventeen (Latino), and Saladhundid David Al Wadud Webb, twenty-seven (black), in a botched robbery. Armed with a revolver and a shotgun, Gomez and Webb concealed themselves in the restaurant bathroom and entered the dining area after the establishment had closed for the night. Gomez ordered Knight and another employee, John Moore, to lie on the floor and announced that a stickup was taking place. In the process of tying Knight up with duct tape, Gomez's gun went off, killing Knight with a shot to the head. Gomez claimed he had cocked the hammer and was kneeling parallel to the victim when the gun fired accidentally. Webb, who was busy grabbing the night's proceeds of $790, raced from the store with Gomez when the gun went off. Both returned to the apartment they shared near the restaurant and changed their clothes. They planned to visit a girlfriend when police pursued them and captured them both at the Robert E. Lee monument in Richmond. John Moore told police that after the shooting Gomez looked at him and said, "I didn't mean to do it," and fled in "a panic." Both defendants were convicted and sentenced to life in prison.

CASE 59 (WHITE/BLACK)

Two brothers, David Starkey, twenty-five, and Daniel Starkey, twenty, both White, were driving on a rural Maryland road when they encountered a car driven by three black women returning from a Christmas shopping trip in December 1999. David Starkey, angered by what he considered to be erratic driving on the part of Michelle Wilson, pursued the black woman's car for twenty miles on the rural, isolated roads, flashing his lights and sounding his horn. He then fired his shotgun at the vehicle, wounding Wilson and fatally injuring her passenger Germaine Clarkson, seventy-three, who died two days later. At his trial Starkey claimed the gun fired accidentally and that the shooting was unintentional. His defense attorney argued that the killer "had an attack of the crazies." The jury convicted Starkey of first-degree murder and sentenced him to life in prison. His brother was also convicted, receiving a sentence of twenty-five years in prison. At his sentencing, David Starkey addressed the Clarkson family, stating, "You have my best wishes and all my prayers."

A review of homicide statistics in any given year also reveals the interaction of race and gender in influencing directly who the victims of murder will be. One's chances of being murdered are not random throughout the population: white females are least likely to be murdered in any given year, while black males are the most likely victims. Table

Table 3.1
Interaction of Gender and Race
Among Homicide Victims—1999

Race/Gender	Rate/100,000
White Female	2.2
White Male	5.6
Black Female	7.8
Black Male	37.5

Source: derived from Table no. 289, *Statistical Abstract of the United States—2002: The National Data Book*, 122nd Edition. Washington, D.C. U.S. Census Bureau, p. 186.

3.1 presents the homicide rate for 1999, broken down by gender and race. The same pattern can be observed in any year where data are available even though the actual number of killings and the actual rate will vary. As these data indicate black males are twenty times more likely to be murdered than white females and almost seven times more so than white males, a tragic pattern repeated year-after-year in the United States.

Socio-Economic Status

Of all the factors related to the incidence of murder in America, few are as obvious as the high concentration of this form of violence among lower-income groups. The vast majority of murders are committed by poor people who kill other poor people. The sociological literature supporting this theory is quite extensive.[9] In his pioneering study of criminal homicide, Marvin Wolfgang found that over 90 percent of Philadelphia murderers in the 1950s were from the lower end of the occupational ladder.[10]

Poor-on-poor murders are so common that few command much media attention. From a human-interest standpoint they are not "quality" killings that attract the public's attention. They frequently involve Latino and/or Black assailants and victims and are not viewed as either shocking or disturbing since they are "expected," not particularly "noteworthy." In order to be considered "noteworthy," murders need to involve middle—or upper-class victims/assailants, multiple victims, young children, public figures, or entail either bizarre methods or circumstances. Without such features the murders of lower-income people are relegated to a few sentences at the back of a major newspaper, pushed to the "crime column" section rather than the front page, or major news sections.[11] They are bumped from TV news by other stories deemed to be more interesting to viewers. Consider the following three accounts of New Jersey homicides that appeared in the *Newark Star Ledger*, the major daily newspaper in the state:

3 Men Killed in Club Gunfight

Two men shot and killed each other and a third man was fatally wounded in a gunfight early yesterday outside a Jersey City nightclub.

Hudson County authorities said Michael Grant, Jackie Bullard, and Terry Jones, all city residents, were killed at 2 A.M., after Grant, twenty-six, and Bullard, 28, became embroiled in a verbal confrontation outside the club Nostalgia.

First Assistant Prosecutor Edward DeFazio said Grant shot Bullard in the chest and stomach, then shot Jones, also 28, twice in the back. At the same time, Bullard who was also armed, shot Grant in the head, said the official.[12]

Newark Man Fatally Stabbed in a Street Dispute

A Newark man was stabbed to death in a fight with another man at Orange and North Fifth Street last night.

John F. Robinson, 34, was stabbed once in the chest at 6 P.M. by his unknown assailant, described by witnesses as a Hispanic, who fled. Robinson died shortly after at University Hospital.

Anyone with information is asked to call Homicide Detective Keith Sheppard or Investigator Kirk Swindel of the Essex County Prosecutor's Office at (201) 733–6130.[13]

Gunfight Kills Man, Hurts Another

A twenty-six-year-old East Orange man was killed and a Newark man was clinging to life last night after being shot in an apparent bar fight in Newark's South Ward early yesterday, police said.

Shyron Mannin was shot twice in the back outside B&E Lounge at 945 Bergen St. said Detective Rocco Malanga, a spokesman for the Newark Police Department. Manning was pronounced dead on arrival at University Hospital in Newark.

Levon Morris, twenty-three, is listed in critical condition at the hospital after being shot once in the head, Malanga said.

Malanga said a verbal dispute in the bar spilled onto the street at roughly 2:30 A.M. yesterday and gunfire erupted.

Police arriving at the scene spotted a car speeding away. During a chase into Irvington, police saw one of the car's occupants toss an object out the window. Police later retrieved a 9mm handgun.

The two people in the car—twenty-five-year-old Akua Hargrove and 18-year-old Nahlah Garretson, both of Newark—were arrested and charged with eluding police, illegal possession of a weapon and possession of stolen property.

Police are performing ballistics tests to determine if the gun thrown from the car was the weapon used in the shooting, Malanga said.[14]

The homicides described above commanded only a few paragraphs each in the newspaper and none of the three were front-page items. The first report of a triple murder in a lower-income neighborhood of

Jersey City would have been national news if the victims were socially noteworthy; instead they were relegated to page 7 of the paper, probably gaining the attention of few readers other than family, friends, and police investigators. The second homicide (John Robinson) invoked even less journalistic interest, and was covered by a brief paragraph on page 21; the third murder (Shyron Manning) received slightly more column inches perhaps because it involved a high-speed chase but was reported on page 36.

Such murders do not command much public interest because homicides among lower-income groups are considered commonplace, ordinary, predictable, expected, and in general, unworthy of the public's attention since they often involve what are regarded as low-life and riff-raff assailants killing each other. Compare the bare minimum of coverage these killings received to the monopolies of both public and media attention that the high profile murders of Nicole Brown, Ron Goldman, Jon Benet Ramsey, Gianni Versace, and Laci Peterson created.

Another illustration of this phenomenon can be found in a series of six deaths that occurred in a lower-income black neighborhood of Washington D.C. in 1997. Over a thirteen-month period, six bodies were discovered either in, or close to, the Petworth area of the nation's capital. At a heated community meeting with the city's police brass, residents of the area complained bitterly that police and the media were uninterested in the safety of the neighborhood and its people. As one resident remarked at the meeting, "We had to call and call and call. We saw nothing in the newspaper until the fifth person was found. Why did it take so long? . . . If five white women had been killed, they would have called out the National Guard by now."[15]

The area's residents pointed out that the slaying of three people at a Starbucks coffee shop in white, upscale Georgetown in mid–1997 attracted national attention and extensive media coverage. All the stops were pulled in the Starbucks case, in contrast to the Petworth killings where subsequent investigations by both district police and the FBI revealed that most of the victims had been linked to drugs and prostitution.

Without detailed information on the socio-economic background of every assailant and victim, it is difficult to determine conclusively their social class. An indirect way of doing so is to ascertain the demographic characteristics of the neighborhood in which the involved parties lived and where the murder occurred. The cases enumerated below, all reported in the crime section rather than in the major news section,[16] took place in low-income areas of Los Angeles and Washington D.C. and are verbatim accounts from the *Los Angeles Times* and the *Washington Post*, and present a fairly typical view of lower-income murders.

The *Los Angeles Times* December 1996 summarized a number of homicides that took place between August 1, 1996, and August 6, 1996.

CASE 60

August 1, 11 P.M.: Near MacArthur Park, at a drug sales corner controlled by 18th Street gang members, Louie Herrera, twenty-seven, is killed in a burst of gunfire. A suspect is identified but charges are dropped after a witness becomes uncooperative, then disappears.

CASE 61

August 4, 11 P.M.: Ricky Delgado Torres, thirty-six, walks along an Azusa alley notorious for drug deals. He encounters two men in a Jeep and smashes a glass beer mug against the side of the vehicle. Torres is shot half a dozen times. One man is convicted of first-degree murder and another is acquitted.

CASE 62

August 5, 8 P.M.: An argument over sunglasses near a drug sales corner in Pico-Union ends with a transient, Ferney Moreno, forty-one, being killed by gunfire. An alleged gang member is convicted of murder and sentenced to thirty years-to-life in prison.

CASE 63

August 5, 9 P.M.: Freddie Donnel Ross, thirty-nine, is shot in the leg after an apparent argument in a South Central Los Angeles home. He bleeds to death waiting for paramedics. The suspect is acquitted of murder and manslaughter charges and the jury deadlocks on an assault charge.

Case 64

August 6, 1 A.M.: Viola Pirtle Woods, fifty-one, mother of a key witness in the 1993 killing of two Compton police officers, is shot on a street near the Nickerson Gardens housing project. Her son contends that the shooting was revenge and sues the police for not protecting his family, but investigators say Woods' death appears to be accidental, the result of gang activity. No arrests are made.

Case 65

August 6, 10 A.M.: A transient, Jamie Garcia, fifty, is stabbed in the neck while standing in a Los Angeles skid row phone booth. With little evidence and conflicting testimony, jury finds another transient, forty-five, not guilty.

The *Washington Post* summarizes crime reports received by the Metropolitan Police Department for Southeast Washington D.C., a predominantly lower-income section of the nation's capital. The first five cases took place on January 29, 1997; the remaining four occurred on February 12, 1997:

Case 66

LIVINGSTON RD., 4500 block, 9:30 P.M., Jan. 9. An unidentified male was found in a car in a parking lot with a gunshot wound to the head. He was taken to D.C. General Hospital where he was pronounced dead at 10:10 P.M.

Case 67

POMEROY RD., 2500 block, 1:55 A.M., Jan. 12. Ronnie Edwards, twenty-two, of the 1300 block of Morris Rd. SE, was found on the sidewalk with multiple gunshot wounds to the back of the head. He was taken to D.C. General Hospital where he was pronounced dead at 4: 10 A.M.

CASE 68

SAVANNAH ST., 2000 block, 9:41 P.M., Jan. 11. Jovan Quick, sixteen, of the 2000 block of Savannah St. SE, was found with several gunshot wounds. He was taken to D.C. General Hospital where he was pronounced dead at 10:09. He was shot during a robbery in which someone attempted to steal his jacket.

CASE 69

TALBERT ST., 1200 block, 4:40 P.M., Jan. 16. David Mitchell, Jr., forty-seven, of the 1200 block of Talbert St. SE, was found in a hallway with a gunshot wound to the head. He was taken to D.C. General Hospital where he was pronounced dead at 7 P.M.

CASE 70

23rd ST., 3200 block, 9:58 P.M., Jan. 12. Michael Bernard Brown, seventeen, of the 2200 block of Savannah Ter. SE, was found in a hallway with a gunshot wound to the chest. He was taken to D.C. General Hospital where he was pronounced dead at 10:30 P.M.

CASE 71

ALABAMA AVE., 2800 block, 2:08 A.M., Dec. 29. Phillip Christopher Carter, twenty-five, of the 5900 block of Southern Avenue SE, was found with a gunshot wound to the upper body. He was taken to D.C. General Hospital where he was admitted in serious condition. He was pronounced dead at 12:45 A.M. Jan. 26.

CASE 72

HARTFORD ST., 2400 block, 7:20 P.M., Jan. 29. Kevin Dennis Brown, eighteen, of the 2800 block of 23rd Place SE, was found on the sidewalk with a stab wound to the chest. He was taken to D.C. General Hospital where he was pronounced dead at 8:18 P.M.

CASE 73

THIRD ST., 4400 block, 10:59 A.M., Jan 28. Steven Antoine Terrell, eighteen, of Clinton, and Anthony Mack Edwards, twenty, of Forestville, were found in a vehicle in an alley with gunshot wounds to the head. Both were pronounced dead by the D.C. Medical Examiner's office at 2 P.M.

CASE 74

MINNESOTA AVE., 1800 block, 3: 10 A.M., Jan. 25. Arthur Curtis Ward, nineteen, of the 2200 block of Prout Street SE, was found on the sidewalk with gunshot wounds to the head. He was taken to D.C. General Hospital where he was pronounced dead at 5: 10 A.M.

Analysis of demographic variables such as age, gender, race, and socio-economic status helps us understand the patterned regularity of the vast majority of murders. What strikes many as a completely unexpected and inexplicable crime may in fact be just the opposite. In fact, most homicides are patterned, rational, and organized in their occurrence. Even the reporting of these crimes follows patterns reflecting the demographic backgrounds of the assailants and victims. Who you are counts not only in life, but also in death (but only collectively—just as you can't predict who will die in car crashes next year, but you can approximate how many will occur, when, and where). Individually they are inexplicable and unexpected; collectively, the opposite.

Notes

1. *Crime in the United States, 2003*—UCR, table 2.5 (adapted).
2. *Sourcebook*, 1995, table 2.37; *Crime in the United States 2002*—UCR, table 2.5.
3. *Crime in the United States, 2003*—UCR, table 2.7.
4. Chilton, 2003.
5. *Statistical Abstract of the United States, 2001*, table 113, p. 86.
6. *Crime in the United States, 1999*, Appendix A, p. 285ff.
7. Sampson, 1987, p. 377–378.
8. Avakame, 1997.
9. c.f Blau and Blau, 1982; Braithwaite and Braithwaite, 1980; Corzine and Huff—Crozine, 1992; Hagan and Peterson, 1995; Lalli and Turner, 1968; Lester, 1991; Liska and Bellair, 1995; Martinez, 1997; McDowall, 1986; Messner, 1982, 1983, 1984; Pallone and Hennessy, 1996; Williams, 1984.

10. Wolfgang, 1958, p. 37.
11. Paulsen, 2003.
12. *Star Ledger*, October 23, 1993, p. 7.
13. *Star Ledger*, March 17, 1996, p. 21.
14. *Star Ledger*, December 13, 1998, p. 36.
15. Wilson, 1997, p. 1.
16. Paulson, 2003.

4

The Geography of Murder

Whereas the demography of homicide illustrates the "who" of homicide (its assailants and victims), the geography of homicide provides us with the "where" of murder—its location in physical space. Murder's geographical distribution ranges from broad macro patterns, which differentiate homicide rates according to regions of the country, states, cities, neighborhoods, etc., to specific micro patterns such as whether the murder occurred indoors or outdoors, where the corpse was discovered, in which room of the house the killing took place, etc. Patterns exist in both macro and micro locational variables, patterns that persist over time and place and help us understand the phenomenon of murder in America more fully.

Those unfamiliar with the patterned spatial regularity of homicide frequently have misconceptions about where killings take place. The public often believes that murders take place only in the back alleys of the seedy areas of our inner cities, areas where "those people" live and congregate. We hear about killings in slum areas and we often accept these incidents as unavoidable realities of modern life. Yet when they occur elsewhere, the public seems stunned. How often have we heard the surprised reaction of neighbors of murder victims who live in upscale areas being interviewed by reporters seeking a response to a killing: "I can't believe it. Things like this never happen in this neighborhood. It's best to keep your door locked and the kids inside. I can't understand why this happened!" How many people realize that some of the most desirable regions of the country in which to reside— namely, the Sunbelt states—are also the most dangerous areas in the nation? Conversely, film audiences who saw *Fargo* in 1996 might think that North Dakota is a dangerous place. In fact, it is not. In 2003 the city of Fargo registered no homicides; the entire state of North Dakota had a total of twelve murders in 2003.

To help clarify possible misconceptions, let us examine the geography of homicide more closely in order to pinpoint more accurately exactly where murders take place.

Regions

The Bureau of the Census and the FBI divide the United States into four regions: Northeastern states, Midwestern states, Southern states, and Western states (see Figure 4.1). The FBI provides a breakdown of murders in these areas on an annual basis, summarized below in Table 4.1.

Clearly, the Southern states command the lion's share of American killings, accounting for 44 percent of all 2003 murders. The Western states place second with 23 percent of all murders. Together, both regions account for 66 percent of the nation's murders even though they contain 58 percent of the country's population. The Northeast and Midwest are relatively under-represented, each having considerably less homicide than statistically expected.

Figure 4.1
FBI/Census Division of U.S.

Table 4.1
Distribution of Murders by Region
of the United States—2003

Region	Population	Percentage of Murder	Murder Rate (per 100,000 inhabitants)
1) Northeast	18.7%	14.5%	4.2
2) Midwest	22.5%	19.5%	4.9
3) South	35.9%	43.6%	6.9
4) West	22.9%	22.9%	5.7
United States	100%	100%	5.7

Source: Index of Crime, Crime in the United States, 2003: Uniform Crime Reports, Washington, D.C.,: U.S. Government Printing Office, 2003, pp 71–72.

States

An analysis of murder rates in each of the fifty states in 2003 helps us to understand regional variations in homicide. Table 4.2 presents the data that clearly show the dominance of the South, and to a lesser extent, the West in the incidence of murder.

Robert Baller and his associates found that homicide is not randomly distributed in space. They discovered that in the 1960–1990 period, a regional pattern emerged wherein counties in the South had higher than average homicide rates, and these homicides formed clusters which were distinct from the non-South areas of the United States.[1]

Of the seventeen Southern States, only five (Delaware, West Virginia, Virginia, Kentucky, and Florida) fall below the national average of 5.7 murders per 100,000 inhabitants. The remaining twelve states, including the District of Columbia (which has a rate almost eight times the national average of 44.2), rank above the national rate. Louisiana's rate of 13.0 (with 586 murders) is the highest of all the states. Clearly, a murder zone exists in the nation, focused primarily on Louisiana, Mississippi, Alabama, and Maryland, as well as the nation's capital, with rates considerably higher than the national average.

The Western states also have relatively high rates. Of the thirteen states in the West, five exceed the national average (Nevada, New Mexico, Alaska, California, and Arizona), while the remaining eight states have murder rates considerably below the national rate.

Of the twelve Midwestern states, only two exceed the national average (Illinois and Michigan), while the remaining ten have rates generally much lower than the national average.

Table 4.2
Murder Rates for 2003
According to State

Northeastern States—4.2

New England 2.2
Connecticut 3.0
Maine 1.2
Massachusetts 2.2
New Hampshire 1.4
Rhode Island 2.3
Vermont 2.3

Middle Atlantic 5.0
New Jersey 4.7
New York 4.9
Pennsylvania 5.3

Midwestern States—4.9

*East North Central 5.6
*Illinois 7.1
*Indiana 5.5
*Michigan 6.1
*Ohio 4.6
*Wisconsin 3.3

West North Central 3.4
Iowa 1.6
Kansas 4.5
Minnesota 2.5
*Missouri 5.0
Nebraska 3.2
North Dakota 1.9
South Dakota 1.3

*Southern States—6.9

*South Atlantic 6.7
 Delaware 2.9
*District of Columbia 44.2
 Florida 5.4
*Georgia 7.6
*Maryland 9.5
*North Carolina 6.1
*South Carolina 7.2
 Virginia 5.6
 West Virginia 3.5

*East South Central 6.6
*Alabama 6.6
 Kentucky 4.6
*Mississippi 9.3
*Tennessee 6.8
*West South Central 7.3
*Arkansas 6.4
*Louisiana 13.0
*Oklahoma 5.9
*Texas 6.4

*Western States—5.7

Mountain 5.4
*Arizona 7.9
 Colorado 3.9
 Idaho 1.8
 Montana 3.3
*Nevada 8.8
*New Mexico 6.0
 Utah 2.5
 Wyoming 2.8

*Pacific 5.8
*Alaska 6.0
*California 6.8
 Hawaii 1.7
 Oregon 1.9
 Washington 3.0

---

*at or above the national rate of 5.7
Source: *Crime in the United States* 2003, Tables 4, pp. 72–81

All the Northeastern states rank relatively low in 2003 murders, with only one state—Pennsylvania even coming close to the national average.

In substance, the incidence of murder is not evenly distributed throughout the fifty states. Instead, it is highly concentrated in certain areas, most notably in the South and in sections of the West. The remaining areas of the Midwest and Northeast all register lower rates, with the exceptions of Illinois and Michigan, where large cities within each (Chicago, and Detroit) comprise the bulk of the states' murders.

Yet even the states with low rates of murder register similar, though not identical, types of homicides. Since their annual numbers are so low, a consistent comparison with states with very high rates is difficult.

Maine provides a good example of a state with a consistently low rate of murder (1.2 in 2003). Though its rate is among the lowest in the nation, the types of killings are not qualitatively different from states with much higher rates. Table 4.3 illustrates this, providing a summary of all the murders (seventeen) that took place in 2003. The assailants were largely male and the victims were both male and female. Domestic violence slayings and acquaintance killings predominate, as does the use of firearms and personal weapons. Absent from these killings are major drug-related factors which play a major role in killings in other states such as California, Louisiana, and New York.

Why the South and the West?

Why do the South and parts of the West display relatively high rates of murder? Aren't these locations considered desirable by people in our nation seeking refuge from crime, cold weather, social disorder, stress, etc.? Isn't the Sunbelt the place to visit, the place to find new jobs, new friends, new lives? Yes and no.

The best answer to questions regarding the South and West's propensity towards homicide relates to the changing demographic characteristics of these regions. To simplify the response, what seems to be occurring in the past twenty-five years is the migration of young males from the Northeast and the Midwest. Many are fleeing the economic hardship of the Rustbelt regions of the old manufacturing centers of the Northeast and Midwest, both low murder regions, seeking new jobs in the newly emerging areas of the Sunbelt. A visitor to such cities as North Adams, Massachusetts, or Camden, New Jersey, or Gary, Indiana,

Table 4.3
Summary of Homicide Incidents Maine–2003*

Age	Sex	Age	Sex	Relationship of Victim to Offender	Circumstances
20	F	28	M	Wife	Victim stabbed to death inside her home. Husband charged with murder.
18	M	20	M	Friend	Victim shot death with shotgun inside his apartment by offender.
43	F	53	M	Girlfriend	Victim was strangled to death inside her apartment. Live-in boyfriend charged with murder.
39	F	45	M	Girlfriend	Victim was shot to death in her home by live-in boyfriend.
22 months	M	29	F	Son	Victim was shaken to death inside his his home by offender.
22	F	30	M	Girlfriend	Victim stabbed to death insider her apartment by her live-in boyfriend, who then stabbed and killed himself.
78	M	53	M	Acquaintance	Victim drank coffee laced with arsenic at church. Offender shot and killed himself.
46	F	44	M	Ex-wife	Victim was shot and killed by ex-husband at her home.
51	M	26	M	Neighbor	Victim stabbed to death in his apartment by offender.
53	M	43	M	Friend	Victim shot to death and buried in woods. Offender was charged with murder.
65	M	—	—	Unknown	Victim found shot to death outside his home.
21	F	47	M	Stranger	Victim, a college student, was abducted and beaten to death by offender.
42	F	40	M	Girlfriend	Victim died from head injuries after being found lying on the road.
23	M	21 20	M M	Acquaintance	Victim shot to death in a remote cabin. Offenders charged with murder.
20	M	30	M	Acquaintance	Victim Shot outside his home. Offender charged with murder.
42	F	41	M	Girlfriend	Victim beaten to death. Longtime live-in boyfriend indicted for manslaughter and assault.
40	M	—	—	Unknown	Victim found shot to death inside his home.

Source: *Crime in Maine 2003 Dept. of Public Safety–UC Reporting Division, August Maine, p.22.

or Youngstown, Ohio, would be struck by the visible economic collapse of the manufacturing sectors of these areas, a late twentieth-century phenomenon which has caused the disappearance of tremendous numbers of unskilled and semi-skilled jobs. Hence, young males have "gone South and West" seeking economic opportunities in Atlanta, Houston, San Diego, Phoenix, Las Vegas, etc. Furthermore, speaking hypothetically, whenever you have a disproportionate number of young males within a population, you will also have disproportionate amount of crime, including homicide. Concentrating large numbers of young adult males (ages fifteen to twenty-four) a given area provides a key catalyst for crime in general, and violent crimes such as homicide in particular.

Subculture of Violence

In addition to the population shift hypothesis, another explanation emerges from the studies: the subculture of violence hypothesis advanced by Marvin Wolfgang and Franco Ferracuti (1967, 1982). This hypothesis argues that the lifestyles and cultures of certain subgroups within the larger population predispose its members towards violent behavior as a normal response to problems they encounter in their lives. These responses are learned within this culture and transmitted from one generation to the next, whereby the youth are socialized into violent lifestyles.

This subculture of violence hypothesis has often been cited to explain the high homicide rates in the South.[2] Its advocates suggest that interpersonal tensions are settled through violence in Southern areas more often than in other area of the country. Why? Perhaps the reasons are rooted in the reality of weak, centralized legal authority that translated into a long-standing belief that differences are settled outside the law, a belief reinforced by the legacy of loss in the Civil War. Many historical and social factors contribute to the strength of this theory: the legacy of resentment against the legal apparatus of Reconstruction implemented by Northern carpetbaggers and Southern scalawags survives; Jim Crow laws and the prevalent segregationist sentiment condoned violence against blacks; black-on-black violence was frequently ignored and even condoned; gun ownership is still considered a mark of pride; personal honor and reputation are prized and defended to the death; and vendettas and retaliatory violence are expected as normal outcomes of interpersonal conflicts. If these factors are real they help explain the high murder rates found in specific areas of the South, not only in the lower-income areas of the cities, but also in certain small towns and rural areas.

Typical areas with high murder rates in 2003 include: Halifax County, North Carolina (rate =14); Birmingham, Alabama (rate =35.4); New Orleans (rate =57.7); Shreveport, Louisiana (rate =21); Alexandria, Louisiana (rate =17.4); Charleston, South Carolina (rate =15.1); Jackson, Mississippi (rate =24.8); Macon, Georgia (rate =18.5); Opa Locka, Florida (rate =39.3). To contrast these rates with the overall U.S. murder rate of 5.7 for 2003 is to acknowledge South's propensity towards murder.

Yet this subculture of violence is hotly debated within the social sciences, since areas outside the Southern states also have high rates of murder (i.e., any of the lower—income sections of our major cities in the West, Northeast, and Midwest). So the hypothetical subculture of violence may not be restricted to Southern areas. Likewise, critics have argued that surveys provide no direct evidence that residents of the South espouse the values of this subculture.[3] Other critics of the hypothesis note that levels of poverty and family disruption explain the variations in murder rates more accurately than do regional criteria.[4] Still others point out that historical rates of homicide were as great, if not greater, in the slums of New York City, Chicago, and San Francisco in the mid-nineteenth century as those of the South.

Community Size

Does the size of a community, as measured by its population, illustrate any patterns in the incidence of homicide? The FBI breaks the United States into three community types: metropolitan areas (large cities and their surrounding suburbs), cities outside of metropolitan areas (generally, small cities), and rural counties. Table 4.4 presents the 2003 Crime Rate by Area data not only for murder, but for other index crimes as well, including those which are regarded as the most serious offenses.

These data clearly show that for all major crimes, the larger the community, the greater the incidence of serious crime. For all categories, metropolitan areas have higher rates of crime than do other cities and rural communities. In turn, these smaller cities have more crime than do rural counties.

Table 4.4
Crime Rate, Area, 2003
(Rate per 100,000 inhabitants)

Offense	Total U.S.	Metro	Other Cities	Rural
Crime Index Total	4,063	4,300	4,533	1,879
Violent Crime	475	517	385	202
Property Crime	3,588	3,783	4,418	1,677
Murder	5.7	6.1	3.8	3.5
Forcible Rape	32	33	38	23
Robbery	142	165	60	16
Aggravated Assault	295	313	283	159
Burglary	741	758	816	555
Larceny/Theft	2,415	2,534	3,132	994
Auto Theft	433	491	200	129
Arson	N/A	N/A	N/A	N/A

Crime Index—statistical summary of major cities, per 100,000 people. These major crimes are: murder, rape, robbery, aggravated assault, burglary, larceny/theft, auto theft, and arson. Arson data are not yet available in index form for the country.
Source: *Index of Crime in the United States, 2003: Uniform Crime Reports*, Washington D.C.: U.S. Government Office, Table 2 and Table 3, p. 71.

There are three exceptions: rape and burglary in the cities outside of metropolitan areas are greater than in either large cities or rural areas; murder rates in rural areas, though lower than those of metropolitan centers, are generally higher than those of smaller cities.

This anomaly for rural homicide appears year after year in the data; 2003 represents a rare exception to this trend. Rural rates for all serious crimes are quite low, with the single exception of homicide. Why? The answer seems to be related to what we have already said about homicide in the South. In the South, an unexpectedly large number of murders occur in rural areas, much more so than in rural communities elsewhere in the United States. Whether this is related to a regional subculture of violence, to disproportionate poverty levels, or to other unknown factors is debatable and deserves further research. For example, why do areas such as Robeson County, North Carolina, have high rates of murder and other rural areas, such as Hancock County, Maine, have very low rates?

A significant proportion of the South's high murder rate is concentrated in certain rural areas with its states. Table 4.5 presents 2003 data for a number of counties in North Carolina that have significant rural populations that exceed the rate for rural communities in country as a whole (national rural murder rate= 3.5) and the total national rate

(5.7). Thus Duplin County's rate (19.8) is almost six times the rural murder rate for the country; as is Robeson County's rate (16) and Bladen County's rate (15.7) far exceed the overall U.S. rural rate. The proponents of the subculture of violence thesis point to this "murder belt" across rural parts of North Carolina and other states in the Deep South as evidence of norms and values supportive of violence in this areas, whereas they are not found in comparable rural areas elsewhere in the nation. Outside of certain areas in the Southern states, rural America is a relatively safe place to live.

Major Cities and Homicide

In the mass media, a great deal of attention is devoted to murder in our cities, and perhaps rightly so, given the above-reported data on homicide in metropolitan areas. Yet, all cities are not equal since certain areas (e.g., Washington, D.C.) have very high rates while others have low rates (e.g., San Diego).

Table 4.5
Selected North Carolina Counties with Major Rural Areas
with High Homicide Rates—2001

County	Population	Murders	Murder Rate/100,000
Bertie	19,746	1	5.1
Bladen	32,376	3	9.3
Brunswick	73,692	5	6.8
Cleveland	97,631	12	12.3
Columbus	54,857	7	13.7
Duplin	49,289	2	4.1
Gaston	189,675	16	8.4
Halifax	57,371	3	5.2
Lenoir	59,515	7	11.8
Martin	25,593	2	7.8
Montgomery	26,902	2	7.4
Robeson	123,989	27	21.8
Sampson	60,517	4	6.6
Scotland	35,841	5	14.0
Vance	3,083	7	16.2
Wilson	72,843	4	5.5
United States Rural Homicide Rate 2001 = 3.7			
United States Total Homicide Rate 2001 = 5.6			

Source: Crime in North Carolina: Uniform Crime Report 2001. Raleigh, North Carolina: State Bureau of Investigation, 2001; pp. 36 and 74–126.
(Rates calculated by author; rounded to nearest whole number)

Table 4.6
Rank Order of Homicide Rates for the
Ten Largest Central Cities in United States with
Population of 1,000,000 or more—2003*

Central City	Population	Murder Rate**	(Actual Murders)
1. Philadelphia	(1,495,903)	23.2	(348)
2. Chicago	(2,898,374)	20.6	(598)
3. Dallas	(1,230,302)	18.3	(226)
4. Phoenix	(1,403,228)	17.2	(241)
5. Houston	(2,041,081)	13.6	(278)
6. Los Angeles	(3,838,838)	13.4	(515)
7. Las Vegas	(1,189,388)	11.9	(141)
8. New York	(8,098,066)	7.4	(597)
9. San Antonio	(1,212,789)	7.0	(85)
10. San Diego	(1,272,746)	5.1	(65)
	Total U.S. Rate—5.7		

*Source: *Uniform Crime Rates, 2003*, Table 6 and Table 8.
**per 100,000 population; recalculated by author

Also, some mid-size cities' (e.g., Baltimore, Miami, Atlanta) rates are much higher than those of much larger cities (e.g., New York City). Table 4.6 ranks the ten largest central cities in the United States according to their murder rates in 2003. These data are only for their respective cities, and do not include their contiguous suburban community rates. Hence the data for New York apply only to its core parts (the five boroughs of the Bronx, Brooklyn, Queens, Manhattan, and Staten Island), and not for the surrounding counties of Westchester, Nassau, etc.

In reviewing these data we might point out that Philadelphia is the leader in homicide among large cities, with 348 murders. Its rate (23.4) is four times San Diego's rate. New York City, which has a high number of murders (597) compared to virtually all other communities in America, is relatively safe when compared to other cities. Its rate (7.0) is considerably lower than those of Chicago, Philadelphia, Dallas, Los Angeles, Phoenix, Houston, and Las Vegas. This generally surprises most people who are convinced, often against all evidence, that New York is not only the most dangerous place in the United States, but also in the entire world!

Another interesting finding in these data is that seven of the ten largest cities listed in table 4.6 are in the Sunbelt, and nine of the ten have rates above the national average (San Diego is the only large city below the 5.7 rate).

Table 4.7 presents another view of homicide in American cities. If one looks at the rates of homicide in cities of less than one million inhabitants, one sees that certain cities have much larger rates than the largest ones. New Orleans, the nation's leader in homicide in 2003, had a rate of (58), almost ten times the overall U. S. rate. Washington D.C., also has a rate very high rate (44), as does Detroit (39). In substance, all of the cities cited in Table 4.7 have higher rates than the national average and some such as Camden, New Jersey (51) and Richmond, Virginia (47), though small, could be considered murder zones because of their rates that are considerably greater than the national average.

Variations within Communities

Just as there are major variations in the incidence of murder in regions, states, and cities, there are also differences within communities. In 2003, New York State had a total of 934 murders, 64 percent of which (597) occurred in one community: New York City; Louisiana

Table 4.7
Rank Order of Homicide Rates for 15 Selected
Cities with less than 1 Million Population—2003*
Other Cities (Selected)**
(less than 1 million population)

Central City	Population	Murder Rate**	Total Murders
1. New Orleans, LA	(475,128)	57.7	(274)
2. Washington, D.C.	(563,384)	44.0	(248)
3. Detroit, MI	(927,466)	39.4	(366)
4. Camden, NJ	(80,132)	51.2	(41)
5. Richmond, VA	(199,968)	46.5	(93)
6. Baltimore, MD	(644,554)	41.8	(270)
7. Atlanta, GA	(431,043)	34.6	(149)
8. St. Louis, MO	(340,256)	21.5	(73)
9. Birmingham, AL	(240,176)	35.4	(85)
10. Newark, NJ	(278,551)	29.1	(81)
11. Miami, FL	(381,651)	19.4	(74)
12. Albuquerqe, NM	(468,764)	10.9	(51)
13. San Francisco, CA	(772,065)	8.9	(69)
14. Boston, MA	(589,795)	6.6	(39)
15. Omaha, NE	(401,692)	3.5	(8.7)
	Total U.S. Murder Rate—5.7		

*Source: *Uniform Crime Reports, 2003;* Table 8, recalculated by author

had 586 murders, 47 percent of which (274) occurred in New Orleans; Nebraska had fifty-six murders, 63 percent of which (thirty-five) took place in Omaha. Consequently, homicide is differentially distributed, with certain sectors of communities having high rates, and nearby areas registering very low rates.

New York City can serve as a useful example of this phenomenon. Table 4.8 presents a list of New York City's police precincts, with the number of reported homicides for each in 2001.

Certain precincts, such as Brooklyn's 67th, 73rd, 75th, 79th, Bronx's 40th, and 52nd, Manhattan's 30th, have very high rates. Contrast these rates with those of other precincts that had no murders in 2001 (Manhattan's 17th and 20th and Brooklyn's 68th). The area that had the greatest number of murders, Brooklyn's East New York section (the 75th precinct) had thirty-six murders. Compare this with the two murders that took place in the neighboring precinct, the 102nd.

In short, the murders in New York City are distributed extremely unevenly, with most areas relatively safe and a few areas very dangerous. This might calm those who are erroneously convinced that New York City is the most dangerous place on earth. This is simply not the case unless you decide to live in Brooklyn's East New York section, Manhattan's Harlem neighborhood, or various sections of the South Bronx.

Variations in Murder Sites

Marvin Wolfgang,[5] in his classic study of homicides in Philadelphia, noted that murders were divided relatively evenly between the home and places outside the home. Homicides that occurred outside the home, or street killings, tended to take place in areas near restaurants and bars. Alexander Pokorny[6] found the same to be true in his study of Houston, Texas, homicides. Kenneth Tardiff and Elliott Gross[7] studied the homicides of 460 males and seventy-six females in Manhattan in 1981 to determine where exactly they took place. They discovered that men tended to be murdered outside of buildings (52 percent) while women were killed inside buildings (62 percent). Many of the women were actually murdered in their own homes (46 percent) or within ten blocks of their home (16 percent). Men, on the other hand, tended to be murdered outside of their neighborhoods (61 percent). Tardiff and Gross also found patterns of victims killed inside buildings: women were more likely to be murdered in the bedrooms or

Table 4.8
New York City Police Precincts and Homicides—2001
(Total—649 Homicides)

Location	Precinct	Homicides	Location	Precinct	Homicides
Manhattan			**Bronx**		
Tribeca, Wall Street	1	1	South Bronx	40	27
Chinatown/Lt. Italy	5	3	Hunts Point	41	12
Greenwich Village	6	1	Tremont	42	18
Lower East Side	7	3	Soundview	43	14
East Village	9	2	Morris Heights	44	30
Chelsea	10	3	Schuylerville	45	5
Gramercy	13	2	University Hts.	44	30
Midtown South	MTS	4	Eastchester	47	17
Midtown	17	0	Fordham	48	13
Midtown North	MTN	5	Baychester	49	5
East Side	19	1	Riverdale	50	8
West Side	20	1	Bedford Park	52	23
Central Park	CPP	1			
Upper East Side	23	10	**Location**	**Precinct**	**Homicides**
Upper West Side	24	3	**Queens**		
East Harlem	25	7	Rockaway	100	1
Mannaside Hts.	26	1	Far Rockaway	101	6
Central Harlem	28	8	Richmond Hill	102	2
Harlem	30	12	Jamaica	103	11
Harlem	32	22	Woodside	104	5
Washington Hts.	33	8	Queens Village	105	17
Washington Hts.	34	7	Ozone Park	106	4
			Fresh Meadows	107	4
Location	**Precinct**	**Homicides**	Long Island City	108	3
Brooklyn			Flushing	109	5
Coney Island	60	11	Elmhurst	110	9
Sheepshead Bay	61	6	Bayside	111	1
Bensonhurst	62	5	Forest Hills	112	0
Flatlands/Mill Basin	63	4	S. Jamaica	113	10
Boro Park	66	1	Astoria	114	5
East Flatbush	67	22	Jackson Hts.	115	5
Bay Ridge	68	0			
Canarsie	69	7	**Location**	**Precinct**	**Homicides**
Kensington	70	13	**Staten Island**		
Flatbush	71	14	St. George	120	7
Sunset Park	72	7	New Dorp	122	4
Brownsville	73	26	Tottenville	123	2
East New York	75	36			
Carroll Gardens/					
Red Hook	76	4			
Crown Heights	77	19			
Park Slope	78	0			
Bedford/Stuyvesant	79	25			
Brownsville/Bed-Stuy	81	18			
Bushwick	83	11			
Brooklyn Hts.	84	3			
Fort Greene	88	11			
Williamsburg	90	12			
Greenpoint	94	5			

Source: data from *Statistical Report: Complaints and Arrests—2001*. New York: New York City Police Department; precinct names from *The Vera Institute Atlas of Crime and Justice in New York City*, 1993, p. 62.

bathrooms; men were killed most often in living-rooms, hallways, bars, restaurants, and in places of work. They discovered that women who had been killed outside were often found in parks, yards, parking lots, etc., while men killed outside were often found in streets, cars, subways and buses, and on roofs.

James Mercy et. al.[8] found similar trends in their analysis of Los Angeles murders (1971–1979): 71 percent of Caucasian women, 71 percent of black women, and 65 percent of Hispanic women victims were killed in their homes; 55 percent of Caucasian men, 50 percent of Black men, and 38 percent of Hispanic men were killed "in the street."

In substance, the gender of the victim tells us a great deal about the probable location of their murder, so much so that oftentimes the very place of the murder can be ascertained with a fair degree of accuracy. Common, predictable scenarios would include women murdered in their own bedrooms and men murdered either in a tavern or in a street adjacent to one. These patterns assist police in solving the crime, since the bedroom victims are often killed by their husbands or boyfriends and the barroom victims are usually murdered by acquaintances with whom they were drinking. Generally, it doesn't take Hercule Poirot or Sherlock Holmes to solve these cases.

If we look at those murders committed outside the home, the work-place must also be considered since these killings entail a significant segment of annual murders.

Of the following seven cases, the first four took place outside; the remaining three occurred inside a home.

CASE 75

In late 1994, in a classic case of "road rage," Donald Graham, fifty-six, used a crossbow to murder Michael Blodgett, forty-two, an emergency medical technician. As both were traveling on I–95 in the New Bedford area of Massachusetts, Blodgett apparently cut off Graham, a retired autoworker and Baptist Church deacon. Graham, enraged, chased Blodgett for seven miles and forced him off the road. As the two men confronted each other, Graham retrieved a crossbow from the trunk of his car, placed a razor-tipped arrow in it, and shot the victim in the chest. Blodgett died of cardiac arrest due to the massive loss of blood. A Massachusetts jury found Graham guilty of first-degree murder and sentenced him to life in prison.

CASE 76

Typical of many murders, the killing of Duren Eldridge, thirty-one, started over a trivial matter. Eldridge was regarded by many as a raucous, beer-drinking bully when he moved into an affluent neighborhood in Leesburg, Virginia, next door to Robert Lorenz, fifty-four, a shy, somewhat cantankerous man who prided himself on his meticulous flower garden in the front of his house. Trouble started the day Eldridge moved in and his dogs urinated on Lorenz's flowers. Feelings of hostility festered between the neighbors and on April 9, 1995, violence erupted. Eldridge, who was drunk, started taunting Lorenz with insults. He urged a teenage friend to skateboard in front of Lorenz's home and the boy allegedly skated on his lawn. Lorenz called the police over the incident and Eldridge berated him and wife, calling them cowards as he approached their front door, taunting Lorenz to come out so he "could kick his ass." Lorenz eventually came out with a .380 semiautomatic pistol and shot Eldridge, killing him. At the trial, a jury acquitted Lorenz, believing that he killed Eldridge to save his own life.

CASE 77

Lawrence Williams, twenty-eight, moonlighted as a bouncer at the D'Cachet nightclub in Northeast Washington D.C., a club which attracted go-go bands and rival gang members to its premises. Go-go is a live funk music characterized by nonstop percussion (drums, congas, etc.) where the beat goes on and on. Williams provided security for one of these bands, the Junk Yard Band, whose appearance several years earlier had sparked disturbances at D'Cachet. At 3 A.M. on Sunday, January 12, 1997, an assailant waited until the club closed and sprayed patrons and security outside the club with automatic fire, killing Williams and injuring seven patrons. Police believe that the shooting took place to avenge insults in earlier Junk Yard Band incidents. Williams had a seven-year-old daughter and was described by family members as hard working, quiet, and well raised.

CASE 78

Hugh Walkup, forty, and John Navin, forty, had been close friends for many years and lived next door to each other in Colorado Springs,

Colorado. On April 21, 1997, the two men argued with each other over whether or not a three-legged dog should be shot in order to put it out of its misery. The dog had been struck by a car earlier that evening. During the ensuing argument outside their residence over what to do with the dog, Walkup fatally shot Navin and was later arrested and charged with second-degree murder. The dog, a Labrador retriever, was reported to be "doing fine" at a local animal shelter. Walkup received a six-year prison sentence after a jury convicted him of manslaughter.

Case 79

Ian Pertos, twenty-two, never denied that he strangled his live-in girlfriend, Kila Blount, twenty-one. The pair had a stormy relationship and on Friday night, August 9, 1997, in Richmond, Virginia, violence erupted. Pertos claimed that Blount was seeing another man and having sex with him. On the fateful night, Pertos recognized his rival's phone and pager numbers on Blount's pager. She went into the bedroom to make a call that he assumed was to his rival. He then took the drawstring from his shorts and started to choke her. He claimed he only wanted to scare her, not kill her. As he was doing this, the pager rang and he thought he saw his rival's number on it and claimed that he simply snapped and killed his girlfriend.

At his trial, the medical examiner testified that it took Blount several minutes to die and that her death was not as quick as Pertos had claimed. Following the murder, Pertos purchased garbage bags, placed the victim in them, and dumped the body in the woods. The next morning he pawned her jewelry for $50 and a few days later withdrew Blount's direct-deposit paycheck of $350 from her account. He then fled to his aunt's home on Long Island, New York, where he was apprehended. The jury found him guilty of first-degree murder, accepting the prosecutor's argument that the crime was cold and calculated and not a crime a crime of passion. Pertos is in prison, and will not be eligible for release until 2036.

Case 80

Donna Bocket, forty-one, knew her killer, Anthony Libardi, fifty-six, quite well. Both were neighbors in their Yaphank, Long Island, community and years earlier Bocket had been a babysitter for Libardi's children. On January 22, 1998, Libardi, who had developed a sexual interest in the victim, waited until her husband and children left her home and then went to visit her. When she resisted his advances he strangled her in her home, put her body in her own car, drove to a nearby supermarket parking area, and dumped her body. He then fled to Las Vegas after he realized that Suffolk County, New York, police suspected that he was the killer. He was arrested in Las Vegas two weeks later and charged with Bocket's murder. A jury found Libardi guilty of second-degree murder. He received a twenty-five-years-to-life prison term.

Case 81

Andrea Will, eighteen, and Justin Boulay, twenty, students at Eastern Illinois University, had been dating for a few months, when Will decided to end their relationship. On February 3, 1998, Boulay went to her apartment in Charleston, Illinois, and strangled her. After the killing he left a note indicating that he had killed her and telephoned his parents in Chicago to tell them that he was in trouble. Police charged Boulay with the murder. Following his conviction on a first-degree murder charge, Boulay was sentenced to twenty-five years in prison.

Workplace Killings

In the past few years the public's attention has focused on a rash of murders in post offices, so much so that a new term has been added to our lexicon—"going postal"—which refers to someone who "goes berserk," "loses it," and kills a number of fellow workers or supervisors. This raises the issue of occupational violence and murder at the workplace, and begs the question: do murders that occur at the workplace play a significant role in the overall patterns of American murders? They certainly do. In 1997, the National Institute of Occupational Safety and Health (NIOSH) reported that an average of twenty workers are murdered weekly in the United States. Homicide is the second leading cause of workplace deaths; only motor vehicle deaths exceed homicides. For females, homicide is the leading cause of workplace fatalities. NIOSH's analysis of these homicides indicates that the primary cause of these killings is robbery related (71 percent); a rela-

Table 4.9
Workplace Violence Rates—1997*

Type of Workplace Most Vulnernable	
1. Taxi Industry	41.4
2. Liquor Stores	7.5
3. Detective/Protective Services	7.0
4. Gas/Service Station	4.8
5. Jewelry Stores	4.7

Type of Occupation Most Vulnerable	
1. Taxicab Driver/Chauffers	22.7
2. Sheriffs/Bailiffs	10.7
3. Police/Detectives	6.1
4. Gas Station/Garage Workers	5.9
5. Security Guards	5.5

*per 100,000; Source: *Violence in the Workplace*, 1997.

tively small number (9 percent) are committed by either a coworker or a former coworker.[9] Table 4.9 lists the workplaces and occupations in which homicides are most likely to occur.

The workplace and the occupation most vulnerable is the taxicab/chauffer industry where the homicide rate of cabbies and limo drivers is sixty times the overall national occupational rate. Table 4.10 shows the annual number of workplace homicides and how they have declined since the early 1990s.

Table 4.10
Annual Number of Workplace Homicides, 1992–2003*

Year	Number of Homicides
1992	1,044
1993	1,074
1994	1,080
1995	1,036
1996	927
1997	860
1998	714
1999	651
2000	677
2001	643 (excludes terror attacks)
2002	609
2003	631 (preliminary)

*Source: U.S. Department of Labor, Bureau of Labor Statistics, *Census of Occupational Injuries, 2003*, p. 5

Why do these places and occupations have relatively high rates of homicide? Jenkins and Castillo suggest that robbery is a primary motive and summarize the research of others, indicating that money exchange, working alone at night in high-crime areas, protecting valuable property, etc., play significant roles in exposing these workers to lethal violence.[10] How often has each of us read about a cabbie shot in his cab, or a convenience store cashier murdered behind the counter, or a police officer gunned down in a narcotics buy-and-bust deal? Clearly certain occupational situations are more susceptible to homicide than others.

CASE 82

At the United States Postal Service Central Office in Milwaukee, Wisconsin, on December 17, 1997, the feud between Anthony Deculit, thirty-seven, and his supervisor Joan Chitwood, fifty-five, reached the violent stage. Deculit had received a written reprimand from Chitwood for sleeping on the job a month earlier; he in turn filed a number of complaints against her. On the fateful day, Deculit arrived at work and after a few hours drew a semiautomatic handgun, shot Chitwood in the eye and then proceeded to shoot Russel Smith, forty-two, in the head, killing him. He then shot another worker, Roderick Patterson, forty-four, as he attempted to flee. Both Chitwood and Patterson survived their wounds. As Deculit fled to another part of the building he was cornered by police, at which point he placed the gun in his mouth and killed himself. After the incident, a co-worker at the facility referred to Deculit as "just a regular guy." Other workers told reporters that they faced considerable stress at their jobs, particularly with the large volume of holiday mail that demanded overtime work.

CASE 83

In 1992, six workers at the James River Papermill plant in Green Bay, Wisconsin, became suspicious of a co-worker, Thomas Monfils, thirty-three, who had anonymously called police to alert them that one of the six, Keith Kutska, forty-four, planned to steal electrical wiring from the mill. Kutska, under the Wisconsin's open-records statute, obtained a copy of the tape of the anonymous call. Monfils was then confronted by Kutska and five fellow workers (Ray Moore, forty-eight; Mike Hem, twenty-five; Michael Johnson, forty-seven; Dale Basten, fifty-three; Mike Piaskowski, forty-six) with a copy of the tape. Prosecutors contended that the men then assaulted Monfils, broke his jaw, fractured his skull and ribs, placed a fifty-pound weight around his neck, and tossed him into a two-story vat of liquid pulp, where he drowned. His body was found the next day after the vat was drained. A friend of Kutska told prosecutors that he had told her, "I am the one that killed Tom Monfils," and that his only regret was that the men threw him in the wrong vat; a second vat would have chewed him up so that the body would have never been found. None of the six men would break their silence as to what happened on that fateful day, though other workers testified that they saw the six men near Monfils at the time of his murder. In the subsequent trial it was revealed that after beating Monfils, the six feared they would be fired for striking another worker and lose their high-paying jobs. All six were found guilty and received life sentences for the murder. Wisconsin then passed what became know as the Monfils Law, which forbids the release of tapes of anonymous calls made to the police. In 2000, one of those convicted, Michael Piaskowski, was released from prison by a federal judge who ruled that there was insufficient evidence linking him to the crime.

CASE 84

On January 19, 1998, Deshon Ellis, fifteen, entered a laundry in Brooklyn, New York, seeking a victim to rob. There he encountered Vitaly Bereslavsky, fifty, a recent Latvian immigrant. Ellis shot the worker in the chest, killing him. He retrieved two dollars in quarters from the victim's pockets and then went to a nearby delicatessen where he spent the money on snacks. When arrested by police shortly after the murder he told them that he shot Bereslavsky because he "was hungry." The murdered man had been widowed after his wife died while giving birth to their son five years earlier. He left behind a nine-year-old daughter. A court found him guilty of second-degree murder, sentencing him to nine years-to-life in prison.

CASE 85

Edilberto Sangco, fifty-five, had been suspended for a week from his job as an electrician at the General Chemical plant in Richmond,

California for failing to follow a normal workplace procedure at the facility. On March 23, 1998, he took his revenge by killing two of his supervisors and then himself. He waited for his victims as they approached the lunch truck outside the plant and shot Dale Laughlin, a production manager, and David Bradley, a maintenance supervisor. He never attempted to shoot any other workers and apparently targeted only those two men. Following the shooting he calmly walked away from the lunch wagon and shot himself.

CASE 86

On March 17, 1998, the office of the Ohio Bureau of Employment Services in Columbus became the scene of a murder-suicide involving two executives of the Bureau. William Evans, fifty-one, the director of business management, and Shasta Dotson, forty, the chief of office services, had been dating each other for over eight years. Dotson, a single mother of two teenage children, broke off her relationship with Evans because she planned to marry another man. Evans, deeply despondent over the breakup, walked up to Dotson as she was speaking on the telephone and shot her three times with a .38 caliber revolver. He then shot himself once in the head. She died at her desk and he died three hour later at a Columbus hospital. Witnesses said that there was no scuffle or argument immediately before the shooting.

Notes

1. Baller, et al., 2001, p. 561.
2. Parker, 1989; Messner, 1982, 1983, 1985; Corzine, Huff-Crozine, and Whitt, 1999.
3. Curtis, 1975; Dixon and Lizotte, 1987.
4. Loftin and Hill, 1974; Sampson, 1987.
5. Marvin Wolfgang, 1958, pp. 120–130.
6. Alexander Pokorny, 1965, p. 481.
7. Kenneth Tardiff and Elliott Gross, 1986, p. 419.
8. James Mercy et al., 1986, p. 433.
9. Violence in the Workplace, 1997.
10. Jenkins and Castillo, 1993, p. 101.

5

Motives of Homicide

Why would one person kill another? What drives one person to use a club to bludgeon an acquaintance in a barroom dispute, another to shoot a convenience store cashier in an armed robbery, still another to stab his spouse in a heated argument?

Murder always has a motive—people do not kill each other without reason. To outside observers these reasons may seem banal, irrational, or even psychotic. Yet to killers, the reasons to commit homicide are very real and their actions are purposeful and self-justified. In the killer's mind, more often than not, the victim deserved to be murdered for a perceived insult or inexcusable behavior. This accounts for the oft-noted lack of remorse on the part of the murderer for his actions and his lack of sympathy for his victim. He dismisses any sense of guilt over the lethal act, an act that took place, often over trivial, ridiculous, and minor perceived provocations. The killer frequently rationalizes his actions by what Gresham Sykes and David Matza termed techniques of neutralization.[1] These techniques are psychological mechanisms by which killers (or any wrongdoers) neutralized their guilt (e.g. "Why should I be sorry for killing her—she deserved it." "Why should I be sorry—I'm glad I killed him for the way he humiliated me." "The knife went into his chest—I couldn't control its direction." "She's a ninety-year-old witch who would have died anyway—I did her a service by strangling her." "It couldn't have been me who killed him—I'd never do anything like that;" etc.) Whatever the rationalization, the killer emerges unscathed in his own mind, his conscience blocked by the techniques that allow him to believe he hasn't done anything wrong. The killer thus neutralizes the shock and disdain directed at him from outside observers. Not only does he refuse to admit to himself that what he did was, on the contrary, wrong, immoral, or evil, but he convinces himself that the act was in fact justified, moral, and good. A guilty conscience simply evades the psychic makeup of most murderers. Homicide detectives frequently remark that the people they arrest for murder often fall asleep in the police station house. Why shouldn't they, since they have already convinced themselves of the merit of their crimes? As Jack Katz has termed it, "A righteous slaughter has been enacted".[2]

Then there are those murders where the killer feels pushed into murdering another. His decision to slay another may not necessarily be due to an inner conscious decision to do so. Rather it may be the response to the physical actions of another who ends up dead in the ensuing struggle or confrontation. Hans Von Hentig, who first investigated this motivation for homicide, termed killings "victims precipitated murders".[3] These occur in a confrontation wherein the victim— the person eventually killed—was the first one to use physical force in the confrontation. A classic example of such a killing would be a drunken husband beating his wife, whereupon she fatally stabs him. Another would be a barroom argument where one drunk patron punches another who in turn slays him. The initial motivation of such killers is neither pre-meditation nor even the intent to kill before the act. It is the victim's aggression that begins the fatal sequence of actions that result in his or her own death. These murders are not classic self-defense, assuming that the killer had a reasonable way out of the initial aggressive encounter (e.g. the beaten wife had a means of exiting the area where she was being verbally and physically assaulted; the patron the bar who had been pushed by the eventual victim could have decided to leave the tavern, etc.). Though physically provoked, the eventual slayer's actions are disproportionate to the victim's prior aggression.

CASE 87

Ryan Winn, sixteen, and Chris Colombi, seventeen, disliked each other intensely. Both had been feuding for several months before their fatal encounter at a backyard beer party on July 4, 1995 in a fashion-

able section of north Phoenix, Arizona. Winn had been a star basketball player at Shadow Mountain High School; Colombi considered
himself a rebel and a gangster and ran with a mostly local gang known
as Piru Blood. He had attended the same school as Winn but trans-
ferred to another because he feared he would be beaten by the jocks at
lunchtime. Weeks earlier, Winn has sought out Colombi to beat him,
but Colombi backed out of the fight. Both vowed that they would fight
to the next time they met. At the party, Colombi and some friends
arrived, uninvited. Winn challenged him and then punched Colombi in
the head. His adversary then pulled out a gun and fatally shot Winn
three times in the chest. Fellow members of Winn's basketball team
including Danny Richardson, eighteen, pursued Colombi and his friends
but could not catch them. Colombi was later apprehended by police;
he cited self-defense as his motive.

Three months later Richardson himself was murdered. On October
2, 1995, he along with his twin brother Paul and two companions,
Patrick McCarville and Jeff Christiano visited the Paradise Valley
Mall. There they encountered three other youths who were total strangers to them—Mike Shoemaker, seventeen, Tommy Lopez, eighteen,
and Greg Acevedo, seventeen. As both groups passed each other in the
mall's food court, Lopez and Christiano bumped shoulders. Lopez
challenged the group and Paul Richardson accepted it. In the ensuing
battle Shoemaker stabbed McCarville and Acevedo stabbed both
Richardson brothers; Danny Richardson died in the attack. The assailants claimed they were first assaulted by the victims who had thrown
the first punches in the confrontation, but eyewitnesses told police it
was mutual combat.

The deaths of Winn and Danny Richardson and the near-fatal wounding of Paul Richardson and Patrick McCarville stunned the local community. Police indicated that both conflicts had more to do with teenage macho and testosterone than with gang violence. A police spokesman stated that "the basketball players brought fists to a knife fight."
Neither group would back down, and risk losing "face" with others.
Chris Colombi received a twenty-two-year sentence. Greg Acevedo
was sentenced to six years for negligent homicide and seven years for
aggravated assault, both sentences to run consecutively. Michael Shoemaker pleaded guilty to reckless endangerment and received a one-
year prison sentence.

CASE 88

Tom Roberts, forty-seven, terrified David Lewis, forty-seven. His defense attorney claimed that Roberts had abused Lewis for many years, that his client suffered from "battered person's syndrome." So frightened was Lewis of Roberts that he carried a 9 mm handgun for protection. In 1996 in Forward, Pennsylvania, near Pittsburgh, Lewis and Roberts confronted each other as Lewis cut wood in a field. Lewis told police that Roberts told him to put the chain saw down or he would "wrap it around your head." Lewis pulled out his gun and warned his adversary to stay away. Roberts refused to do so and picked up a tree limb, coming toward Lewis who then shot him, twice in the head, once in the stomach, and once in the back, killing him. He then burned his victim, according to Detective Chris Kearns, and drove Roberts' truck to a lonely section near Rastraven, Pennsylvania, punctured a tire to make it appear that Roberts had abandoned it and simply disappeared. A few days later he told police what happened and led them to the burned body. He pleaded self-defense, but prosecutors disputed this, indicating that the bullet in Roberts' back contradicted a self-defense argument. At his trial in February 1998, Lewis pleaded guilty to third-degree murder, and received a five-to-ten year prison sentence.

CASE 89

Scott Falater, forty-three, claimed that he loved his wife Yarmilla and never would harm her, yet in 1997 he stabbed her forty-seven times and dumped her body into their swimming pool of their Phoenix, Arizona, home. He indicated to police that he had no memory of the murder, which his lawyers said took place during a sleepwalking episode. He claimed that he and Yarmilla had enjoyed a near-perfect twenty-year marriage, with two wonderful children. Falater testified in a court "I loved her . . . There's no way I could do that, not intentionally". Prosecutors argued otherwise, saying that the marriage between Scott and Yarmilla was far from perfect, that Yarmilla had complained to neighbors about the strains in the relationship caused by the demands of her husband's Mormon faith and beliefs, a faith to which she had earlier converted but was now reconsidering. Prosecutors further argued that the defense claim of Falater's sleepwalking was ridiculous since his actions at the time of the murder were quite deliberate and calculated. They cited the testimony of the next door neighbor who observed Falater go inside his home after the attack, wash his hands, command his dog to lie down, then push his wife's body into the pool and held her head under water. A jury refused to believe the sleep-walking defense, convicted Falater of first-degree murder in June 1999 and sentenced him to life in prison.

CASE 90

Leo Wright, thirty-eight, told Washington D.C. police in his December 2000 taped confession that he had not planned to kill Bettina Pruckmayr, twenty-six, a human rights lawyer. On December 16, 2000, he abducted Pruckmayr in her car and drove her to her local bank where he tried unsuccessfully to use her ATM card. He claimed he needed money for drugs. He then stabbed her thirty-eight times with a hunting knife, killing her. Arrested soon after, Wright told police, "It's not like I stabbed her on purpose. Everything just went haywire . . . I panicked and we just got into a tussle." Convicted of a previous murder of a cabdriver in 1976, Wright used similar words in his rationalization of that killing: "We were tussling and I shot him." He served seventeen years for that murder, released on parole in 1993. After repeated violations of parole, and a drug distribution arrest in 1995, Wright remained on parole until his fatal encounter with Pruckmayr. At his trial, Wright pleaded guilty to murder and received a life sentence, without possibility of parole.

So what lies behind the reasons people commit homicides? What sets off the chain of events that leads to a fatal encounter between the assailant and victim? Generally, the motives for murder directly relate to the emotions and urges of the human condition. Homicide investigators find that people kill each other for the same reasons now as they did decades ago, a century ago, millennia ago. Cain killed Abel out of envy; David had Uriah killed out of lust; John Wilkes Booth assassinated Lincoln out of ideological fury and malice. People still kill each other in fits of rage, jealousy and revenge over real or perceived insults. They murder to improve their economic standing, to advance their status and prestige within their group, to act out their lust and sexual passions, and to mollify their fears and anxieties.

Occasionally they may even kill in self-defense, protecting either themselves or others from the predatory attacks of potential murderers. Often they kill in what D. Cohen[4] describes as a culture of honor, and what K. Polk terms honor contests, defending what they deem as their honor or dignity which another allegedly has trampled or sullied,[5] a thesis questioned by C. Loftin and D. McDowall (2003).

The *Uniform-Crime Reports* compiled by the Federal Bureau of Investigation provide a generalized glimpse of the motives and circumstances of thousands of murders committed in any particular year. Table 5.1 presents these circumstances for 2003.

Table 5.1
Murder Circumstance, 2003

Circumstances	
Total*	14,408
Felony type total:	2,359
Rape	43
Robbery	1,056
Burglary	93
Larceny-Theft	22
Motor Vehicle Theft	30
Arson	77
Prostitution and commercialized Vice	16
Other Sex Offenses	10
Narcotic Drug Laws	666
Gambling	6
Other—not specified	340
Suspected felony type	88
Other than Felony type total:	7,070
Romantic Triangle	98
Child killed by babysitter	29
Brawl due to influence of alcohol	128
Brawl due to influence of narcotics	53
Argument over money or property	220
Other arguments	3,806
Gangland killings	115
Juvenile gang killings	819
Institutional killings	13
Sniper attack	2
Other—not specified	1,787
Unknown	4,891

*Total number of murder victims for whom supplemental homicide information was received.
Source: *Crime in the United States—2003—Uniform Crime Reports*, Table 2.11 (abridged)

A cursory glance at the circumstances reveals that many of them involve motives that spring from the volatile nature of the human condition. Human weaknesses and foibles account for much of the criminal behavior and social chaos that are a part of daily life in America.

There are few innovations in the human tragedy; centuries ago philosophers and theologians sought to categorize the evils in the world. John Cassian (c. 420 A.D.) enumerated eight such dispositions or vices which are the source of all other evils. Pope Gregory the Great (c. 590 A.D.) took Cassian's list as well as the lists of other theologians (e.g., St. Cyprian and St. Columbanus) and reduced the vices to the seven with which we are now familiar. Thomas Aquinas (c. 1250 A.D.) combined pride and vainglory from earlier versions and made the final list of the seven capital sins: pride, avarice, lust, anger, envy, gluttony, and sloth. These seven capital, or deadly, sins eventually became part of the Christian heritage, particularly in the Western world. They are depicted in literature (Chaucer, Dante, Shakespeare), art (Michelangelo, Breughel, Bosch), and, in a less sublime fashion, current cinema as in the 1995 film *Seven*, directed by David Fincher.[6] The efforts of scholars and writers have enriched our understanding of sin and evil by categorizing the causes of human suffering.

Terms such as "sin" and "evil" are generally avoided by sociologists and criminologists; they are relegated to the glossaries of disciplines, such as theology, literature, and philosophy, simply because they do not fit into empirical positivistic models of inquiry. Yet how else are we to explain the behaviors of notable killers, such as Jack the Ripper, Ted Bundy, Edmund Kemper, John Wayne Gacy, and hundreds of others who defy the conventional stock explanations of the sources of deviance—poverty, broken homes, psychosis, racism, low intelligence levels, educational failure, etc. Their murderous acts are not covered by the usual "scientific" explanations of why we, as human beings, act the way we do. Environmental and social determinism scarcely help us understand the decision-making process of a killer in deciding to commit murder. Such determinism can never convincingly deal with the free choice a person exercises in pursuing crime. Perhaps Cassian, Gregory, Aquinas, Dante and other medieval observers knew more about the human condition than modern social scientists care to admit.

As one reviews the scenarios of the thousands of murders that occur annually in the United States, one cannot help but be struck by the presence of these vices in the etiology of the homicide act. The seven deadly sins are not misnamed, for their presence in the human heart predisposes the killer to commit a murderous deed. Let us examine each of these sins in detail, realizing that they often overlap and complement each other, wreaking havoc on individuals and communities.

Pride

Often regarded by medieval philosophers and theologians as the cardinal sin, the "queen of all the vices," pride traditionally tops the list of the deadly sins. The excessive love of one's own perceived excellence allows the proud man or woman to bask in self-exultation and self-adulation while simultaneously refusing to recognize or submit to the realistic assessments of others. The proud individual refuses to recognize any defects, faults, or limitations. He magnifies his own attributes and qualities and ignores or greatly minimizes his shortcomings. Arrogance, vainglory, self-centeredness, crass ambition, and feelings of superiority over others are all byproducts of pride, blinding the proud individual to reality as he or she strives to achieve their unrealistic goals and pretentious aims. They constantly seek what is beyond their capacity, yet they fail to grasp the futility of such actions. Proud persons do not back down during arguments or allow others to disparage their honor, sexuality, superiority, or assessment of a given situation. The proud individual looks down on others and assumes that they can be used or abused as need be. Essentially, the proud are trapped in their own dungeon of self-delusion and fantasy.

Pride is easily observed as a motivating factor in a substantial number of homicides. All too often, the thing that triggered the murder is pride: "he insulted me at the party"; "she just cast me aside for another"; "he tried to get ahead of me on the line"; "the jerk insulted my favorite team"; "he mocked my clothes," etc. The event which precipitated the murder often strikes outside observers as trivial and ridiculous, yet the killer, due to his or her pride, does not view it in that light. Rather, the killer's self-delusion and perceived superiority over others magnify a relatively small encounter into a major confrontation that must be mastered: "What will people think if I back down to that bum?"; "Who is she to insult me and tell me what to do?"; "I'll destroy him for trying to embarrass me in front of others"; "How dare he think he's better than me!" What is a molehill for others becomes an Everest for the proud. Truly, "pride cometh before the fall."

CASE 91

In 1993 Joey Fischer, eighteen, broke up with his girlfriend Cristina Cisneros. This was unacceptable to Cristina's mother, Dora Cisneros, sixty, the wife of a prominent Brownsville, Texas, physician. The mother plotted revenge for the dishonor done to her daughter, and ten months later she commissioned her seventy-seven-year-old fortuneteller, Maria Marting, to cast a spell on Fischer. The fortuneteller refused but did provide Cisneros with information on where she could hire an assassin to kill Fischer. As he washed his car before going to school, two Mexican hitmen killed him. Cisneros was sentenced to life in prison in 1993, but that verdict was overturned in state court because the jury did not receive sufficient instructions from the judge. In May 1998 Cisneros received a new trial and was again convicted in her murder-for-hire scheme and again received a life sentence. The hitmen were convicted of the charges in Mexico and are serving fifteen-year sentences there. The fortuneteller received a twenty-year prison term in a Texas prison.

CASE 92

Quentin Carter would have been thirteen years old if had not been murdered by Brian Wright, sixteen. In July 1995 in New York City, Wright demanded a quarter from Carter in front of Carter's friends. Carter refused to give Wright the money and sneered at him. Insulted, Wright told Carter, "I guess you're gonna die," to which Carter replied, "I guess you're gonna have to kill me." The following evening Wright found the boy, chased him, and shot him five times, killing him. Instead of preparing for his birthday, Carter's mother, aunt, five sisters and brother had to prepare for his funeral. His family had that day purchased a birthday cake to celebrate his first day as a teenager. Convicted of second-degree murder, Wright received a twenty-five-years-to-life sentence.

CASE 93

Ronald Shanabarger, thirty, was devastated when his father died in October 1996. When his girlfriend Amy, twenty-nine, refused to cut her vacation cruise short to comfort him, his pride was demolished. He decided to punish her for treating him so callously. The following May he married Amy and fathered their child, Tyler, whom he later killed "to make Amy feel the way he did when his father died."

Shanabarger had waited until the eve of Father's Day 1999 to exact his revenge. He entered his seven-month-old son's room in their home in Franklin, Indiana, and smothered the boy in his crib. Amy discovered the boy's body the next morning. Police and family assumed, as the coroner indicated, that Tyler had died from SIDS (Sudden Infant Death Syndrome), but they also noticed that Shanabarger was cold and aloof, offering no comfort to his distraught wife. After Tyler's funeral Shanabarger told his wife that he smothered the baby. When arrested, he told police officers that his plan of vengeance for Amy's insult to him three years earlier included marrying her and getting her pregnant. He then "allowed time for her to bond with the child, and then took his life." He also begged the police to shoot him for his deed. A court sentenced Shanabargar to a forty-nine-year prison term.

Avarice

Avarice, or greed, is the inordinate desire or love of riches. Pope Gregory the Great viewed avarice as the well from which flowed violence, fraud, deceit, perjury, and hardening of the heart towards those in need.[7] This vice forces the greedy into viewing the obtaining and keeping of money and possessions as the main purpose of life. Money and possessions are seen as the ends to live (and die and even kill!) for. Greed involves more than the accumulation of wealth so as to purchase or obtain material possessions; rather, it relates primarily to the accumulation of wealth as an end in itself. Other sins and crimes are committed in the pursuit of avarice that becomes the incentive for perpetuating all sorts of injustices. Greed is ultimately insatiable. The avaricious person never has enough and is obsessed with the fear of losing what he or she has accumulated.

The greedy individual seeks to hold onto possessions no matter what the cost. These possessions may be substantial, as in the case of the very wealthy who are inordinately attached to their millions, or insignificant, as in the case of the poor who cling tenaciously to what the few possessions they have even though they may be worthless or valueless in the eyes of others. All too often, people kill for what strikes others as inconsequential amounts of money or trivial material possessions. Whether rich or poor, the hoarder's obsession focuses almost entirely on material items and the means of either attaining or keeping them.

CASE 94

In March 1995, Joshua Torres, twenty-three, Nicholas Libretti, nineteen, and Jose Negron decided to kidnap Kimberly Antonakos, twenty, and hold her for $75,000 ransom. Libretti and Negron abducted the woman from her Brooklyn, New York, front yard and held her for three days in an empty, unheated Queens apartment where they tied her to a pole. The trio placed a call to the woman's wealthy father's answering machine and demanded the ransom. Unknown to the kidnappers, the machine failed to record the repeated demands. After no response from the victim's father, Torres doused Antonakos with gasoline, set her on fire, and burned her alive. Torres was found guilty of murder and was sentenced to fifty-eight years in prison. He was also charged with the murder of his accomplice Negron, allegedly because he feared that Negron would tell police about Torres' role as the mastermind of the crime. Torres was later acquitted of that murder. Libretti was found guilty of kidnapping and murder and sentenced to fifty-eight years in prison.

CASE 95

In February 1999, Michael Cole and his cousin Alexander Hall were driving together in a car in Lauderhill, Florida, when they began to argue. According to police the dispute arose over who owned tickets to a Super Bowl concert. As they argued, Cole shot Hall, who ran from the vehicle and collapsed in the parking lot of a nearby firehouse. Police indicated that Cole calmly walked up to Hall and shot him again, killing him. Cole was charged with first-degree murder. Following his conviction on second-degree murder, Cole was sentenced to life in prison.

CASE 96

In April 1999 in Hillsborough County, Florida, Gene Sexton, thirty-seven, and his half-brother Archie Yohn, thirty-five, argued over an

$80 loan. As the argument escalated, police indicated that Sexton picked up an aluminum baseball bat and hit Yohn in the head, killing him. Sexton later told the arresting officers that he killed his step-brother in self-defense, but investigators found nothing to substantiate his claim that the victim had attacked him. Sexton received a twenty-five-years-to-life sentence after his conviction of second-degree homicide.

CASE 97

Willie Mitchell, fifty-five, had fallen on hard times. A recluse, Mitchell had served in the military and worked steadily, but his ambition faded as he grew older. He lived in rusting trailer in Broxton, Georgia that had not had electricity or water for years. He had not paid his rent and his home was about to be hauled away. On January 4, 2000, a police officer, James Bryant, thirty-five, and a sheriff's deputy, Almond Merritt, fifty-three, arrived at the trailer for what they believed would be a routine eviction. Mitchell first shot Bryant and then later shot Merritt when he attempted to rescue the police officer. Mitchell later surrendered to police and was arraigned on two murder charges. One of his neighbors, Patrina Porter, stated, "He used to work until a few years ago. After that, he just let things go down. His pickup stopped running. He was probably just protecting his house because that's all he had left."

Lust

Lust can be described as the overwhelming and inordinate craving for carnal pleasure. Perhaps the most common of the deadly sins, it affects not only individuals, but communities as well. The pleasure derived from this vice leads to other forms of behavior which are judged to either be criminal, immoral, or both: fornication, adultery, rape, sodomy, and incest. This vice is hard to contain even though societies throughout the ages have always attempted to do so through laws, marriage arrangements and norms, and religious imperatives. Lyman describes lust as "a mysterious stranger who lodges in us but remains alternately unpredictable, cunning, foolish, and knavish. Always it moves or fails to move without notice or apology. Such a phenomenon was truly wondrous as well as troublesome".[8] Lust is difficult to control because it exerts such a strong grip on those within its grasp, and those within its grasp are legion.

In the criminal realm, many of the crimes against persons are directly related to lust, including forcible rape, prostitution, commercialized vice, pornography, sexual abuse, and certain types of aggravated assault. Most seriously, lust leads to homicide, either alone or in combination with other vices, such as anger, hostility (towards women in particular), revenge, sadism, perversion, etc. The media frequently describe incidents of children murdered by their abusers, prostitutes and homosexuals killed by their customers or lovers; wives and girlfriends slain by their husbands "in the heat of sexual passion"; women victimized by men who stalk them; children and women murdered by "sexual predators" who scarcely knew them—innocent bystanders killed by those covering up previous sexual crimes—all precipitated by the lustful craving for self-gratification, no matter what the cost or consequences to others.

Case 98

In the Watts neighborhood of Los Angeles, California, in August 1996, a group of seven young boys accosted a thirteen-year-old girl. They took her to an abandoned building where they raped and tortured her in an hour-long ordeal.

After their crimes the boys decided to conceal what they had done by locking the girl in a room and starting a fire to burn the building with her in it.

The house adjoining the abandoned building belonged to Viola McClain, an eighty-two-year-old grandmother and popular neighborhood figure. When her grandson Dumar Starks heard the commotion next door, he confronted the seven boys and told them to stop playing with fire. One of the youths pulled out a handgun whereupon Starks returned to his grandmother's house to get his own gun. Meanwhile, Viola McClain went out the front door to see what was happening and was struck dead by a stray bullet fired from the gun of a fifteen-year-old boy, who was subsequently charged with the shooting. The rape victim escaped the burning building and reported the entire incident to the police who apprehended the remaining youths (Boy Held in Shooting Death . . . , 1996). The killer was convicted of the murder and received three life sentences plus thirty years, but because of his age, he could be released when he turns twenty-five. He also had been found guilty of killing Patrick Birdsong, twenty-five, two weeks earlier.

CASE 99

When William Bosko, nineteen, returned to Norfolk, Virginia, after a week-long Navy cruise, he found his newlywed wife, Michelle Moore-Bosko, eighteen, dead in their home. She had been raped and stabbed multiple times. Daniel Williams, twenty-six, lived in the same apartment building as the new bride and told police investigators that he was obsessed with her. On July 8, 1997, Williams and six friends decided to rape her and then murder her to conceal the crime. They broke into her apartment and took turns raping her. To make sure none of the seven implicated the others if caught, each stabbed the woman so that each was equally culpable. Williams then strangled her. All seven were either in active service or had served in the Navy at the time of the murder. Williams pleaded guilty to rape and murder and was sentenced to life without parole as part of a plea that spared him the death penalty. Omar Ballard, twenty-two, received two life terms in prison. Joseph Dick, twenty-one, also received a life sentence, as did Derek Tice. Charges of murder against the other defendants were dropped or reduced to other crimes.

CASE 100

A jury in Valparaiso, Indiana, took just two hours to convict David Malinski, thirty-four, of the murder of Lorraine Kirkley, even though her body was never found. Malinski and Kirkley were co-workers in a local hospital and prosecutors claimed that Malinski tortured his victim before killing her in July 1999. They stated that Malinski was obsessed with her and had stalked her for months before the homicide. Malinski's defense lawyers claimed that he was only cooperating with Kirkley in a plot to fake her death so she could get out of an unhappy marriage and marry him, and that she was alive somewhere. The prosecution countered these claims with pictures of Kirkley naked and bound in handcuffs and bindings. They stated that Malinksi had burglarized the Kirkley home twice and had stolen and burned her car. On the day of her disappearance police found signs of a struggle in her kitchen, one lens of her eyeglasses under the stove, blood on the floor, and her asthma and thyroid medicine, which she would have taken with her if she were walking out on her husband. Friends and family testified that her marriage was in no danger of collapse and that she and her husband were moving to South Bend, Indiana, to start a family. Malinksi's obsession with her changed those plans.

Anger

Anger is the desire for revenge, a hatred directed at another as one seeks vengeance for some perceived wrong. In this context we are speaking of anger which is inappropriate for the situation, not anger which is justified or tempered in order to impose restitution for some prior evil deed. Thus, a person who hates another and wishes him or her evil would be included under the umbrella of the deadly sin of anger; one who seeks to punish another reasonably for a wrongdoing in order to correct bad behavior and restore justice would not be so included.

Anger refers to a disordered state of mind in the person seeking revenge on another, with the accompanying hatred and deliberate desire to harm the other. People in such a state of rage at others lash out in unreasonable ways and vent their anger on persons and things inappropriately. Those afflicted with this vice are quarrelsome, vengeful, malicious in speech and action, easily incensed when things do not go their way, furious when crossed, and unrestrained in their wrath. Perhaps the common idiom "fit to be tied" best describes the individual ensnared in the vice of anger.

When the inappropriate rage reaches its zenith or climax, violence against other people ensues. Table 4.10, which was cited earlier and categorizes the circumstances of murders, would reveal the precipitating influence of anger. Approximately one-third of all murders are due to arguments. As elaborated in our discussion of the seven sins, the circumstances that elicit homicidal rages are often petty and insignificant in the eyes of objective observers, yet they govern the subsequent homicidal act of the killer.

CASE 101

A series of four murders in Pennsylvania in 1995 began with an argument over a gerbil. Mark Spatz, twenty-three, was sleeping when the young son of his brother's fiancée placed his pet gerbil close to Spatz's head. Awakened and enraged, Spatz argued with his brother Dustin, twenty-five, who subsequently stabbed Mark. Mark Spatz then shot Dustin twice, killing him. The killer then fled to Schuylkill County. The following day police found the body of June Ohlinger, fifty-two, near her home in Pine Grove; she had been shot in the head and her car was missing. A day later Penny Gunnet, forty-one, was discovered shot and run over near North Cordorus. The last victim was found a day later near Carlisle. Police apprehended Spatz with his seventeen-year-old girlfriend, Christine Noland, in a Hanisburg motel. Noland was charged with the murder of Ohlinger and Spatz with the other murders in the killing spree.

Case 102

As Ernest Comegys, seventy, watched the 1996 Republican National Convention in his Dallas, Texas, home, he became enraged when Senator Bob Dole received the presidential nomination. After viewing the proceedings he retrieved a handgun from his bedroom and returned to the living room where he repeatedly shot his cousin Elbert James, seventy, killing him. He also wounded his stepdaughter, Gwen Nelson, who survived the attack, and then killed himself with a shot to the head. Police indicated that Comegys suffered from depression due to his terminal illness—cancer—and believed that Senator Dole's nomination was the spark that ignited the rampage.

Case 103

Haminder Sing Virk, fifty-four, was convicted of first-degree murder in the shooting death of his daughter Ranjit, eighteen. On May 13, 1999, in Kent, Washington, the father found his daughter asleep at the kitchen table where she was supposed to be studying for her driver's license examination. He later claimed that she had "made a face" at him and "curled her lip" when he woke her. Incensed, he retrieved a handgun and shot her five times in her body, reloaded, and shot her twice in the head. He turned himself in to police later that evening. At his trial his attorneys argued that he killed Ranjit because she wanted to break away from the strict rules of the Sikh religion of his homeland, India.

Envy

Envy, or jealousy, is resentment over the good fortune of another. The envious torture themselves by recognizing the success of another and creating an unrealistic and intemperate desire to attain similar good fortune, even by unjust or criminal means. The jealous feel that their own superiority is threatened by the material possessions of others or by their good reputation, health, security, or psychological well-being. Yet this good fortune is often beyond the reach of the jealous individual. Sadness, resentment, and a brooding hatred of the successful individual often result and take root if the envy is not controlled or contained.

The misfortunes of another cause a perverse joy in the jealous person, *schadenfreude* to an unhealthy degree. In extreme cases, the envious may seek to destroy the object of envy by ruining a good name, reputation, and even a life.

Unlike anger or lust, envy is an internal vice "more often experienced in isolation from one's associates, or as a secret sin to be hidden from view. . . Envy is likely to reside in a heart of darkness, a secret sharer as well as a corrosive product of the sorrow and anguish of unregulated desire".[9] It is no wonder that St. Augustine considered envy as the diabolical sin—a sin (unlike the other capital sins) that provides no pleasure to the envious. Hence, the envious are constantly attuned to the material possessions and social status of others. "Keeping up with the Joneses" assumes monumental significance, and the envious feel that they are lowered in the eyes of others if they do not have similar cars, clothing, beauty, status, etc. Resentment and brooding result, and the envious person does what has to be done to gain this esteem and status, sometimes through criminal means.

Thus the success of another constitutes a failure to the jealous individual—"If he rises, I fall"; "If I can't have her, no one will." Violence, assault, and even murder can spring from the jealous mind that has run amok.

Case 104

Felecia Scott, thirty-one, had a hysterectomy in 1991 and was obsessed with having a third child, which was impossible. In 1996 her envy led her to befriend Carethia Curry, seventeen, when she learned that the teenager was pregnant. On January 31, 1996, the two women went for pizza in Tuscaloosa, Alabama, and returned to Curry's apartment where Scott shot the expectant mother. She then cut out the full-term baby and stuffed Curry's body in a garbage can and discarded it in a local ditch. Scott pretended that the baby girl, who survived the ordeal, was her own child. Scott was arrested and convicted of the murder and received a life sentence in 1998. Her boyfriend, Frederick Polion, received twenty years for assisting in the kidnapping. At the time of the trial in 1998 the girl was $2^1/_2$-years-old and was living with her father.

CASE 105

Dr. James Kartell, fifty-nine, established his reputation as a respected plastic surgeon at Holy Family Hospital in Methuen, Massachusetts. His fellow doctors elected him as president of the hospital's medical staff on two different occasions. On February 23, 1999, Kartell decided to visit his estranged wife, Susan Kamm, who was a patient in the hospital. When he entered her room he found Janos Vajda, fifty-six, who was believed to be his wife's new boyfriend. An argument between the two men ensued and Kartell pulled out a revolver and shot Vajda in the head, killing him. Kartell was later admitted to the hospital's cardiac unit and was arraigned on murder charges in his hospital bed. Kamm, his estranged wife, also remained in the hospital recovering from her medical condition.

CASE 106

Elizabeth Otte, nineteen, a former honor student from Lanexa, Virginia, often had "jealous spells." She lived with Joseph Martinez and their one-year-old son Joseph. In September 1999 she was charged with the first-degree murder of young Joseph. According to friends Otte was jealous of the love Martinez displayed for their baby. Steve Walker, a neighbor of the young family, told police, "We'd go long spells without seeing her. She was jealous over the baby. She wasn't getting enough attention. She felt the baby was getting it all." The baby's father also indicated that Otte was jealous of their son.

On September 24, 1999, the baby's father awoke and could not find his son in his crib. The mother said she did not know where the baby was. Frantic, Martinez called family members who searched the house and property, as did local police. Finally the baby's aunt, Alina Martinez, found young Joseph in the microwave oven. The medical examiner stated that the burns on the boy's body were consistent with microwave burns. Otte claimed that she had suffered an epileptic seizure that morning and thought she was placing the baby's milk bottle in the microwave for heating. A Hanover County jury convicted Otte of involuntary manslaughter and the judge sentenced her to ten years in prison, with five years suspended.

Gluttony

Gluttony, perhaps the most ignoble of the seven deadly sins, involves the excessive and inordinate indulgence in food, drink, or other substances in such a manner as to be injurious to the health and well-being of oneself or others. In addition, the excessive ingestion of these materials may actually impair the glutton's mind and his ability to reason properly, as can be seen in the case of alcoholics and narcotic addicts.

Addiction characterizes the physical and emotional state of the glutton. Fueled by an insatiable desire, the glutton's thoughts are always focused on the next meal, the next drink, or the next fix. Aptly, the actions of the glutton are often compared to animals in pursuit of nourishment: "She eats like a beast"; "He pigged out"; "They wolf down their food"; "He drinks like a fish." Overeating, drunkenness and drug use are stigmatized by society either as a moral failing or as a disease not only because of what they do to the glutton, but also because they often lead to other vices which follow in gluttony's wake and further entrap the person afflicted with this vice. Lust and greed have traditionally been associated with gluttony since the pursuit of engorging oneself physically spills over into craving and hoarding the means to satiate other physical desires. Whether voluntary or involuntary in its etiology, gluttony is a vice despised by the larger society.

The negative social and criminal ramifications of gluttony are readily apparent in contemporary life. The chronic overeater certainly endangers himself and can be considered, at least indirectly, to be engaging in a slow form of self-destruction. The person who drinks and drives is a threat to the entire community, as are crackheads and heroin addicts in pursuit of their next high. Gluttony may be a personal vice, but its repercussions are social and catastrophic when the repercussions surrounding the inordinate desire for food and drink lead to lethal violence. The excessive desire for satiation can have fatal consequences.

CASE 107

In June 1995 John Fearance, Jr., forty, died of a lethal injection in the Huntsville, Texas, State Prison for the stabbing death of a neighbor, Larry Faircloth, in 1977. He stated that he had returned home from his job at a car repair facility and discovered that his wife had cooked a casserole for him with meat in it. He stated that he liked his meat on the side of the casserole, not baked in it. Enraged, he broke into two houses in his Dallas, Texas, neighborhood, one of which was Faircloth's. He stabbed Faircloth nineteen times. Fearance had been arrested previously once for rape and twice for larceny-theft. At his execution he told the warden and witnesses, "I don't have any hate towards humanity. I didn't mean to and I'm ready to go meet my Maker." His last words before his death were, "Hail Mary."

CASE 108

On June 22, 1996, Kiev Rouse, twenty-six, was having pizza with Tammy Allison and her twenty-month-old son James. When the boy was bringing a slice of the pizza to Rouse, he accidentally dropped it on the kitchen floor. Enraged at the child for ruining his supper, Rouse struck James several times on the head and then slammed him against the wall with such force that pieces of the boy's hair were embedded in the wall. Rouse then put the boy to bed and did not allow Tammy Allison to care for him or give him any medical attention. The next morning the boy was dead. An autopsy revealed that he died of blunt trauma to the head. Evidence suggested that the child suffered from prior physical abuse. At his trial Rouse said, "I really believe that I will never do this again." He received a twenty-eight-year prison sentence.

CASE 109

John Grace, fifty-two, awoke hungry from his nap in Fort Lauderdale, Florida, on March 21, 1999. He decided to eat a steak that his girlfriend had cooked but discovered that she had fed the steak to her two children. Outraged that they had eaten his steak, he began to beat the children and argue with their mother. In the ensuing confrontation his girlfriend picked up the steak knife and stabbed him in the chest.

CASE 110

When a fifteen-year-old boy returned to his Staten Island, New York, home one day in April 2000, he told his mother that his jacket had been stolen. His mother took him to report the crime whereupon he was arrested for the murder of Sarif Saed, eighteen, a clerk at the Second Eden delicatessen in the neighborhood. Police reported that the fifteen-year-old had been in the process of stealing snack foods when Saed caught him. The boy then shot Saed dead and wounded two other store employees, Susaim Mused, forty-one, and Shawn Heyes, twenty-eight. In the confusion surrounding the shooting, the killer inadvertently dropped his coat outside the convenience store. The mother had no idea that her boy had shot anyone when she took him to the police precinct.

CASE 111

Hunger motivated five youths—Darryl Tyson, seventeen, Jamel Murphy, seventeen, Stacy Royster, seventeen, James Stone, sixteen, and Robert Savage, fourteen, to kill Jin-Sheng Liu, forty-four, a father of two children, an immigrant from China, and owner of the Golden Wok Restaurant in St. Albans, Queens, in New York City.

On September 1, 2000, the five teens finished a Chinese meal they had purchased at another take-out store when they decided to get more to eat. Having no money, they plotted to order $60 worth of shrimp and chicken from the Golden Wok and ambush Liu when he delivered the meal. Royster phoned the order on her cell phone and requested that it be delivered to an abandoned building in the area. When Liu arrived with the order the youths rushed him, threw a blanket over his head, and beat him to death with a brick. The five assailants then ran off to Tyson's house where they calmly ate the food. Police arrested all five when they traced the phone order to Royster's phone. In custody, each of the youths accused the others of the killing. All were charged with second-degree murder, robbery, and weapon possession. The lawyer for Savage, who reportedly killed Liu with the brick, stated that his client told him that he didn't hit anyone; he dropped it without hitting Liu. Stone received a seventeen-year prison sentence, Tyson, sixteen years, Savage, seven years to life.

Sloth

Sloth refers to the avoidance of effort with an indifference to work, exertion, or fulfilling one's duties and obligations, a disgust for what is noble and good in life. It is characterized by a hostility and resentment towards what one should be doing because the effort to do so is perceived to be too great and time-consuming. Sadness, melancholy, pusillanimity, laziness, boredom, and despair replace joy, hope, and the pleasures of life in the spirit of the slothful individual.

One form of sloth leads to profound cowardly inaction, a failure to do what is good when required to do so. In effect, the lethargy and silence of the slothful person permit evil to proceed, for the mental fatigue and spiritual inertia preclude any meaningful defense of evil tendencies. Sloth allows evil to happen while the person does nothing to intervene. The slothful sit and do nothing as their world crumbles around them, paralyzed by their own apathy. Indeed, idleness is in fact the devil's workshop.

How often have we read of horrifying crimes that resulted from the mental paralysis of those who could have prevented them? How often has this melancholy or sadness or despondency led to the slaughter of entire families? Sloth runs much deeper than the clinical depression that also produces paralysis of action. Sloth targets one's duties and obligations that are either avoided or ignored. In other areas of behavior the slothful appear quite "normal." Yet sloth should not be confused with clinical depression. Clinical depression is all-encompassing and pervades the entire personality, paralyzing its victims and behavioral responses of those afflicted; sloth's devastation remains more circumscribed and more easily masked from the view of others. The slothful person may be actually busy and occupied, for inactivity alone does not constitute sloth.

CASE 112

Patricia Mudd, twenty-seven, had a history of abusing her children. In 1988 she had spent four months in prison for attacking her young daughter and fracturing her ribs. In 1992 she locked her 7-month-old son Trevor in a car for eight hours while she worked in a Jacksonville, Florida, fast-food restaurant. The windows were left closed and Trevor died in the hot vehicle. Mudd told police she could not find a babysitter and that she needed the income from her job. She pleaded guilty to manslaughter and must serve a minimum sentence of five years. Her two other children have been adopted.

CASE 113

When he died of starvation in 1998, Zechariah Mayer, almost three years old, weighed only nineteen pounds, the same amount he weighed when he had seen a physician two years earlier. Charged with his murder were his San Diego, California, parents David, thirty-two, and Jennifer, twenty-three. David Mayer spent most of his time drinking, smoking marijuana, and watching his big screen TV. His son lived in a darkened bedroom on a mattress on the floor in clear view of a fully stocked refrigerator. Neither parent offered any plausible reason for their son's death. The father received a twenty-five-years-to-life sentence in his first-degree murder conviction; the mother was convicted of second-degree murder in a separate trial and faces a fifteen-years-to-life sentence.

CASE 114

Maurita Sublitt, twenty-three, worked as a clerk for the Colorado Springs Police Department. On April 30, 1998, she was charged with first-degree murder in the starvation death of her 2-year-old son Rashad. She was also suspected of child neglect in connection with her three-year-old daughter's hospitalization for malnutrition. She often left the two children home alone when she went to work. When arrested, Sublitt told police that she reduced food purchases so that she could pay off her credit card debt. The landlord of her apartment indicated that her apartment was neat and clean and that she paid her rent on time. When police discovered Rashad he was "very thin with rib cage showing, knee sockets bulging and wearing extremely dirty clothes." His sister smelled of vomit and urine and was also wearing soiled clothes.

Another specific form of sloth was named *acedia* by the scholastic philosophers and theologians of the Middle Ages. Acedia refers to a sadness of the soul that weighs a person down and prevents doing good or performing virtuous acts. Acedia constituted a serious affliction to monks and other clerics, especially in cloistered orders during the medieval period. The "joie de vivre" of those in monastic life was sometimes replaced by a sadness and melancholy that had the potential to wreck entire communities. Lyman analyzes acedia in its contemporary manifestations beyond the cloisters and monasteries. As he notes, acedia can have horrifying consequences since the "kinetic component of the sin of acedia consists precisely in those terrible and terrifying acts that are generated to relieve or remove the gnawing corrosiveness of the spirit. To put the matter bluntly: "Boredom begets aggression, and aggression releases the victim of acedia from its prison house of torments".[10] Acedia thus leads to those evil acts that are viewed by others as senseless, incomprehensible, heinous, and so on.

Here we see murders that were committed by those who were "bored" or "looking for excitement and thrills." One cannot help but be struck by the hollowness, profound sadness and self-absorption of the lives of these murderers before they killed others, whether they were poor and impoverished or affluent and spoiled. In each case we see a restlessness and a despair which seek out lethal violence "just for the hell of it." Murder becomes a means of confronting and undoing the emptiness of their lives, an expression of anger and hatred against the estrangement they feel towards themselves and, by extension, everyone else. Their violent behavior gives them the recognition they crave from a world that has ignored them. They are mesmerized by the newfound attention of the media and bask in the limelight of public recognition, with no concern or remorse for their victims. Theirs is a "say anything you like about me but spell my name right" mentality.

The seemingly random and meaningless homicides that result illustrate Lyman's observations about acedia. Senseless murders that defy the conventional explanations of causation stem from the inner corrosive spirit of the killer afflicted with acedia, which seeks release through violence. Often the killer does not have any real idea of the true motives that led to the murder, claiming that he did not know why he killed. His inner despondency, boredom, and despair seek outlets in aggression. The resulting crimes represent a crude attempt to relieve the frightening despondency and emptiness of the killer's inner self. Persons afflicted with acedia do not always recognize this tendency towards violence. In their own minds they are not intending to commit murder. Rather, they are satisfying the need for a "thrilling experience" or the desire "to see what it feels like to shoot someone."

The sensational 1924 Leopold-Loeb case comes remarkably close to illustrating the inner spiritual and moral vacuum inherent in acedia. Richard Loeb, eighteen, and Nathan Leopold, nineteen, (the "poor little rich kids") came from prominent, wealthy Chicago families. Convinced of their intellectual superiority and bored with their privileged but meaningless, existence, they plotted the perfect crime with the intention of killing "for fun." They kidnapped an acquaintance, Bobby Franks, fourteen, and quickly murdered him. Their incompetence in the execution of the murder and the discovery of incriminating evidence led to their quick arrest. At their trial both Leopold and Loeb openly joked in court and mocked the proceedings. Both were found guilty but were spared the death sentence only by the brilliant defense work of their attorney Clarence Darrow. Loeb was later murdered in prison during a homosexual brawl. Leopold was eventually remorseful for his crime and lived an exemplary prison life. Released in 1958, he became a social worker in Puerto Rico and died in 1971.

Truman Capote's 1962 book *In Cold Blood* also depicts the ravages of acedia. Capote vividly depicts the hollowness and inner superficiality of Richard Hickock and Perry Smith, which culminated in the murders of four members of the Clutter family in Kansas in 1959. The banal and senseless nature of their crimes is best reflected in the comment of Smith to police: "Clutter," Smith said "was a nice gentleman. . . I thought so right up to the moment I cut his throat."[11] The murderers were methodical and totally unemotional in their killings. Smith was particularly respectful of his victims before the murders: he provided pillows and mattresses for them, talked kindly to them, and took care not to damage furniture. They were not murdered "in the heat of passion."[12] Following the slaughter the murderers concealed evidence in a methodical, deliberate fashion. No fits of rage or explosive release of anger emerged from either killer. Capote's title, *In Cold Blood*, aptly describes the murders.

CASE 115

Scott Mickler, thirty-one, a quadriplegic since a 1978 auto accident, died in Moore Haven, Florida, in 1990 from a massive infection a few hours after he was rushed to a hospital by emergency medical technicians.

At her trial in 1995, his wife Cheryl received a fifteen-year prison sentence for allowing her husband to die of decay. When medical personnel came to their home, Scott was covered with rotting, gangrenous flesh. His heels and toes were falling off as he lay in a pool of body fluids and waste. When they tried to move him the flesh separated from his body. Due to his condition, EMT could not take his pulse or blood pressure.

At her trial, Cheryl claimed that she did not notice that he was rotting from gangrene until she tried to turn him the night before he died. At her sentencing she showed no reaction to the fifteen-year sentence, the maximum allowed by the court. She received $1.5 million, the remainder of her husband's $3.5 million settlement for the accident that crippled him. At the sentencing hearing his mother, Mary Mickler, told the court that Cheryl chose death for Scott rather than help him in his paralyzed condition, and that she should be held accountable for her actions. The court agreed.

Case 116

Truman Capote's *In Cold Blood* served as an inspiration to Bradley Price, twenty-three, and Jesse McAllister, twenty-one. They repeatedly watched the film version of the book. On July 14, 1997, both men were walking on the beach at Seaside, Oregon, when they encountered a couple—Gabriella Brooke Goza, twenty-six, and Frank Nimz, thirty-six. Goza and Nimz were fatally shot as they watched the sunrise. The killers and victims were complete strangers to each other. Like the killers in Capote's book and film, Price and McAllister fled to Mexico but were captured a year later.

At his trial, Price claimed that his partner had an intense desire to kill someone just to see what it felt like. In defending his part in the "thrill killings," Price indicated that he did not believe that his friend would ever kill someone, even though he had purchased the murder weapon and knew of McAllister's intention to kill as they walked on the beach. Both were found guilty in June 1999 and both received two consecutive life sentences.

Case 117

Todd Rizza, twenty, of Waterbury, Connecticut had an ongoing interest in serial murderers, particularly Jeffrey Dahmer, the Milwaukee, Wisconsin, killer who murdered his victims, cannibalizing some of them. On September 30, 1997, he invited his neighbor Stanley Edwards, thirteen, to come to his yard to hunt for snakes. When Edwards arrived, Rizza hit him thirteen times with a three-pound sledgehammer. When questioned by police as to his motive, Rizza stated that he just wanted to know what it felt like to kill someone. A Connecticut jury found him guilty of first-degree murder and recommended a death sentence.

CASE 118

According to prosecutors, Robert Neville Jr., twenty-five, and Michael Hall, nineteen, methodically planned the abduction and torture-murder of a co-worker from an Arlington, Texas, supermarket. On February 15, 1998, both men kidnapped Amy Robinson, nineteen, as she bicycled to her job. They took the mentally retarded woman to a field where they used her for target practice with a pellet gun before they killed her with a rifle. In written and videotaped confessions, Hall told police that both he and Neville "just burst out laughing" as Robinson died. Neville told police that he was frustrated over losing his supermarket job and stated to Hall, "I would like to kill somebody because I am just pissed off." At his trial Neville told the court that they had both killed Robinson "for the adrenaline rush." The prosecutor, Alan Levy, read a letter written by Neville wherein the defendant referred to himself and Hall as "sociopaths." He continued, "That means a person who has no respect for the people they kill. We are cold-blooded and ruthless as my doctor would put it." The jury found Neville guilty of capital murder and sentenced him to death. Hall also received the death sentence in a separate trial.

CASE 119

Kimberly Dotts, fifteen, had trouble making friends. Short, overweight, and learning disabled, she was quite happy when she was invited to the home of another teenager in May, 1998. When she arrived she went with a group of other teenagers whom she scarcely knew into the woods in the Clearfield area of Western Pennsylvania. While there, the group discussed plans to run away from their families to travel to Florida. One in the group complained that Kimberly might reveal the group's plan and get them in trouble. Two of the teens, Jessica Holtmeyer, sixteen, and Aaron Straw, eighteen, put a noose around Kimberly's neck and twice hanged her from a tree; when her body, still alive, dropped to the ground, Holtmeyer smashed the victim's head with a large rock, laughing at the incident and indicating that she wanted to cut up Kimberly's body and keep a finger as a souvenir. Straw and the other accomplices eventually testified against Holtmeyer who was found guilty of murder, conspiracy, and aggravated assault. She was sentenced to life without parole; Straw received the same sentence in a separate trial.

Whatever the actual immediate cause for a specific killing may be, the actual internal motivation may never be known. Does the motivation lie in the biochemical makeup of the killer? Is it environmentally produced? Pallone and Hennessy[13] have argued that much of impulsive violence is neurogenic in origin, calling it tinder-box aggression. They propose a stepwise progression from the neurogenic impulsive behavior to the final outcome of criminal violence. Their thesis clearly argues for the possibility that a great deal of violent criminal behavior is, in fact, rooted in organic, physiological origins more than in environmental factors only. Their research vividly demonstrates how complex the actual motivation for murder may be. The jury is still out on whether the actual precipitating causes for killing lie in physiological disturbance, or in environmental factors, or some poorly understood combination of each.

Notes

1. Sykes and Matza, 1957.
2. Katz, 1988, chap. 1.
3. Von Hentig, 1948.
4. D. Cohen, 1998.
5. Polk, 1999.
6. Himes, 1989; "Sin," *Catholic Encyclopedia*, vol. 14:5.
7. Lyman, 1978, p. 235.
8. Lyman, 1978, p. 55.
9. Lyman, 1978, p. 186.
10. Lyman, 1978, p. 14.
11. Sifakis, 1982, p. 155.
12. Katz, 1988, p. 277.
13. Pallone and Hennessy, 1996.

6

The Chronology of Murder

Historical Trends in Murder Incidents

A review of long-term historical rates of homicide almost inevitably leads to several questions. Are the current murder rates higher or lower than those of eras past? Are the current chances of being murdered greater today or less than fifty years ago, 200 years ago, 500 years ago? Are our communities safer or more dangerous places than in times past?

Not having reliable historical homicide data, we find these questions difficult to answer. Systematic collection of homicide data in the United States began only in the 1930s when the FBI undertook the responsibility of categorizing criminal data in what would eventually become the *Uniform Crime Reports*, or UCRs. In most parts of the world today, there is no such systematic documentation of homicide, and many nations in Africa, Asia, and Latin America even today do not have accurate information of their homicide incidents.

Other problems in homicide accounting abound, particularly when we try to fathom the frequency of the crime: How is murder defined? Are infanticides and abortions included or excluded in the counting? What about justifiable and excusable homicides that, technically, are not crimes? How many jurisdictions report or fail to report murders to official agencies? Even though we may know the actual number of murders in a given community, can we accurately compute a rate if we are unsure of the total population of that same area? Are multiple murders that occur at the same time treated as one incident or multiple incidents? These are questions that compound the difficulties in gathering reliable, scientific data on lethal violence. If they are trouble-some in our modern era, imagine the difficulties entailed in determin-ing rates 500 years ago.

With these caveats in mind we can conclude that murder was a major problem in medieval Europe. The distant past illustrated, at least for sections of Europe, a time period when lethal violence oc-curred much more often than in the recent past. James Sharpe[1] cites evidence from England that Oxford's homicide rate in the 1300s was approximately 110 per 100,000 inhabitants. Elias and his associates argues that violence and murder were far too common in medieval Europe and only subsided in later history as a result of the introduc-tion of civilizing manners such as using a knife and fork, avoiding public urination and other modes of behavior that moderns take for granted.[2] Citing earlier research on homicides in Sweden and Holland from the fifteenth century to the present, Eric Johnson and Eric Monkkonen[3] also conclude that murder was far more prevalent then than now.

Table 6.1 summarizes the research of Eva Osterberg on Scandina-vian murder rates and Pieter Spierenburg's study of homicide in Hol-land, clearly confirming the view that homicide rates in the past clearly exceed those of later eras. Marvin Wolfgang[4] also confirms this find-ing, citing Victorian and pre-Victorian England as an example. He discovered that Victorian England had substantially higher rates than

Table 6.1
Estimated Annual Homicide Rates in
Sweden and Holland (15th to 20th Century)

Century	Amsterdam	Holland	Stockholm	Sweden
15th	50.0	—	42.5	33.0
16th	20.0	—	28.0	30.0
17th	7.5	—	34.0	30.0
18th				
first half	8.0	—	—	16.5
second half	2.0	0.5	0.7	—
19th	1.4	—	3.0	1.5
20th				
first half	—	0.5	0.6	—
second half	6.0	2.5	0.8	—

*data revised by author to reflect rates per 100,000 inhabitants; current data: Holland, 1985–90; Amsterdam 1987–90; Stockholm, 1966–70.
Source: Johnsons and Monkkonen (1999: 9).

contemporary England and infers that the murder rate was even greater in the period preceding the nineteenth century.

Even in the United States, there is a surprising lack of objective data from the seventeenth and eighteenth centuries. Nevertheless, direct and indirect information from nineteenth century suggests a high incidence of homicide, particularly in the lower—class sections of rapidly growing cities and in the frontier towns of the West. Though far from scientific, Asbury's journalistic accounts of murder and mayhem[5] in cities such as New York, New Orleans, and San Francisco suggest a high level of homicide and gang warfare in the mid-to-late nineteenth century, a view confirmed by others.[6] Likewise, the large number of homicides in the South, particularly in the rural sections of the Deep South, has been well documented by historians and social scientists.[7] James Inciardi[8] confirms this conclusion of high homicide rates for the nation, especially in the 1880s. Citing *Chicago Tribune* data, he demonstrates the high murder rates of that era that are considerably higher than the current national rate.

Table 6.2
Homicides in the United States, 1881–1900

Year	Rate/100,000
1881	2.47
1882	2.79
1883	3.16
1884	2.67
1885	3.22
1886	2.61
1887	3.98
1888	3.64
1889	5.82
1890	6.85
1891	9.24
1892	10.42
1893	14.47
1894	15.22
1895	15.13
1896	13.28
1897	8.36
1898	8.36
1900	10.87

Source: Figures complied by Chicago Tribune and reported in J. Inciardi, Reflections on Crime, New York: Holt, Rinehart and Winston, 1978, p. 51.

On the other hand, Eric Monkkonen[9] also cites high, but fluctuating, rates in the nineteenth century in New York City, even though the rates then were still considerably lower than the rates for the 1970s to the 1990s.

Not all historical observers agree. Margaret Zahn and Patricia McCall analyze murder rates over a long period (1900–1996) and find a fluctuating level of lethal violence, high in the 1930s,1970s, and 1980s; low in the 1940s and 1950s. Interestingly, their data for the year 1900—approximately 6.4—differ substantially from Inciardi's *Chicago Tribune* rate of 10.9 cited in table 6.2. Such a discrepancy underlines the illusive nature of historical homicide rates.[10]

The data from 1940 to the present are much more reliable, particularly with the publication of the *Uniform Crime Reports* by the FBI that summarize the occurrence of murder in an accurate and systematic fashion.

Table 6.3 presents the annual homicide rates from 1940–2003. These data indicate that the low point in the post World War II era occurred in the 1950s and the high point in the 1980s. The U.S. rate at the beginning of the twenty-first century indicates a return to the less violent trend of forty years ago.

Table 6.3
Homicide Rates: 1940–2003

Year	Rate	Year	Rate	Year	Rate	Year	Rate
1940	6.3	1956	4.6	1972	8.9	1988	8.4
1941	6.0	1957	4.5	1973	9.3	1989	8.7
1942	5.9	1958	4.5	1974	9.7	1990	9.4
1943	5.1	1959	4.6	1975	9.6	1991	—
1944	5.0	1960	4.7	1976	8.8	1992	9.3
1945	5.7	1961	4.7	1977	8.8	1993	9.5
1946	6.4	1962	4.8	1978	9.0	1994	9.0
1947	6.1	1963	4.9	1979	9.7	1995	8.2
1948	5.9	1964	5.1	1980	10.2	1996	7.4
1949	5.4	1965	5.5	1981	9.8	1997	6.8
1950	5.3	1966	5.9	1982	9.1	1998	6.3
1951	4.9	1967	6.8	1983	8.3	1999	5.7
1952	5.2	1968	7.3	1984	7.9	2000	5.5
1953	4.8	1969	7.7	1985	7.9	2001	5.6
1954	4.8	1970	8.3	1986	8.6	2002	5.6
1955	4.5	1971	8.5	1987	8.3	2003	5.7

Source: *Historical Statistics for the United States: Colonial Times to 1970*, Series H 971–986; F.B.I. *Uniform Crime Reports*, various years (1970–2003) Table 1.

CASE 120

John Billington, a ruffian from the slums of seventeenth Century London, sailed with the original Pilgrims on the *Mayflower* in 1620 to settle in Plymouth. On board, he constantly provoked the other passengers and crew to the point that the eventual military leader of Plymouth Colony, Myles Standish, had him hogtied to protect all those on board. His abusive and violent behavior continued for the next decade in the new community, with Billington quarreling with neighbors and authorities alike. One of his neighbors, John Newcomen, particularly irritated him and both men constantly argued with each other. In 1630 Billington waited in ambush for his rival and shot him, mortally wounding Newcomen. Quickly apprehended and tried, Billington was hanged by colonial authorities and gained the notoriety of being the first killer juridically indicted and executed killer in the American colonies.

CASE 121

In 1723 a young couple, Peter and Judith Dutartre, came under the spell of a charismatic religious preacher, Christian George, who established a love commune in the Orange Quarter near Charleston, South Carolina. George preached free love to the citizens of Charleston and mesmerized a number of them, who joined his community. Shortly thereafter, Judith Dutartre gave birth to George's child, known to the residents of Charleston as "the Devil's Child." Outraged citizens, under the leadership of Justice Symmons, formed a posse to attack the commune. In the resulting conflict Judith Dutartre's husband, Peter, shot Justice Symmons dead with a musket. In the trial that followed, not only was Peter Dutartre found guilty, but so too was Christian George, who had not taken part in the killing. Both were hanged the next day and the commune was burned to the ground by the outraged citizens of Charleston in 1724.

CASE 122

John Miller and Mary Jane "Bricktop" Jackson terrorized New Orleans in the 1850s and early 1860s. Jackson, nicknamed "Bricktop" because of her red hair, pursued a violent, criminal career, killing four men in different confrontations and maiming countless others in the tough dancehalls of the French Quarter of the city. One of her victims, "Long Charley," said to have been seven-feet tall, argued with her as to which way he would fall if stabbed; she stabbed him with a special knife, one that she had specially ordered. Another, Laurent Fleury, objected to her obscene language at a local restaurant and was knifed to death by Jackson and three other notorious women—Briget Fury, America Williams, and Ellen Collins. All four were acquitted of the murder since the coroner could not decide the cause of death and subsequently ruled it a heart attack (Fleury had been stabbed six times!).

In prison, Bricktop met John Miller and the two became inseparable, even though they constantly fought and argued. Miller, a tough gangster, had previously lost an arm in a knife fight. When the stump healed, Miller fastened an iron chain and ball to it, ruling the underworld of Gretna, a town across the river from New Orleans. He served two years in prison for murdering a man in a fight in the French Quarter and was released in 1857. He and Bricktop Jackson lived together and constantly fought. In 1861 she slashed Miller and left him, only to return after his impassioned pleas. When she returned however, Miller felt she needed a good beating and attacked Jackson with a whip, which she grabbed from him. Attempting to hit her with his ball-and-chain, he was repeatedly stabbed by Jackson who had managed to grab the ball in mid-air. Miller died from his wounds. The *Picayune*, in its report of the killing, stated: "Both were degraded beings, regular penitentiary birds, and unworthy of any other notice from honest people." Jackson spent less than a year in prison when she was released by the Military Governor of Louisiana, General George Shepley, in blanket pardons of the entire penitentiary.

The broad historical overview of homicide in the past suggests that the motives behind murders were scarcely different than they are today. People kill each other out of anger, for revenge, for honor, and so forth. Historical analyses suggest a high incidence of family killings and murders that occur during arguments over small matters. The passage of time has influenced the volume of murder in different geographical settings, but it has not changed the nature and motivations of murder. In this regard, the human condition has remained surprisingly constant since the days of Cain and Abel.

The chronology of homicide includes not only the broad, macro-level approach entailed in historical incident research, but also the micro-level analysis of the actual time of the homicide act. Specific repeated patterns manifest themselves on this level as well.

Time of Homicide

Those familiar with the Old Testament can probably recall the well-known verses: "All things have their season, and in their time all things pass under heaven—A time to be born and a time to die. . . A time to kill. . . A time to destroy".[11] The time frame for murder clearly fits into this description, since the temporal incidence of homicide follows clear-cut patterns in relation to months, days of the week, and hours of the day of occurrence.

Month of Occurrence

With respect to the seasonal variations of homicide, Table 6.4 clearly demonstrates that murder occurs more often in the summer than in other seasons.

July and August can be described as the killing season, while Feb-

Table 6.4
Months with Highest and Lowest
Percentages of Murders in USA, 1988–2003

Year	Month—Highest Incidence	Month—Lowest Incidence
1988	August (9.5%)	February (7.2%)
1989	July (9.1%)	February (7.1%)
1990	July (9.6%)	February (7.0%)
1991	August (9.4%)	February (7.0%)
1992	July/August (9.1%)	February (7.5%)
1993	July (9.3%)	February (6.7%)
1994	August (9.2%)	February (7.6%)
1995	August (9.9%)	February (6.8%)
1996	August (9.0%)	March/April (7.6%)
1997	July (9.0%)	February (7.3%)
1998	August (9.2%)	February (7.2%)
1999	July/August (9.1%)	February (7.1%)
2000	August (9.4%)	February (7.3%)
2001	July (9.5%)	February (6.2%)
2002	July/September (9.6%)	February (6.8%)
2003	July (9.3%)	February (6.9%)

Source: Crime in the United States (volumes 1989 thru 2003), Table 2.3.

ruary is the "safest" month. Even correcting for days each month (July and August both have thirty-one days, February only twenty-eight), this pattern still holds.

What accounts for a consistent pattern of July/August slayings? Is it the hot weather? High humidity? Short tempers? Sociological research has not, perhaps cannot answer these questions. Perhaps common sense provides us with the best answer. In American society the summer months are considered a time for relaxing and socializing with family and friends. It is a time when most jobs go into a less hectic mode, with vacations and leisure activities replacing the usually frenetic pace of work. It is a time for family celebrations, picnics, weddings, graduation parties, Fourth of July festivities, etc., at a time when alcohol and camaraderie mix and, at times, create havoc.

The data on who kills whom are quite unambiguous: the vast majority or victims are murdered by people whom they know, sometimes very well. These killers are often close friends, family members and acquaintances. What occurs in a significant number of killings is that friends and families get together, drink too much alcohol, confront each other in petty quarrels, attack each other, and finally kill someone. No one planned the murder. In most cases no one had the intent of doing harm before the fatal encounter. Instead, the plan was simply to get together with some friends, have a few beers, shoot the breeze, and kill some time. In too many instances it is not the breeze that is shot, nor time that is killed.

Such homicides, as we noted, are more frequent in the summer months than in the dead of winter when there are fewer viable opportunities for social occasions. In February, more people are struggling to get through the winter rather than engaging in outdoor social activities. It may be as simple as noting people do not even *see* each other in February, let alone kill each other (the one notable exception—the 1929 Chicago St. Valentine's Day Massacre allegedly orchestrated by the Capone mob against "Bugs" Moran's mob).

Case 123 (February)

On February 9, 1998, Christopher Churchill, sixteen, killed five people, beating them to death with a hammer in their home in Nobel, Illinois. Bludgeoned were Debra Smith, thirty-five, her three children, Jennifer, twelve, Korey, ten, and Kenneth, 8, and Churchill's half-brother Jonathan Lloyd, seventeen. Four days later the bodies discovered by neighbors who became suspicious when they saw no activity in the home. When arrested for the killings, Churchill told family members that he murdered the victims because he was "just angry."

CASE 124 (February)

In Little Rock, Arkansas, Quinta Matthews, sixteen, and her younger sister, thirteen (whose name was never released because of her age), argued with their father, Larry Matthews, forty-six, about difficulties they had been having in school. On February 16, 1998, the girls became so enraged that the younger sister obtained a can of gasoline and poured some outside her parents' bedroom as Quinta watched. She then ignited the fuel. Her father died of burns and her mother, Shirley Matthews, forty-five, was seriously injured from smoke inhalation. The thirteen-year-old confessed to police that she had started the fire. She will be detained in a juvenile facility until her eighteenth birthday.

CASE 125 (August)

The bodies of Jennifer Wicks, twelve, and Cassandra Frolek, thirteen, were discovered in a drainage pipe in a park in Milford, Michigan, on August 27, 1995. The two girls left a slumber party where they met two men in a parking lot who bought them beer and took them to the park to drink. The two assailants, twenty-one and twenty-eight, later told police that they had had sex with the girls. One became concerned that he might be charged with statutory rape; the other said that he committed the murders so that he would be returned to jail, since he was unhappy working and living in the local woods. One of the suspects reported the crime to police, led them to the scene, and told them where the murder weapon—a knife—could be found. Both victims had been stabbed to death.

CASE 126 (July)

In San Francisco on July 24, 1997, a waitress, Helen Menican, forty-seven, in a popular diner was shot and killed by Hashiem Zayed, fifty-nine, a cook who had earlier been criticized by her. The victim had worked with Zayed at the diner for more than twenty years. On the fateful July day, Menican berated Zayed in front of customers, telling him that he could not make poached eggs because they were not on the menu. Apparently this was too much for the cook who told another waitress that he was going to kill Menican, but she did not take the threat seriously. A few minutes later Zayed and Menican argued again, at which time he pulled out a gun, shot her multiple times, killing her. When police arrived at the diner, Zayed surrendered peacefully.

CASE 127 (August)

As John Devanney, a self-employed roofer, was driving on Interstate 64 near Chesterfield, Missouri, on August 15, 1997, he suddenly braked to avoid hitting a car that had cut him off. In the process, he spilled hot coffee on himself. Enraged, he sped after the "offending" driver, Jennifer Hywan, twenty-two, and cut her off, forcing her into oncoming traffic where she was hit, thrown from her car, run over by another car, and killed. He fled the scene but later turned himself over to police who charged him with involuntary manslaughter and leaving the scene of an accident.

Day of Occurrence

Marvin Wolfgang[12] demonstrated in his Philadelphia study that murders occur primarily on weekends, with 66 percent of all murders taking place on between Friday and Sunday; 32 percent of all murders occurred on Saturday. This finding was replicated by Henry Bullock[13] and Robert Bensing and Oliver Schroeder[14] in their analyses of Cleveland murders, as well as by Hugh Bartlow,[15] confirming Wolfgang's findings. On the other hand, Kenneth Tardiff and Elliott Gross[16] did not find such a clear-cut pattern. In their analyses of New York City homicides, they found that Monday registered the highest rate of occurrence, yet they pointed out that this reflects discoveries of bodies on Monday, rather than the time of the actual killing. An analysis of 2001 New York City homicides confirms that 51 percent of murders (for which the time of incident is known) occurred on either Friday, Saturday or Sunday, or in the composite weekend catagory.[17]

The prevalence of crack cocaine in the 1980s altered the pattern, as noted by most observers. The epidemic of drug-related homicides in the 1980s reflected a different temporal sequence. These killings tend to be more business-motivated crimes revolving around disputes over territories, eliminating rivals, disagreements over profits, costs, etc. They do not fit the usual definitions of crimes of passion that are characterized by interpersonal relations, drunkenness, spur-of-the-moment violence, and so on. These drug related homicides are often premeditated assassinations of fellow drug dealers and could occur, and often did occur, outside the weekend context. Furthermore, the autopsied victims in these drug-related murders often did not have drugs in their systems, confirming the view that these killings were business-oriented rather than fitting the stereotype of one "drug crazed" addict murdering another. One can only speculate what will happen to this temporal pattern of homicide as the crack epidemic winds down in our major cities, whether we will return to the prevalence of weekend killings or witness some new day of the week pattern.

Case 128

It's a long way from the Denver area to California and Dudley Stephensin, twenty-two, and his wife Bree, nineteen, desperately wanted to go there, but they had no way of doing so since they were both unemployed and lacked cash. Instead, they stole Bree's mother's car and drove to Cedar Creek County in Colorado to inspect a sports utility vehicle advertised in *The Denver Post* by its owner, David Green, fifty-one. On Saturday, February 2, 1998, they looked at the vehicle, and realizing that Green was alone, lured him into his home where Dudley shot him in the head with a gun they had obtained earlier that day. Both were apprehended shortly after the murder and confessed that they originally planned only to steal the vehicle, but later decided to kill Green so that there would be no witnesses to their crime. In their haste to flee Green's home they had left Bree's mother's car and took off in Green's car. Shortly after, the couple split up and Bree confessed to the crime to her mother who then called the police. First-degree murder charges were filed against the couple. Bree Stephenson received a fifty-six-year prison term; Dudley Stephenson was sentenced to life without parole.

Case 129

On Friday evening, January 25, 1998, in Boulder, Colorado, Donna Gladwell, fifty-nine, was murdered by her seventeen-year-old grandson, Leon Gladwell. According to police the two became engaged in a heated argument and the grandson assaulted the victim, who died from blunt force skull and brain injuries. He then fled the scene in the victim's car with a friend, a male juvenile runaway. After witnesses reported the stolen vehicle driving erratically on an interstate highway near Boulder, police apprehended Gladwell who was charged with first-degree murder, aggravated assault, robbery, and motor vehicle theft.

CASE 130

On Friday, January 30, 1998, an unidentified male, thirty-one, was shot eight times inside a pizza shop in North Philadelphia. He died at 4:42 P.M. at the Temple University Hospital. A suspect was arrested for his murder. That same night, at 7:45 P.M., another killing took place. Kenneth Williams was shot and killed in another section of North Philadelphia. According to police the shooting took place in a local store following an argument between Williams and his killer.

CASE 131

On Sunday afternoon, February 1, 1998, Michael King, nineteen, pulled his car over in front of the home of Kenneth Smith, twenty-seven, in Clayton, Georgia, and proceeded to urinate on Smith's lawn. King, who was drunk, argued about the incident with Smith's eight-year-old stepson who ran into the house to tell his parents. In the argument that followed King went to his car, retrieved a baseball bat, and beat Smith to death. He then fled the scene but was soon apprehended by police. The local sheriff, Roger Grayson, said later, "This is easily the most senseless crime of any kind on any level."

Hour of Homicide

Patterns of homicide regularity also extend to the hour of the day in which murders take place. Both Wolfgang[18] and Bensing and Schroeder[19] state that the greatest number of killings take place between 8 P.M. and 2 A.M. Tardiff and Gross confirm this finding, stating that the typical homicide of New York City occurs between 8 P.M. and 1 A.M. Hugh Bartlow[20] indicates that most murders take place during the evening hours, as other researchers report. New York City Police Department data for 2001 confirm that the greatest number of homicides (for which time of the incident is known) occur between 4 P.M. and midnight (42 percent).[21]

CASE 132

Tom Overstreet, twenty-two, and his wife Iliana, twenty-one, had been high school sweethearts prior to their marriage in 1992. Their relationship had been a stormy one. Police responded on numerous occasions to complaints of domestic violence in their Island Park, New York, two-room basement apartment, which they shared with their four-year-old daughter.

Tom had previously been assaulted by his wife and had obtained a court order of protection from her after she had stabbed him and was arrested in April 1996. Following this, Iliana had been arrested twice for violating the court order. Things came to a head on Friday, January 23, 1997, when Nassau County police responded to a domestic disturbance incident at the Overstreet home at 1:30 A.M. Both husband and wife informed officers that there was no order of protection, when in fact a Family Court order was still operative. Two hours after the police left, Iliana stabbed Tom, who staggered to a neighbor's house and asked for assistance. He died shortly thereafter. Iliana fled the scene and jumped into a nearby canal and was later found wandering the streets wet and cold. She was arrested for second-degree murder.

CASE 133

Terry Daniels, twenty, had been homeless, living on the streets of Gary, Indiana, estranged from his family. On Saturday, September 27, 2003, he went to his family's home and shot five members of his family execution-style as they slept. He then turned his 9 mm gun on himself, committing suicide. Killed in his attack were his mother, two-year-old nephew, his sister, eighteen, and his brother, seventeen; Daniels' eighty-two-year-old grandmother survived the shooting and called police. Other family members indicated that Daniels had a history of mental illness. They were uncertain whether he had been taking medication that would have controlled his mental illness.

The chronology of homicide demonstrates clear-cut patterns of occurrence, both on the macro-historical level and on the micro-temporal level. Even though the long-term historical data are sparse, what does exist shows that high murder rates are not confined to the present and that we are not living in the most violent period of human history. The current data on hour/day/month of occurrence show that homicide is quite patterned and regular; not only do we kill those we know and love, but we do it on a regular and patterned basis. We know the who, what, when, and where on a regular basis; we don't know how many killings will take place from year-to-year.

Variations in Homicides

Why do homicide rates vary so dramatically from one time period to another? Experts disagree as to any decisive common factor in exploring such fluctuations, but most offer one, or a combination of the following explanations: demographic factors (i.e., percentage of adolescent and young adult males in the populations, sex ratio variations favoring excess males); socio-cultural factors (i.e., proportion of dysfunctional families in a given area, single family households, degree of economic disenfranchisement and poverty, racial and ethnic prejudice, waxing and waning of the crack epidemic, cultures of poverty, subcultures of violence, etc.); law enforcement strategies (i.e., death penalty provisions, tough law enforcement, crime preventative techniques, gun control laws, etc.). Hypothetically, increases and decreases in the historical incidence of homicide have been, and continue to be, explained by sociologists utilizing these factors which can be overlapping and are not necessarily mutually exclusive.

In recent years, the decrease in the rate of homicide in the United States has been dramatic. The current rate (5.7 in 2003) is considerably lower than the 1993 rate (9.5). Whether the current rate will continue to remain relatively low is anyone's guess, yet a 70 percent decreased in less than ten years is rather starling. What explains such a decline?

A partial answer lies in the experience of New York City, which witnessed a phenomenal decrease in homicides within a short time frame. In 1990, homicides in New York City peaked at a total of 2,262. In 2002, that number fell to 580, a 74 percent decrease. While New York City certainly does not represent the United States, its approach to reducing crime has resulted in major declines in its homicide rate and cities across the nation have begun to implement similar strategies to reduce homicides.

In 2002, New York's Borough of Manhattan had eighty-two murders, the lowest number in any year since the end of the nineteenth century. Contrast that number with the 661 murders in Manhattan in 1972, and the 503 in 1990. What tactics, policies or socioeconomic conditions helped to create this dramatic decline?

In 1994 New York City Mayor Rudolph Giuliani and his Commissioner of Police, William Bratton, implemented revolutionary changes in how the city's police responded to crime. They relied heavily on James Q. Wilson and George Kelling's broken window thesis.[22] The thesis argued that just as a unrepaired broken window signals to a community that no one cares, so also does disorderly social behavior left unattended signal that no one cares, and leads eventually to much more serious crime. These unaddressed "minor" offenses (i.e., vandalism, street prostitution, public urination, subway fare beating, street "squeegie" windshield cleaners, minor street drug dealing, graffiti, panhandling, etc.) lead inevitably to major crimes which eventually destroy the cohesive fabric of urban neighborhoods. Responding quickly and forcefully to these "broken windows" will nip more serious disorders before they can mature.

Beginning in 1994 Giuliani and Bratton concentrated on cracking down hard on these minor offenses, arresting those who engaged in them. Using legal "stop-and-frisk" procedures on these offenders, police soon discovered that many of those apprehended had violated more serious laws (i.e. outstanding arrest warrants, illegal hand gun possession, drug possession, etc.). Soon the quality of life in the city improved markedly as these behaviors were no longer tolerated.

Simultaneously, Giuliani and Bratton instituted other overlapping procedures which held local police commanders accountable for the crime in their precincts. Using an innovative computer program COMPSTAT, Bratton and his aides had weekly computer reports of all crimes in the city—where they occurred, what time they took place, and how serious they were. Precinct commanders, notified only thirty-six hours in advance, had to appear before an "inquisition board" at police headquarters to explain the crime in their precincts and what measure they were taking to counteract it—all of which were highlighted on computer screens before the top brass of the department.

Those who were reluctant to change old ways or who offered feeble excuses that "crime just happens" found themselves demoted or forced into early retirement. By late 1995, Bratton had replaced half of all precinct commanders in the police department. The days of 9–5, Monday-Friday leisurely approach to policing were numbered. Anxious commanders returned to their precincts and alerted their subordinates that the old approaches were out, new and proactive strategies were in. Using COMPSTAT, drug hot spots were identified and rendered inoperative; illegal handgun arrests skyrocketed, and homicides with handguns plummeted; when questioned many of those arrested for minor offenses revealed details about other criminals, unsolved murders, and new details about car theft rings, drug gangs, and drug sales. Civil libertarians argued that these tactics bordered on harassment; police officials responded that the tactics are legal and the resulting decrease in crime has made New York City livable for the first time in decades. The never-ending debate continues on the legality and ethics of these new procedures.[23]

On a personal note, I found this change highlighted in one of my criminology class field trips to high crime areas in Brooklyn. Each spring I take my criminology class to the neighborhoods of Williamsburg, Bedford-Stuyvesant, Bushwick, and East New York to talk to police, crime victims, streetwalkers, gang members, and local residents. In 1996, our bus, with forty-five students and two NYPD homicide detectives, stopped at a tenement in Bushwick; the detectives asked two men who had just been released from Attica prison for armed robbery to speak to the students which they gladly did. When I asked them about the extent of crime in the area, both said it was "way down." I asked why. Both simultaneously responded "Giuliani!" Interestingly, they said this was a good thing because they "felt safe" in this former high-crime area, whereas "before Giuliani," they never did! The benefits of the tough NYPD approach seemed to please even the "bad guys."

But are there other explanations for the impressive decline in murder rates, not only in New York City, but in other cities which implemented similar crime-control procedures? Anthony Harris and his associates offer one interesting alternative. Analyzing lethal criminal assaults over a forty-year period (1960–1999) they argue that improved medical care throughout the nation has dramatically lowered the homicide rate; better ambulance response time, timely 911 dispatches, and excellent trauma care in inner-city emergency rooms have saved thousands of lives that would have been lost without such care. Harris and his associates concluded that the homicide level would have been triple its current rate were it not for the superior emergency room care victims now receive.[24]

Some might argue that New York City's application of the "broken windows" thesis does not explain the murder decline whereas the Harris et al. hypothesis does. If that were true, then the data for New York City should show a large increase in aggravated assaults and other violent crimes since those whose lives were spared because of medical attention now become aggravated assault statistics, robbery statistics, or rape statistics rather than murder statistics. The data from New York City do not support this assertion: between 1994 and 2001 overall crime fell 57 percent, shootings declined 75 percent, robberies declined 63 percent, and in that time period 90,000 illegal guns were take off the streets.[25] Clearly the anti-crime procedures led to a decline in all crimes, not only homicides. If the ambulance / emergency room successes were the only explanation, then all other types of non-homicide crime should not have declined so markedly. In the first year (1993–1994) of the new approach, murders declined 18 percent and robbery 16 percent. Clearly better medical care alone can not account for such dramatic decreases.

Notes

1. James Sharp, 1996, p. 22.
2. Elias, et. al., 2000; chap. X.
3. Eric Johnson and Monkkonen, 1999, pp. 8–9.
4. Marvin Wolfgang, 1986, pp. 404–405.
5. Asbury, 1929, 1968A, 1968B.
6. Graham and Gurr, 1969; Hofstadter and Wallace, 1971; Fried, 1980; O'Kane, 1992.
7. Hackney, 1969; Courtwright, 1996.
8. James Inciardi, 1978, p. 51.
9. Eric Monkkonen, 2001, p. 16.
10. Zahn and McCall, 1999, p. 12.
11. Ecclesiastes 3, p. 1–3.
12. Marvin Wolfgang, 1958, pp. 106–107.
13. Henry Bullock, 1955, p. 566.
14. Robert Bensing and Oliver Schroeder, 1960, pp. 8–10.
15. Hugh Bartlow, 1984, p. 139.
16. Kenneth Tardiff and Elliott Gross, 1986, p. 419.
17. Statistical Report—NYPD, 2001, Section II.
18. Wolfgang, 1958, p. 96ff.

19. Bensing and Schroeder, 1960, pp. 8–10.
20. Hugh Bartlow, 1986, p. 139.
21. Statistical Report—NYPD, 2001, Section II.
22. Wilson and Kelling, 1982, p. 31.
23. Anderson, 1997.
24. Harris, et al., 2002.
25. Giuliani, 2002, p. 77 and Appendix A

7

Domestic Murder—Intimate Partners

For most, the family is the primary place where they can feel safe and secure. The family is a haven, a safe harbor from the tensions and turmoil in a world that often seems uncaring, unpredictable, and hostile. Within the family we expect to love and to be loved, to nurture and to be nurtured, to appreciate, care, and respect loved ones and to have them do the same for us in return.

Yet the prevalence of domestic homicide and other forms of violence challenges this idyllic picture. All too many families experience violence and abuse: spouses kill their mates, children murder parents, parents murder children, siblings kill siblings, lovers slay each other, former spouses murder those that they once loved, and in turn, frequently kill themselves. Domestic homicide is the standard fare of media reports such that readers and viewers have became accustomed to the "routine" carnage within the home. The prevalence of this type of homicide unveils itself year-after-year in the FBI's *Uniform Crime Reports*, where roughly one of every seven homicides involves one family member killing another (in 2003, 13 percent of all murder victims were related to their killer).[1]

Lethal violence within the family takes many forms, and distinctions between these types help explain why one family member murders another.

Spouse and Intimate Partner Murders

Within family killings, the most common type is the murder of one intimate partner by another. This includes spouse murders, which comprised 39 percent of all family killings in 2003; of these, husbands kill their wives 82 percent of the time and wives killed their husbands the remaining 18 percent.[2]

If the category is expanded to include *partner homicide*, which Browne et al. define as "homicide occurring between current or former dating, cohabitating, common-law, and formally married heterosexual couples"[3], then the percentage of spouses/partners, murdered approaches 60 percent of all family killings.

Why do men and women slay the intimate partner? Why would spouses who had vowed their love and care for one another turn on each other so violently? The reasons are, of course, varied. Some kill for profit, for insurance money or inheritance rights. Some feel trapped in their current marriages or relationships and kill out of desire for another. Some kill when their mate threatens to leave, or actually does leave the relationship. Some kill because they feel tied down by their partner's demands or by family obligations, such as raising their own children or their mate's children by a previous partner. Highly publicized and sensational murders highlight some of these motives:

CASE 134

Paul Fried's 1978 murder mesmerized the residents of Philadelphia. Fried, sixty-one, had been a prominent gynecologist. Found dead on his bedroom floor, his death was considered a suicide since a scribbled note to that effect was discovered near his body.

Eventually his wife Catherine, thirty-two, was convicted of his murder: she had suffocated him by sitting on a pillow over his face so as to collect one-third of his estate, valued at $450,000. Shortly before his death she had learned that he was about to divorce her.

CASE 135

The notorious murder of Carol Stuart stunned not only Boston, but the entire country. In 1989 her husband Charles placed a frantic cell phone call to Boston police saying that a black carjacker had shot him and his pregnant wife, Carol. This phone call horrified all who heard and believed it. He survived the attack, but his wife and unborn child did not. Later, to the shock of the nation, police discovered that he had staged the incident and shot his wife because she refused to have an abortion, which he had demanded. He believed that the impending birth would hinder his career aspirations and his chances for future wealth. When the hoax was discovered, Stuart committed suicide.

CASE 136

In 1997, Craig Rabinowitz, thirty-four, a bankrupt Pennsylvania man, strangled his wife Stephanie, twenty-nine, so as to collect on her $1.8 million insurance policy. Rabinowitz had been deep in debt, spending over $100,000 to finance his sexual escapades and lavish trips with an exotic dancer named "Summer," with whom he had become romantically obsessed. Initially, he told police that his wife had fallen in the bathtub and drowned. However, police noticed that she died with her jewelry on, and autopsy reports indicated that she had been dragged to the tub and that she may have been drugged. Rabinowitz finally confessed after claiming that his dead wife told him, in a dream, to admit his guilt. The court sentenced him to life in prison.

Virtually all spouse murders motivated by profit are first-degree murder cases since they are premeditated and planned; many include the hiring of another to do the actual killing and resemble fictional murders depicted in mystery novels. The same would be true of spousal revenge killings wherein one party kills another for some alleged or real act of infidelity, betrayal, or insult.

Other less notorious, less publicized, yet still tragic cases illustrate the determination of spousal and partner killers to fulfill their desires for revenge, for money, or for dozens of other motives known perhaps only to them.

CASE 137

John Patton, ninety-nine,, confided to Rev. Billy Simon, the pastor of the Greater Poplar Springs Baptist Church, that he believed his wife Lillie, sixty-seven, had been cheating on him. Patton worked as a part-time handyman and deacon of the church and related well to everyone there. On February 2, 1996, in Jasper, Florida, he shot and killed his wife with a .22-caliber rifle in their home and then rode his bicycle to the local sheriff's office to confess his crime. Initially, Sheriff Harrell Reid didn't believe that Patton was in his right mind and told him to return home but the sheriff did drive to the house where he and another officer discovered Lillie's body. Patton was later arrested at a local drug store where he was paying his utility bill. Regarding the possible infidelity of Lillie Patton, the Baptist pastor stated that this was probably only in John Patton's mind.

Case 138

Robert Wheeler, forty-one, of Highland Township, Michigan, placed a home-made pipe bomb under the seat of his wife Rhonda's car, fatally injuring her when the bomb detonated in suburban Toledo, Ohio, on April 8, 1996. Wheeler claimed he owed $14,000 in gambling debts and admitted placing the car bomb so that he could collect $17,000 in car insurance. He claimed he had no plans to kill Rhonda. Federal officials argued otherwise, indicating that he killed his wife to collect $100,000 from her life insurance policy. He eventually pled guilty and faced a life sentence.

Case 139

The Hrickoses had been having marital problems. To patch up their relationship, Kimberly, thirty-three, a medical technician, and Stephen, thirty-five, a golf course superintendent, decided to go to a resort in St. Michaels, Maryland, for a romantic St. Valentine's Day getaway in February 1998. In a case of life imitating art, they watched a play, "Mafia Wedding," a whodunit wherein the groom sips champagne which had been poisoned and drops dead at his own wedding reception. Stephen Hrickos was unaware that before the night was through he too would be poisoned by Kimberly.

Following the play, the couple fought. Kimberly claimed that Stephen had been drinking heavily and that she left the room to visit a friend. When she returned their room was engulfed in smoke and Stephen was dead. She told police that he smoked in bed and probably set the room on fire in his drunken state. An autopsy suggested otherwise; tests indicated that he had been dead before the fire had started and that no alcohol was present in his system. In addition, the cause of his death was poisoning. by an injection of succinylcholine chloride which stopped his breathing. Friends told police that the husband did not smoke and that a year earlier Kimberly offered a coworker $50,000 to murder her husband. She had asked Stephen for a divorce but he refused. She was also the beneficiary of his $400,000 life insurance policies. A jury convicted Kimberly of first-degree murder in January 1999, the ultimate act of "life imitating art."

These sensational cases, as well as the less well-known cases reported above, constitute only one type of spousal murder. The typical mate slayings are often less bizarre and often include partners with histories of physical abuse (particularly to the female partners) and parties angered by extramarital and relationship, separation, monetary discord, and perceived or actual sexual rivals.

Carolyn Block and Antigone Christakos[4] provide an interesting glimpse of what has been happening with spousal/intimate partner killings over a twenty-five-year period (1965–1990). Examining Chicago partner homicides, they found that males have been just as likely to have been murdered by their partners as females (see table 7.1). Yet, even though this may have been true in the period studied, current data show a growing gender gap since females have become less murderous over time, as indicated above in 2003 *UCR* data. Browne et al. attribute this declining rate of female violence to the greater prevalence of legal and extralegal resources currently available to women in abusive situations which provide them with an exit strategy which does not entail the murder of their spouses. Interestingly, the same is not true for males killing their female partners; their rates have declined only slightly. Hence, we have the current scenario wherein female victims represent three quarters of all victims killed by their partners.[5]

Block and Christakos explore intimate partner homicides further by looking at ethnic/racial characteristics. Analyzing victimization rates, they discovered that among whites and Latinos, the risk of intimate partner murder is greater for women than for men; among blacks, the risk is reversed; it is greater for men than women. This has been true since 1970 in Chicago; Wilson and Daly found similar results in surveys of other large cities.[6] Block and Christakos attribute the high victimization rates for black men to the repeated abuse of the women who eventually murder them, to the presence of alcohol in the confrontation, and to the males' past arrest records for violent offenses.[7]

Does the stability of the marriage bond relate to intimate partner homicide? In his study of domestic homicide Todd Shackelford[8] ana-

Table 7.1
Definition of Intimate Partner Used in the Analysis
Gender of Victim/Offender by Type of Union (Percents)
Chicago Homicide Victims, 1965–1990

Type of Union	Man Kills Female Partner	Women Kills Male Partner	Gay Couple
Spouse	39.1%	35.6%	—
Ex-Spouse	3.5%	1.7%	—
Commonlaw		27.4%	36.9%
—			
Ex-Commonlaw	1.8%	0.8%	—
Boyfriend/Girlfriend	24.6%	22.2%	
—			
Ex-Boyfriend/Girlfriend	3.7%	2.9%	—
Gay Couple, Male	—	—	89.1%
Gay Couple, Female	—	—	10.9%
Total Percents	100.1%	100.1%	100.0%
Total Homicides	1,180	1,145	46

Source: Block and Christakos, 1995: Table 1, p. 146.

lyzed partner killings by women according to whether or not they were cohabiting or married to their male partner. He found that men in cohabiting relationships were ten times more likely to be murdered by their partners than were married men, and the greater the age difference between these partners, the greater the probability that the male will be killed.[9] His research replicates a growing body of evidence that demonstrates that both men and women in cohabiting relationships are at greater risk of being murdered than married men and women.[10]

What factors help explain these patterns of violence? The predominant motivation for these intimate partner homicides relates to changes in the actual relationship between the partners. Men kill their partners when they suffer an actual or perceived loss of power and control over them, particularly when the woman has left or is about to leave the relationship. Women kill their partners in situations where they feel there is no realistic alternative; when they believe their lives or the lives of their children are actually threatened by a violent and abusive mate. These are often violent households, inhabited with violent people. In their Chicago sample, Block and Christakos found that 40 percent of the men and 18 percent of the women who killed their partners had previously been arrested for a violent offense.[11] Naturally, not every partner murder fits this description, but many, if not most, spousal killings entail some variation of this emotional and physical disintegration of a relationship, whether in a cohabitating one, or in a disintegrating marital one. Either planned or spontaneous, these killings illustrate the psychological rage generated in the collapse of what had been a once meaningful union of two individuals.[12]

Male Killers

For males, estrangement (the time period between the actual separation and the eventual divorce of the two partners) plays a key role. Wilson and Daly studied spousal murders in Chicago, Canada, and Australia, found that the highest rate of male-precipitated partner homicide occurred among husbands estranged from their wives. Almost 90 percent of these murders took place within a year of the separation.[13] Other studies confirm this finding and indicate that those women who had lived in a common-law relationships before separation stand an even greater risk of lethal violence from their former partner.[14] Additionally, women who live with men who are not the biological fathers of their children are at a greater risk than women whose partners fathered their children.[15]

The male killer in these situations refuses to accept the decision of his former partner to leave the relationship. From his perspective, the intended or actual departure of the woman is the "last straw," an unforgivable affront to his sense of power and control over her, an act of actual betrayal that can be avenged only by killing her. The previously abusive and violent relationship now turns lethal—"If I can't have her, no one will:" "How could she humiliate me in front of our friends?"

The actual murder displays an intense rage towards the former partner, reflected in what police term "overkill," where excessive and redundant force, far beyond what is necessary to kill a human being, is used by aggrieved husbands. It is common for enraged husbands to stab their ex-wives twenty or thirty times, shoot them multiple times, bludgeon them, strangle them, beat them, and otherwise assault them in a lengthy, gruesome, and tortuous fashion. In many of these homicides, the murderers use multiple methods to literally stamp the life out of their former partners. Overkill thus proclaims the psychological rage of these husbands, and is common in male murderers, though rare in females who kill their former mates.[16]

The violent nature of these intimate partner homicides reflects the background of these males. Often raised in abusive households, these killers have histories of violent crimes against their wives and others, with numerous restraining orders issued against them, as well as violations of these orders.[17] Whether this propensity towards violence caused the woman to leave the relationship, or whether her departure triggered the resulting violence, is an open question; either way, the homicidal result remains the same.

Case 140

Forest Fuller, twenty-eight, and Jodie Myers, twenty, had been dating each other for three months following Fuller's separation form his wife. In the fall of 1994, Myers ended their relationship and started dating other men. On Thanksgiving eve Fuller strangled Myers and then stabbed her multiple time in his home in Pemberton Township, New Jersey. Placing the bloodied body in his car on Thanksgiving Day, he traveled aimlessly and telephoned Myers' mother. He told her that he intended to marry her daughter and would dress her in a wedding gown and place a wedding ring on her finger. To prove that he had done so, he promised to sever the corpse's finger with the ring attached and mail it to the mother. Arriving at the Last Stop tavern in Fairmont, West Virginia, Fuller told the barmaid that his dead girlfriend was outside in his car. Police arrived and discovered the bloody body wrapped in blankets in the backseat. They also found a wedding dress in the trunk of the car.

Case 141

James and Lisa Dawn Hayes, both twenty-three, frequently quarreled and fought with each other over money and James' use of marijuana. When Lisa discovered that she was pregnant, the couple got married on July 6, 1995, in Winchester, Virginia. Six days later the husband, together with Anna Oakes, the couple's roommate, murdered Lisa. Hayes smothered his wife with a pillow while Oakes held the victim's legs as she struggled for her life. Hayes then washed his wife's body, dressed her, put her in their car and drove to Abrams Creek, where the killers tried to stage what would appeared to be an accident. Wedging a stick against the accelerator, they pushed the car down a seventy-five-foot embankment. They neglected to remove the stick however, and eventually police ruled the death a homicide. Realizing he was the main suspect in his wife's death, Hayes planted a bogus confession and suicide note from a friend, Brian Kisler, whom Hayes claimed had had an earlier affair with Lisa. The note suggested that Kisler had murdered Lisa and then committed suicide. The note was discovered to be fraudulent when police noticed that "Brian" was misspelled. Anna Oakes eventually confessed to the murder and testified against Hayes. She received a six-to-fourteen year sentence; Hayes received a life sentence.

CASE 142

Richard Lynch, forty-five, and Roseanna Morgan had been having an affair, but Morgan broke the relationship off in order to return to live with her husband in March 1997. Lynch, unemployed, had gone to the Morgan apartment in Sanford, Florida, to collect money that he claimed she had charged on his credit cards while they were living together. He waited there for her with her thirteen-year-old daughter Leah Caday. When she arrived she refused to enter the apartment, whereupon Lynch shot her, he later claimed, accidentally. Morgan was shot three times and her daughter once, in the back. Both died at the scene. When questioned as to how he could have done this accidentally, he claimed that he shot his former lover "to put her out of her misery." Lynch was charged with two counts of first-degree murder.

Female Killers

For female killers, the homicidal act often involves the slaying of family members and other intimate partners. Browne et al.[18] report that 63 percent of the homicides committed by women involve family members and relationship partners; approximately 40 percent of their victims are their intimate partners.[19] Typically, women who kill do so in their home and without much prior planning or premeditation.[20] These homicides tend to be are impulsive acts arising out of the volatile circumstances of the moment.

These volatile circumstances often involve long-term abusive relationships between the woman and her male victim. This past and current pattern of abuse plays a crucial role in these spousal/intimate partner slayings.

Victim precipitation plays a central role in the vast majority of murders where the woman kills her male partner; Mann states that these comprise over 80 percent of such cases.[21] Victim precipitation refers to a situation where the victim—in this case the male—first use physical force against the female, who then kills him in the confrontation. These killings are typically reactive acts by the wife, ex-wife, or common-law partner. In a few instances women killers are just as violent as their male mates and only chance determines who will be killer and who will be victim. Yet for most, this is not the case; 70 percent of female killers had no prior violent history.[22] Typically, these women sought only to defend themselves at the time of the incident and had previously suffered severe, life-threatening violence and additional threats of further violence from their partners.[23] Browne[24] points out that these women kill primarily when they believe that their lives are threatened, when they see no realistic hope that their conditions will improve, where they feel that there is no safe escape for either themselves or their children. Leaving the relationship, as we have seen, may actually exacerbate the danger.

Courts and juries usually to be into account this reactive stance of the female killer to a violent and abusive male partner who, more often than not, had been intoxicated during the confrontation. As Mann indicates, though 90 percent of these women were initially charged with murder, only 28 percent were actually tried on a murder indictment; of these, only 37 percent were sentenced to prison, with the majority (75 percent) spending fewer than ten years in jail.[25]

CASE 143

When Maria Blackburn purchased an abandoned storage box at the Stor-King Storage Company auction in Upland, California, in 1997, she never anticipated its contents. When she opened the box she found the body of Robert Bourk, twenty-seven, along with wedding pictures and champagne glasses. His wife, Darlene Bourk, thirty-one, was arrested and charged with murder. Detective Anthony Yoakum of the Upland Police Department indicated that the couple lived in an abusive relationship, with the husband frequently abusing his wife physically. In December 1997, in a violent encounter, Darlene shot her husband twice, killing him. She then stored his body in the Stor-King facility. When she failed to meet two $25 storage payments, the facility auctioned the box to Blackburn. When the killer received a letter from the facility stating that her box had been sold, she panicked and left notes at Stor-King indicating that she would "give anything, anything to get the storage back." Darlene Bourke was convicted of second-degree manslaughter and received a prison sentence of eighteen years.

Case 144

For months Alwyn Chan, forty-five, stalked his former girlfriend Aliceson Haile, thirty, and frequently harassed and beat her. The two had dated for two months in 1998 in Brooklyn, New York. Neighbors of Haile said that she had endured regular mistreatment by Chan, who would sometime shower her with presents and apologies. When Haile started dating former boyfriends the relationship between the couple quickly deteriorated. On February 1, 1999, Chan attacked his former girlfriend and beat her severely. She had him arrested for assault and obtained a restraining order, but Chan was released on bail. Three weeks later Chan came to Haile's apartment, pushed his way in, and attacked her with a three-foot-long sharpened stick. In addition, he repeatedly slammed her head against the kitchen window's iron security gate. Haile grabbed a kitchen knife and stabbed Chan, killing him. The Brooklyn District Attorney's Office declined to prosecute Haile since she acted in self-defense against an assailant who should not have been in her apartment.

Notes

1. *Crime in the United States*, 2003, Figure 2.4.
2. *Crime in the United States*, 2003, Figure 2.4 revised.
3. Browne et. al., 1999, p. 150
4. Carolyn Block and Antigone Christakos, 1995.
5. Brown et. al., 1999, pp. 150 and 160.
6. Wilson and Daly, 1992.
7. Block and Christakos, 1995, pp. 147–148.
8. Todd Shackelford, 2001.
9. Shackelford, 2001, p. 253.

10. Daly and Wilson, 1988; Wilson, Johnson, and Daly, 1995.
11. Block and Christakos, 1995.
12. Block, et al., 2000, p. 92ff.
13. Wilson and Daly, 1993.
14. Wilson, 1995.
15. Daly et al., 1997.
16. Browne et al., 1999.
17. Langford et al., 1999, p. 58.
18. Browne et. al., 1999.
19. Browne et. al., 1999, p. 150.
20. Peterson, 1999, p. 30.
21. Mann, 1988, p. 36.
22. Pollock, 1999, p. 32.
23. Smith and Zahn, 1999, p. 158.
24. Browne, 1997.
25. Pollock, 1999, p. 32.

8

Domestic Murders—Children and Families

Child Victims

In 1999, five juveniles per day were victims of homicide in the United States.[1] No other type of murder creates more anger and disdain in the public's mind than the killing of children. Infanticide (the killing of infants) and feticide (the killing of young children) differ from other types of homicide precisely because the victims are so small, so defenseless, and so vulnerable to attack from others. The murder of these most precious of human beings instantly commands our attention and receive top priority in the media witness the sensational attention to the murder of Jon Benet Ramsey. Who is not horrified when parents, particularly mothers, murder their own children?

The shock over Susan Smith's murder of her two sons (Michael, three, and Alex, one) in South Carolina in 1994 accomplished by strapping them into their car seats, rolling the car with them inside into a lake, consequently drowning them, and blaming a supposed African-American carjacker for the crime—the shock of it still remains years later, as does the callousness of her motivation, namely her desire to continue her relationship with her boyfriend who she believed would never marry her if he had to raise her boys. To Smith, her children constituted so much excess baggage that had to be jettisoned. She received a life sentence in a South Carolina prison. Likewise the horror over Andrea Yates' killing her five sons in Houston, Texas in 2001 still permeates the nation's psyche. Methodically luring them to the bathtub in her home, she drowned each in turn and then calmly telephoned her husband to tell him to come home. Debates continue to rage as to her sanity, yet she had been judged competent to stand trial, found guilty of their murders, and is serving a life sentence in a Texas psychiatric center.

Other types of murder (robbery killings, drug killings, bar fights turned lethal, lovers' quarrel killings, etc.) though rarely condoned, are reasonably comprehensible to the public. Not so the murder of children. Few, if any, justify the killings. Even hardened criminals detest such acts and loath child murderers, so much so that they have to be segregated in prison for their own protection. Prison guards and inmates alike regard to such killers as the "bottom of the feeding chain." Child murderers have crossed a tabooed line, and they will be attacked and murdered by other prisoners if left unprotected. Few were surprised when fellow prisoners murdered Jeffrey Dahmer, the incarcerated serial killer who cannibalized his young adolescent male victims. Few voiced any regret over his murder or mourned his passing.

In my contact with active and retired homicide detectives from New York City Police Department's Brooklyn North Homicide Task Force, I have been struck by the emotion these seasoned professionals convey when they speak about the child murders they have investigated. Years later they still speak with heartfelt sympathy for the victims and with anger and utter disdain for the killers. More than any other types of murder they investigate, these detectives pursue these cases with a determination that amazes even themselves. The professional, dispassionate, objective approach to the "ordinary" killings they handle still applies to the search for child killer, but added to it is an almost obsessive drive to find the killer, to do justice to the young, innocent victim.

The late detective Paul Weidenbaum's ingenuity and professionalism illustrate such dedication to the solution of child homicide. In December 1988 he and fellow homicide detectives from Brooklyn's 90th Precinct received a call from the attending physician at the Pediatric Emergency Room of Woodhull Hospital to come to the view the body of Jessica Cortez, five years old. In what eventually became a sensational case in New York City, Detective Weidenbaum quickly determined that the child had been murdered. The physician thought that the scars on her buttocks resulted from a hot iron, but Weidenbaum said that they had been ulcerated lesions caused by long-term, repeated, severe beatings. As Weidenbaum told me, "there wasn't a part of her body that was not scarred or beaten." Even the inside of her mouth had ulcerated, gangrenous sores in it." Jessica's mother, Abigail Cortez, twenty-five, and her boyfriend, Adrian Lopez, twenty-seven, had called 911 and had Jessica brought by ambulance to the hospital. Weidenbaum interviewed each adult separately in the hospital waiting area. They claimed the girls natural father, Anthony Cortez, had taken Jessica for the weekend and did not return her. The mother and her boyfriend then went to Cortez's apartment at 20 Green St., Brooklyn, discovered the girl and called for assistance. Weidenbaum ordered police to transport the mother and Lopez separately to the precinct, allowing no conversation between them. As he drove past 300 Bushwick Avenue, another detective pointed out that it was where the mother and the boyfriend lived. Weidenbaum immediately recognized the building—he had arrested the natural father, Anthony Cortez, a year earlier for the murders of two transsexuals. He then knew that he could not have killed Jessica since he was in prison awaiting trial for the two murders. Furthermore, the patrol offices on the case told Wiedenbaum that there was no such address as 20 Green Street.

Detective Weidenbaum then confronted Abigail Cortez stating, "Don't you remember me? I locked up your husband for two murders and he's in jail!" She had not, in fact, even recognized him. After reading her the Miranda Rights, he confronted her with her lies and she began to crack, admitting some involvement in the killing. Wiedenbaum then interrogated Lopez after reading him his rights and told him that Jessica's mother said he killed the child. As Detective Weidenbaum said to me, "I told him that I understood parents sometimes lose their cool. I informed him that I also have kids and they sometimes get to you. He took the bait and opened up. You see, you have to give a suspect a face-saving way out, so he can begin to tell you what happened. I then asked Lopez why he hit Jessica. He answered that she wet her bed. Then, with the girl's mother helping him, he beat her with a rope, a belt and a hanger and told me where these instruments were located in the apartment." Detective Weidenbaum then left to interrogate the mother who confirmed everything her boyfriend said. Both were then charged with second-degree murder in Jessica's death.

After obtaining a search warrant, Weidenbaum and fellow detectives returned to the Cortez-Lopez apartment to collect the murder instruments. Upon opening a closet they found a nine-year-old boy, Nicky Alvarez, lying huddled on the floor unable to stand or walk.

The boy was Abigail Cortez's son from a previous boyfriend. They rushed him to Woodhull Hospital where doctors found he had ten separate broken bones. The flesh between his nose and upper lip was missing; the rest of his body was bruised and lacerated. Weidenbaum confronted the couple who finally admitted to assaulting Nicky. Weidenbaum indicated to me that, "the son-of-a-bitch Lopez punched the kid repeatedly; he crushed the boy's left hand by placing it on the table and hitting it with a baseball bat; he made the poor boy kneel for half an hour on a serrated cheese-vegetable grater; he couldn't even remember how he broke the kid's feet. I felt like reaching over and ripping his throat out, but I didn't because we'd lose the case and no justice would be done for either Jessica or Nicky. When we prosecuted the case to the Grand Jury, we showed them the pictures of what this creep had done. They were so gruesome that the Prosecutor, Mary Jane Fisher, broke down and had to leave the chamber."

The case was eventually tried in New York Supreme Court by Judge Ruth Moskowitz and both Abigail Cortez and Adrian were convicted of second-degree homicide and received life sentences (at that time, New York State could not indict a suspect on first-degree murder since there was no capital punishment).

Looking back over his twenty-two years as a homicide detective, Paul Weidenbaum, now deceased, told me that he had investigated thousands of homicides, but the case of Jessica Cortez and Nicky Alvarez was the only one that brought tears to his eyes.

Similar dedication fueled the activities of another member of Brooklyn North's Homicide Task Force, Detective Dave Carbone. In 1993, he and fellow homicide investigators were called to the garbage compactor room in the basement of a public housing project in the East New York section of Brooklyn, where they discovered the body of a four-year-old boy in a bag of garbage. The boy had been beaten and strangled, and he had died before being thrown in the garbage. As Detective Carbone told me, "It was sad to see this poor little kid thrown out with the garbage, like so much junk. I was determined to find the . . . animal who could do this." At that point, no one knew the child's identity, and a check of the project's resident records indicated that no young boy had been reported missing. The police circulated a photo of the child's face to the press. Eventually police in Jersey City, New Jersey contacted NYPD about a missing four-year-old boy. They reported that Stephan Poole had assaulted and stabbed his wife Dana

Blackledge Poole and drove away with young Kayesean. Visiting Dana Poole in the hospital, Carbone showed her the picture of the dead boy whom she identified. She also told him that Kayesean was her adopted son. Carbone then searched for Stephan Poole. Since the car was missing and presumed stolen, Dana Poole agreed to allow Carbone to put out a stolen car alarm; he in turn put the plate numbers on a national computer database.

Stephan Poole called Detective Carbone to find out how, if he surrendered, he would be charged, but revealed nothing, always hanging up before a meeting could be arranged. Said Detective Carbone, "I had him on the line a couple of times but couldn't keep the jerk on long enough to trace the call. I always kept my cool and talked to him politely but matter-of-factly so he would turn himself in. No such luck though." Police had no idea where he was hiding. In re-interviewing Dana Poole, Detective Carbone was stunned to learn that she had had a sex change operation and was actually the granduncle of young Kayesean. Advertising that she was a transsexual in personal dating columns, she met Stephan Poole and eventually married him. During a sexual escapade he stabbed her and fled with the little boy. Monitoring Dana's bank accounts and tracing Stephan's telephone calls to her family, Detective Carbone and fellow detectives chased the suspect from Queens, New York, to Clearview, Florida, to Biloxi, Mississippi, and finally to Walker County, Texas, where he was arrested for driving a reported stolen car (his own!). Detective Carbone related to me the details of this chase with all the gusto, animation and enthusiasm for which he is well known in the NYPD. He felt "like a hunter after his prey who couldn't wait to catch this miserable animal son of a bitch."

In this interrogation Detective Carbone set aside his desire to attack Poole for what he had done to young Kayesean. Instead, he calmly spoke to him, befriended him, told him that he understood how someone could get angry at young kids and do something he really didn't want to do. Poole eventually confided in Detective Carbone, admitting to killing Kayesean because the boy was hungry and wouldn't stop crying. He choked him "a little bit" and he went limp. Discarding the victim in a garbage chute in Brooklyn, he then fled to Texas where he thought he would get a job at Six Flags Great Adventure Park. Poole was found guilty of second-degree murder and received a twenty-five-years-to-life sentence.

Detective Carbone later related to me how, from his first glimpse of the body he swore to himself he "was going to catch that miserable piece of shit who would throw a little boy down a garbage compactor." Almost ten years later, he still has nothing but contempt for Stephan Poole. His anger, like that of Detective Paul Weidenbaum, is typical of homicide investigators who have to murders of children.

Research into child homicide shows that the most likely killer is a family member or close acquaintance. Stepparents are the most common killers of young children, and children in homes with stepparents are 100 times more likely to be killed than children living with both biological parents.[2] Smith and Zahn argue that stepparents do not have the strong genetic attachment to the children of their partners and when stressed, such individuals are more likely to abuse and in extreme cases kill their mate's children. Smith and Zahn point out that genetic fathers often kill their children in the context of their own suicide whereby they seek to release their children from perceived difficulties so they kill them and often themselves. Stepparents, on the other hand, most frequently kill in a situation of violent rage , often beating them to death.[3] The same pattern emerges for the boyfriends and other intimate male partners who, in a generalized manner, might be considered "stepparents" of the children they murder.

Yet males do not comprise the majority of child killers. J. Dawson, using Uniform Crime Reports data, indicates that 55 percent of those arrested for killing children are women and that women are more likely to kill their sons than their daughters.[4] Finkelhor and Omrod report that female killers overwhelmingly kill very young children, with 75 percent of their victims under age 6.[5] In an early study in 1969, P. Resnick found that mothers were twice as likely to murder their children as the children's fathers.[6]

The reasons for killing are varied: insanity, financial burdens, release from suffering, social stigma of out-of-wedlock births, revenge towards spouse, inconvenience to one's lifestyle, gross endangerment, neglect, etc. Mothers who murder infants frequently do so intentionally and deliberately, often under the pressure of social and financial burdens, as in the case of single, unwed mothers; mothers who murder older children typically do so unintentionally through loss of control, by hitting them, shaking them, etc.[7] Whatever the reason the causative motive seems to be changing from past years. Holmes and Holmes sadly state,

Today the stresses that lead to the murder of children appear to have changed. For example, in recent interviews with women in the United States who have killed their children, the primary reason appears to be not financial hardship, as in other countries, but inconvenience. These women believe that, with children, they are no longer attractive to men, and the children's care appears to get in the way of their social lives.[8]

These mothers who see their children as obstacles to their future life chances are rarely remorseful after the killing, and rarely attempt suicide, nor do they show signs of psychological defects following the killings, unlike those mothers who kill in a violent rage.[9] Hardened and determined, they willingly and knowingly eliminate the impediments to their selfish and evil desires.

CASE 145

In April 1998, police in Middletown, New York, arrested Tracy Ann Irwin, twenty-seven, her boyfriend William Banker, thirty-three, and their landlord, Jeanna Lyn Lester, thirty-one, in the beating death of Irwin's son, 3. The child had been repeatedly beaten, scalded with hot water, burned with cigarettes, and thrown down flights of stairs. The terrible beating left him with a broken jaw, a broken arm, a lacerated liver, and a collapsed lung. Earlier photographs of the boy show him smiling, but with what investigators said was cigarettes burns on his forehead. He died of his injuries in St. Frances Hospital in Poughkeepsie where he had been airlifted. Police indicated that the brutal attack began after he had taken some candy from one of the three defendants. Both Irwin and Banker were charged with first-degree murder; Lester was charged with second-degree murder.

CASE 146

Rosanna Hooper separated from her husband George in 1995 and subsequently lost her job as a data entry clerk. She then used credit cards to pay the rent and other expenses, running up $50,000 in debts. Even after the couple reconciled, she "cried all the time" about their financial situation, upset that she and her husband could not adequately provide for their eleven-year-old son, Daniel. In Los Angeles, California, in May, 1997, the mother strangled young Daniel with a pair of pantyhose. After his death, she drove to a nearby park where she and her son frequently visited, climbed down a hill to the metrolink train station, and stepped into the path of an oncoming train, and was killed instantly. Her husband indicated to investigators that his wife constantly blamed herself for their financial difficulties. He stated, "Daniel was her life. She would never be happy, never be able to live with herself if she couldn't give him everything he wanted."

CASE 147

William McClellan, forty-two, suspected that his wife, Juanita McClellan, was a lesbian since he noticed that she was regularly on the Internet with a woman from Texas. His wife worked as a computer specialist at the Free Library in Philadelphia. On January 7, 1998, he killed his two children, Will, five, and Patrice, eight, as they slept in the family home. McClellan stuffed socks in each child's mouth and then stabbed each. Following this he stabbed himself, but the wounds were superficial. He told the police that he didn't want them to learn that their mother was a lesbian stating, "I figured if I didn't take them and myself out of here, they would be in her hands." The prosecutor in the case, Assistant District Attorney Judith Frankel Rubino stated, "This is an absolutely horrendous case . . . Even if it was true, you don't kill your kids over it."

Children Who Kill Within Families

The literature discussing very young children who kill others is relatively sparse, most likely due to the extreme rarity of pre-adolescent murderers.[10] When they do kill however, the deed receives a great deal of attention; the statistical rarity of such murders command instant attention from the public and the news media. What can be more disturbing, more bizarre than a seven year old killing a five year old? We assume that these children have no real understanding of the finality of their act, and don't know why they killed another. Typically they have severe mental disabilities.

Older youths, typically adolescents, constitute a more diverse population, and their murderous acts vary from killing parents, particularly fathers, to gang killings, to more recent school shootings. Sometimes they act alone. At other times they act in concert with accomplices each supporting the other with appeals to the higher loyalties of their close friendship, the loyalty to their gang, neighborhood turf, and so on.

Within the family, youths who kill one parent or both constitute less than 2 percent of all homicides in the United States. Generally, these killers are white males with severe mental problems, though most have no prior involvement with the criminal justice system.[11] This latter point is debated by other researchers. The motives in killing parents or stepparents are varied, but the most common reason relates to a real or perceived fear that the victim planned to harm them in some way, either physically or by curtailing their lifestyle and its privileges. Parental victims have been murdered because of their physical, mental and sexual abuse of the young assailant and/or because they complained about the killer's friends, music tastes, clothing styles, or any number of attitudes or behaviors which the killer felt were part of his or her persona and which could not be challenged, let alone altered. Commonly, the homes and families in which these killings occur are dysfunctional. Almost without exception, researchers report that these killers have been raised in broken homes where drugs, alcohol, violence and abuse are common.[12]

Similar to their adolescent counterparts who have killed fellow students in highly publicized mass killings such as Columbine High School in Colorado, or gangbangers who kill in the gang war zone of South Central Los Angeles, these youth family killers show little or no remorse for their violence; they have settled scores and exacted revenge for alleged wrongs done to them by those who would beat or challenge them.

Case 148

Robert Dingham, eighteen, of Rochester, New Hampshire decided to murder his parents, Even and Vance Dingham, because of their decisions to ground him due to his poor grades and their refusal to get him a cell phone. On the night of February 5, 1997 he approached his brother Jeffrey, fifteen, asking him to join him in the killings. The younger brother finally agreed to go along with the plan even though "it was kind of drastic." At midnight both agreed they were too sleepy to kill their parents and postponed it to the next afternoon when the boys shot each parent multiple times as each returned from work. After cleaning the crime scene in their home, the boys left the house to party. Both boys were arrested when police found the parents' bodies wrapped in plastic in the home's attic. A New Hampshire jury sentenced Robert Dingham to life without parole; his brother received a lesser eighteen-to-thirty-year sentence since he was testified against his older accomplice.

CASE 149

An eleven-year-old Minneola, Florida boy, Patrick Boykin, became enraged at his thirteen-year-old sister, Constance, because he had been beaten twice by his mother for arguing with the sister. On January 25, 1999 the boy shot his sister multiple times as she stood in the kitchen of their home. Both parents were at work at the time of the incident. The young boy, sobbing, told the 911 dispatcher, " I shot my sister . . . I got whipped twice . . . I got real mad." Later, when interviewed by detectives, the young boy indicated that he had been hearing voices from the Devil telling him to kill his sister. He claimed the shooting was accidental and the voices stopped after he shot his sister. In August 1999 a judge ruled that the boy was incompetent to stand trial and sentenced him to a mental institution.

CASE 150

Conan Pope, fifteen, eventually received a four-year sentence for killing his father, Frank Pope, during a family argument in their Las Vegas, Nevada home on January 6, 2000. He pleaded guilty to a voluntary manslaughter charge, thus avoiding a trial on the more serious charge of murder. The teenager told the court that his family was a violent one, where drugs, guns, and abuse were rampant. At the time of the shooting, the boy's father became enraged when he returned home to find dirty dishes piled in the kitchen sink. When the father attempted to swing a broom at the boy and his sixteen-year old sister Desiree, Conan shot him. His defense attorneys argues that the teenager had shot his father in self defense, that the victim had physically and sexually abused his son for years. The father had earlier, in 1962, been convicted of manslaughter in the torture slaying of an infant daughter, serving four years in prison on that charge. Conan Pope, tearful, told the court that even though he was afraid of his father, he wished he was still alive. He read a letter in the courtroom to his sister stating, "To my sister above all, I'm sorry. This was not supposed to happen."

CASE 151

In May 2001, in Rochester, New York, a group of young children were playing baseball when a three-year-old boy threw a stone which hit his six-year-old brother. The older child then hit the three-year old with a brick and then proceeded to beat him in the back and abdomen with a baseball bat. The other children did not intervene and no adults were present during the assault. The two children returned home where their babysitter, the mother's boyfriend, stated that the beaten child seemed lethargic. He bathed both children and put them to bed. The mother returned at midnight, and the next morning she found the boy dead and called police. The Monroe County Family Court ordered the young killer to be placed in a foster home until a decision as to what should be done with him. Under New York State Law, a six-year-old cannot be held criminally responsible for a death. The Family Court which handles such cases, typically seals its proceedings and does not comment upon them.

Family Annihilators

Family annihilators—familicide—typically involves one member of family murdering multiple members of his or her family. Fathers and stepfathers wiping out their wives and children, mothers killing all their children, children killing not only their parents, but siblings and relatives as well—all comprise this type of lethal domestic violence.

What possesses an individual to annihilate his or her family? The reasons are varied. Often the murderous rampage results from a desire to exact revenge, to punish other family members for some real or perceived hurt done to the killer.

Husbands, for example, kill their wives because they believe their wives have wronged them in some unforgivable way; the children are also murdered, either as a way of hurting the wife even more, or because the killers actually feel their lives would be unbearable without the mother he has murdered or a father who either kills himself or will be imprisoned for years to come. Oftentimes these male annihilators are autocrats who believe they are in complete control of their partner and their children, and the destiny of others is in their sole control. When that control is threatened by separation, divorce, economic loss, or unemployment, the killer feels there is no viable future for either him or the family. In his mind, they are "better off dead," freed from the concerns of this world. Some, locked in custody battles for their children kill their spouse and children out of spite: "If I can't have them, no one will." Others fear the family is breaking up anyway as did Ronald Simmons in Arkansas who in 1987 murdered fourteen family members in the largest family massacre in United States history. He believed his children were insubordinate and that his wife planned to leave him and take the children with her.

Children who murder members of their own family often do so to protest what they perceive as excessive control from their parents. They believe that their parents dominate them, allowing them no room to achieve their own goals and wishes. In some cases, the parents, particularly the fathers or stepfathers, are domineering; in other cases the child killer believes them to be so, even if outsiders view the behavior as normal parental concern and responsible control. In either scenario, the parents and the other family members are murdered to allow greater freedom to the killer.

Women who kill all their children often do so for one of many reasons. Generally they kill to make their lives easier, to unload the "baggage" of children who, they believe, hinder their chances of future marriage, or impede a desired lifestyle. They also kill when the future for themselves and their children appears hopeless—"better they die so they can live in heaven as angels than suffer on this hellish earth." In rare cases, they kill for the attention the tragic deaths of their children will bestow on them. Often, in following the pattern termed "Munchausen Syndrome by Proxy," these mothers will kill their own children over a period of years, masking their deaths as rare medical conditions such as SIDS (Sudden Infant Death Syndrome) and as a result receiving a great deal of sympathy and attention from other family members, neighbors and the local media. In Schenectady, New York, Marybeth Tinning over a period of twelve years, lost nine of her children to what appeared to be SIDS. In 1985 authorities finally became suspicious and she was convicted of murder by suffocation. Apparently she craved the attention she invariably received when each child died, and her need to be the center of attention precipitated each murder.

These family murders are not necessarily rare. In the United States since the 1970s, there have been about eight mass slayings of four or more family members per year. The precipitating factor in the majority of these murders is some stressful event, particularly a woman seeking an end to a relationship, with her killer exacting vengeance on her for such a "betrayal." Yet, as noted above, the precipitating event can be anything which sets off the eventual killer, or which the killer perceives as either bringing harm to him or her, or bringing disgrace and attention from the outside community.

CASE 152

Two days before, Mark Clark, thirty-two, from Essex, Maryland had talked to neighbors about killing his family , but no one believed he was serious about the threat. On September 11, 1995, he lured his estranged wife, Betty Louise, and her three children to the Middlesex Shopping Mall near Baltimore where he promised to buy clothing for the family at Newberry's department store. As all five sat in the Ford station wagon, he ignited a bomb which blew apart the vehicle, killing himself, his wife, and the children, Krysta Clark, four, their daughter, and Ricardo Valdez, six, and Melissa Ray, eleven, children of Mrs. Clark from previous relationships. Mrs. Clark had begun a new relationship with Mark Weitzel who later told police, "Yesterday I had a family—a girlfriend and three kids. Now I have nothing." The explosion sent debris half a mile away and knocked out electrical power near the mall.

CASE 153

Joshua Jenkins, fifteen, from Vista, California apparently suffered from emotional difficulties and had difficulty accepting the fact that he had been adopted by George Jenkins, fifty, and his wife Lynn, forty-eight. His parents told neighbors that they feared that he might kill them at some point. On February 16, 1996, he did just that, stabbing and bludgeoning not only his parents but also his grandparents Bill Grossman, seventy-eight, and Ellen Grossman, seventy-four. The next day he took his sister Meagan, ten, shopping to buy an axe which he then used to murder her. He dragged the five bodies to his grandparent's home and set it afire. Firefighters discovered the bodies.

He then disappeared in the family's Mercedes-Benz car. Two days later Jenkins was spotted in the area filling the tires with air and was arrested by police. A jury found the killer guilty and sentenced him to 114 years in prison for the killings to which he confessed.

CASE 154

Sandi Nieves of San Fernando, California felt wronged by her two ex-husbands and was bent on getting revenge for their alleged mistreatment of her. In 1998, she gathered her four daughters ages five to twelve and her son, thirteen, in the kitchen of their home for a slumber party, and instructed them not to leave the kitchen. She then set fire to the house, killing all four of her daughters; the son survived. At her trial where she was convicted on four counts of murder, prosecutors argued that she killed the children to instill guilt in the ex-husbands, to get revenge on them. One husband had fathered two of the daughters; the second husband—who was also the killer's stepfather—fathered the two youngest girls. Her defense attorney argued that Sandi Nieves had been raised in a dysfunctional family and that jurors convicted her on only limited information.

CASE 155

Between 1949 and 1968, Marie Noe of Philadelphia, Pennsylvania bore ten children, none of whom survived to their second birthday; one was still born, another died in the hospital shortly after birth. The remaining eight died mysteriously, and investigators originally believed that the cause of death was SIDS—sudden infant death syndrome, or crib death. Marie Noe received a great deal of sympathy and publicity over these tragedies which were featured in national news media, including *Newsweek* and *Life* magazines. By the 1990s, however, researchers hypothesized that many crib deaths were homicides masked as SIDS. In 1998, Philadelphia police reopened the eight cases and ruled them homicides, arresting Noe, then sixty-nine years old, charging her with first-degree murder. Eventually she confessed to suffocating four of the children with a pillow. Her husband, Arthur Noe, seventy-seven, refused to believe his wife could have murdered the children. Following her indictment for murder, he contemplated suicide, claiming that authorities had ruined his life: "They took my life and my memories. I don't have anything here anymore, except for my dog." He believed that his death would once again enable him to see his babies who never grew up. Prosecutors believed that the deaths were cases of Munchausen Syndrome by Proxy. Marie Noe, in poor health, received a sentence of twenty years probation, with five years of house arrest. She also agreed to an extensive psychiatric study to help determine why she murdered eight of her children.

Notes

1. Finkelhor and Ormrod, 2001, p. 1.
2. Daly and Wilson, 1998, 1996, p. 80.
3. Smith and Zahn, 1999, p. 65.
4. Dawson, 1994.
5. Finkelhor and Omrod, 2001, p. 9.
6. Resnick, 1970.
7. Holmes and Holmes, 2001, p. 122.
8. Holmes and Holmes, 2001, p. 120.
9. Holmes and Holmes, 2001, p. 126.
10. Heide, 1999, pp. 222–223.
11. Hillbrant, et al., 1997.
12. Smith and Zahn, 1999, p. 225.

9

Multiple Victim Homicide

Perhaps the most frightening type of homicide a society encounters are those murders where the killer or killers slaughter many victims whom they do not know. Three general types of homicides constitute this pattern: mass murder, spree murder, and serial murder. Mass murder involves the killing of at least three victims at one time. Spree murder involves the killing of three or more people over a longer period of time, from different times in the same day to a period of a month, but at different locations. Serial murder refers to the killing of three or more victims over an extended period of time, sometimes even years, at different locations. These three types constitute a temporal continuum, ranging from mass killings to spree killings, to serial killings, each delineated by the interval or lack of interval between the murders. Obviously these types of murder command enormous public attention, as do terrorism and genocide which can be considered as types of mass murder event though they can occur at one point in time (e.g., World Trade Center and Pentagon disasters in 2001) or over an extended period of time (e.g., Nazi death camps in 1930s and 1940s). Also attracting attention are professional contract killings and drug gang killings that, because of their volume and temporal occurrence, can be considered types of serial murder. Each of these types rightfully terrifies the public and are categorically different from what might be termed "ordinary " or "typical" murders, those killings which are more routine and predictable (e.g., husbands killing wives, robbers murdering store owners, drinking buddies killing each other in bars, etc.).

While these "ordinary/typical" killings are shocking and tragic, they do not elicit the same degree of societal concern as do the mass, spree, and serial murders. In these routine murders, most of us are removed from the scene and circumstances of that killing. Realistically, we do not regard ourselves as potential likely victims of the killer who stabs a friend at a house party, or the victim of an assailant who shoots another in a drug transaction. We are sheltered in our safe world; they are trapped in their dangerous world. For the most part, therefore, we read and hear about these killings in a detached manner. Sorry though we may be for these victims, they remain distant and foreign to us, mere stories on the ten o'clock television news.

Mass, spree and serial murders constitute a different story. For the most part, the victims of these types of murders are arbitrary and random. None of the twenty-one victims of James Huberty's murderous rampage at a McDonald's Restaurant in San Ysidro, California, in 1984 ever believed they were at risk as they sat down to a meal. Who among Ted Bundy's dozens of victims considered the danger that she would be murdered in such a violent manner? The statistical possibility of being a potential victim of mass, spree or serial murders is considerably smaller than that of an "ordinary " killing, yet the pubic feels far more threatened by these killers precisely because of the supposed random nature of such violence. The mass murder-terrorism of the tragic events of September 11, 2001, created thousands of victims in New York City, Washington D.C. and rural Pennsylvania who did not know their murderers or that they would be chosen to fulfill terrorists' goals. Yet to the mass killer, these victims are not random at all. They are chosen with at least some rationale, as the terrorists believe they are paying "them" back for past hurts and injustice done.

Though there are obvious differences between the backgrounds, personalities, and psychological composition of terrorists, mass murderers, spree killers and serial killers, they share certain features in common. Whether organized or disorganized, sane or insane, privileged or dispossessed, these killers view their victims in a depersonalized manner, as mere objects that can be manipulated and eliminated to accomplish the killer's goal. Workers in the World Trade Center, Holocaust victims in Nazi death camps, children of family annihilators, students at Columbine high school in Colorado, prostitute victims of sadistic serial killers—all are pawns in the killer's mind as he seeks to eliminate his victims for political or monetary gain, or to exact

revenge for some perceived wrong done to him. His victims are eliminated coldly and methodically, either quickly and horrendously, as
with the terrorist and professional assassin, or slowly and sadistically,
as with the serial sexual sadist. Whatever the method, the killer seeks
to assert his full control over the unknowing victim. They are his to
dispose of in whatever manner suits him, so much "stuff" to be dis-
patched at his command, expendable detritus in the killer's world of
life and death. The victims are in the wrong place at the wrong time
and are at the killer's disposal to satiate and satisfy his desire for
revenge, financial gain, lust, notoriety, political agenda, or any con-
ceivable motive deemed adequate by him.

To the world outside, these murders are the incomprehensible and
inexplicable work of a madman who has suddenly gone berserk; to the
killer, the crimes are logical, rationale, and moral, fitting retribution
against his enemies or those who are surrogates for his enemies. In his
murderous acts, he is in total control, perhaps for the first time in his
life.

Mass Murder

Though there is some debate as to the actual number of victims
needed to defined mass murder, most observers agree that it entails
the killing of at least three people in one place and at one time.[1]
Oftentimes, mass murder involves many more murders, as, for example, Julio Gonzalez's 1990 massacre of eighty-seven victims in the
South Bronx, New York City Happy Land Social Club which he
firebombed to get back at his girlfriend who had broken off her relationship with him. Ironically, his intended victim survived the attack
and named him as the culprit responsible for igniting the fire in the
crowded club.

As we will point out shortly, mass murder differs from serial murder not only in the time and place sequence of the killings, but also in
the motivation and methods through which the murders are conducted.
Mass murders are also different from spree murders, which refer to the
murders of multiple victims over a longer period of time in different
locations; spree murders may involve as many victims as mass murder, but they are scattered rather than concentrated in one area, and
killed over a longer time frame.

Numerous classification systems exist for types of mass murders, and there is no consensus as to these types. Park Dietz identifies three types: family annihilators (discussed in the previous chapter), pseudocommandos (those preoccupied with guns and military tactics and who kill in commando-style types of attacks), and set-and-run killers (those who seek, plan, execute, and leave the scene of the killings, invisible and undetected, as for example, food tamperers and those who plant a bomb in a public place to explode after the bomber has successfully left the killing site.[2] Holmes and Holmes add two additional types: the disciple killer (the killer whose charismatic qualities attract a cult-like following who kill for their leader's cause, as in the case of Charles Manson and his followers), and the disgruntled employee (those who retaliate against supervisors who have either mistreated them or fired them from their jobs).[3] Thomas O'Reilly-Fleming adds a sixth category, the mentally disordered killer whose psychiatric condition erupts in a violent, murderous rage.[4] To extend the list further, I would add the robber-assassin type who kills witnesses to his crime so as to prevent his later identification by them (c.f. Michael Kelleher, for a different classification schema[5]).

With the obvious exception of the mentally deranged psychotic killer, these various types of mass murderers plot their killings beforehand in a reasonably organized fashion. Even though they may not be emotionally stable in the view of the general public, they know exactly what they are doing. Some are paranoid, feeling mistreated and persecuted by others. Some feel they have reached the end of the line in their jobs, or in their family life. The catalyst may be a demotion, a divorce, a bankruptcy, or any similar event that triggers the slaughter. Some, like the robber-assassin, are anti-social personality types whose sociopathic behavior manifests itself in their emotional and moral indifference to the massacre of the witness to their crime. Whatever their mental state, mass killers display some ability to plan and organize their lethal deeds as they coldly and methodically seek out their victims to exact vengeance.

Virtually all of these killers displayed signs of serious emotional problems long before the rampage, but few outsiders picked up on the warning signs. They often talked openly of killing others and frequently stockpiled weapons for this purpose. They did not snap or "go postal" without warning signs. The triggering event is merely the straw that broke the camel's back.

Their victims may be complete strangers to the killer, as were those of George Hennard whose 1991 rampage in Killeen, Texas, killed twenty-three customers in Luby's Cafeteria as he drove his pickup truck through the restaurant's window and then proceeded to shoot patrons indiscriminately. Yet other mass killers know their victims, as in the case of family annihilators, whose massacres account for almost 40 percent of all victims of mass murder in America. So also in the case of workplace massacres where the killer singles out those who he believes persecuted him in some way, as did Joseph Wesbecker when he killed eight employees at the Standard Gravure Printing Company in Louisville, Kentucky, in 1989 after he had been placed on disability leave for psychiatric problems. Others may be victims of upset clients who seek revenge for what they regard as fraudulent or poor professional services; Gian Ferri walked into the San Francisco law firm of Pettit and Martin in 1993 and fatally shot six people whom he believed had failed to give him proper legal counsel in his failed trailer park business. Still others may be victims of killers who seek to avenge the insults, real or perceived, which they have suffered from others, as did Eric Harris and Dylan Klebold, in their 1999 massacre of thirteen fellow students at Columbine High School in Littleton, Colorado. Similar revenge mass killings occurred in numerous other school shootings throughout the country.

Finally there are those innocent victims who may have been acquainted with their killers, but who were killed to prevent them from telling police about the crime. These "leave no witnesses" killers often execute multiple victims in armed robberies of commercial establishments. The Wendy's Restaurant massacre of five employees in Queens, New York City, in May 2000, serves as an example of this type. John Taylor and Craig Godineaux gagged and herded seven employees into the store freezers, shooting them execution-style , one-by-one; only two survived the ordeal. Taylor and Godineaux killed the employees who could identify them, covering up their robbery of $2,400 from the eatery.[6]

Firearms are the weapons of choice of mass murderers since it is difficult to kill large numbers at one time by means of knives, strangulation, beatings and so forth. Other weapons include fire, bombs and explosives, and vehicles such as planes and buses that, in effect, become lethal weapons in the hands of mass murderers, and terrorists in particular.

Qualitatively, mass murderers differ in many ways from the "typical" or "ordinary" killer. In a study of 102 rampage killers over a fifty-year period, the *New York Times* discovered that rampage killers are older, better educated, more likely to be unemployed, and more likely to kill themselves than typical killers. Also they tend to be overwhelmingly male, White, have military experience, kill during the day, and fail to get away after their rampage. Of the 102 rampage murders, sixty-five had killed three or more victims, classifying them also as mass murderers.[7]

CASE 156

Andrew Kehoe, a farmer, served as the treasurer of the Bath Consolidated School in Bath, Michigan in 1927. Angered by the increase in local taxes to support the new school, Kehoe spent weeks storing dynamite in the school's basement, stringing electric wires throughout the building that fateful spring. His fury stemmed from his fear that his farm would be foreclosed because he might not be able to pay the new tax assessment. Kehoe also wired his farmhouse to dynamite stored there. Shortly after 9:45 A.M. on May 18, 1927, as Kehoe was seen running from the school's premises, a giant blast destroyed the north section of the school. After the explosion, Kehoe returned to the schoolyard where terrified students, teachers, and parents had assembled. There, he called the school's superintendent to his car, spoke to him, and then fired a gun into the back seat of the vehicle, igniting still more dynamite, killing himself and the superintendent. In total, in the two blasts thirty-eight children, two teachers, the superintendent, two onlookers, and Kehoe perished. When police arrived at his farm they discovered that Kehoe had killed his wife and blown up six of the buildings on his farm, all timed to go off simultaneously that morning. On the fence near his farmhouse. Kehoe had painted a sign which read, "Criminals are Made, Not Born." The day of the massacre was the last day of school before summer vacation.

CASE 157

William Lembcke, sixteen, became angry when his father reprimanded him for not assisting in bringing firewood into their Addy, Washington, home. On December, 23, 2000, the teenager waited until his father came out of the shower and shot Robert Lembcke, forty-nine, point-blank range in the head. He then executed his mother Diana, forty-three, who suffered from multiple sclerosis, his sister Jolene, eighteen, and his brother Wesley, twelve. He attempted to conceal his rampage by cleaning the house and painting the walls which had blood splattered on them. He dumped the bodies in a ditch near the house, telling relatives that the family had taken a trip to California. When he finally confessed to the killings a week later, he told police that he killed his mother, sister and brother so as to leave no witnesses to the crime. A jury convicted Lembcke on all four murders and the Stevens County judge sentenced him to life in prison.

CASE 158

Ki Yung Park, fifty-four, had been acting strangely. He operated his Houston, Texas convenience store somewhat erratically; on some days he would open and close several times during business hours; on other days he wouldn't open at all. Park suspected another business owner, Chong Chang, fifty-eight, of having an affair with his estranged wife, Byong Sun Park, forty-two. On January 9, 2001, Park entered Chang's business the Amko Trading Company, and shot him, his wife Hyon, fifty-four, and their daughter Kathy, twenty-three. When Houston police arrived at the murder scene, Park shot himself fatally. On searching Park's convenience store hours later, investigators found his estranged wife's body in the freezer. Friends of the gunman indicated that Park not only believed that Chang and Byong Sun were having a relationship behind his back, but that Change was trying to destroy his convenience store business. In his shooting rampage, Park carefully singled out his victims, ignoring the other employees and customers. Witnesses indicated that before he shot the Changs he stated, "They murdered my family, and now I'm going to murder them."

Spree Murders

The spree killer murders three or more people at different locations over a more extended period of time than the time frame of the mass killer. In some cases, the differences between these two categories of murder are difficult to discern: how long must the interval between murders be?; how far apart must the locations of each killing in the rampage be? In 1949, in Camden, New Jersey, Howard Unruh murdered thirteen people in less than fifteen minutes as he killed victims in a shoe repair store, a barbershop, an apartment over a drug store, and pedestrians walking on Camden streets. A World War II veteran, Unruh believed his neighbors laughed at him behind his back. When he discovered that someone had stolen the gate to his front yard fence, his rampage began, he specifically searched for Rose and Charles Cohen who had earlier complained about Unruh's loud radio. After shooting the Cohens, he planned to decapitate them but later admitted that he forgot to bring his machete with him. Finally surrendering to the police, he was diagnosed as a paranoid schizophrenic and committed to a state mental institution.[8] Should Unruh be classified as a spree killer or a mass murderer? Technically he fits the criterion of multiple murders over time, but the time frame is quite compressed. His selection of targets in different locations fits the definition more closely than does the temporal aspects of his crime. This suggests that the locale of each of the spree murderer's killings assumes primary importance in determining whether the killings are mass or spree murders. However, these distinctions are probably meaningless for most killers, and the families and friends of those murdered as they try to deal with the ravages of such rampages.

The sensational murder of Gianni Versace, the internationally known fashion designer in Miami, Florida in July 1997 clearly fits the spree murder scenario. His killer, Andrew Cunanan, began his killing spree three months earlier, eventually killing five people as he moved across the country, murdering former homosexual lovers and complete strangers. He began his killing spree in San Diego, California, moved to Minneapolis, Minnesota, then to Chicago; from there he traveled to Pennsville, New Jersey where he continued his rampage and finally stopped in Miami, Florida killing Versace and where he eventually shot himself in a stolen houseboat on July 23, 1997. His murder spree lasted weeks, and geographically traversed the nation.

Typically, spree murders entail hit-and-run tactics as the killer moves from one target to the next. He seeks to elude capture and the rampage only stops when he has no escape as police move in, often by his own suicide. Unlike the mass murderer who stops when he has exacted vengeance on his victims, the spree killer keeps going until he literally can't continue. Cunanan reached the end of the line in the Florida houseboat and killed himself; Unruh surrendered in his own house in Camden when police laid siege to it.

Similar to mass murderers, spree killers tend to choose victims known to them. Like Unruh and Cunanan, they retaliate against people they have known well, or at least with whom they are acquainted. Other victims can be total strangers to the spree killer; two of Unruh's victims were young children; one of Cunanan's victims was a cemetery worker whose truck he commandeered. These strangers literally illustrate the "wrong place, wrong time" phenomenon. Yet there are notable exceptions. As in the case of mass murders involving robbery, the spree killer often selects victims who are virtual strangers to him, but massacres either individuals or groups of robbery victims so that no live witnesses remain to identify him to police.

CASE 159

Douglas Gretzlen, forty-seven, had been Arizona's death row longer than any prisoner in the state's history. After twenty-five years in prison he was executed by lethal injection in June, 1998. Before his execution he said he was sorry for his crimes and extended his love to his family and friends. Gretzlen received the death sentence for two of the seventeen murders committed by him and his accomplice, Willie Steelman, in their month-long murder spree in Arizona and California in November, 1973. Steelman died in prison of liver disease, escaping execution. The pair began their crime spree by robbing their victims, but later decided to kill them so as to avoid being identified to police. In Victor, California they executed nine people: Walter and Joanne Parker; their children Robert, nine, and Lisa, eleven, the family babysitter, Debra Earl; her parents, brother and boyfriend. All were tied up in a closet and shot in the back of the head. The proceeds of this robbery-murder netted $4,000. In his final statement, Gretzlen stated, "from the bottom of my soul I am so deeply sorry and have been for years . . . I apologize to all 17 victims and their families." He also thanked his family and friends "for life's lessons learned."

CASE 160

Mark Barton, forty-four, suffered major financial losses totaling almost $500,000 in his stock day-trading activities conducted through two Atlanta, Georgia investment firms: All-Tech, and Momentum Securities. In a single day in 1999 he lost $150,000. In his suicide note he vowed vengeance on those who he believed had ruined him, writing, "I don't plan to live very much longer, just long enough to kill as many of the people that greedily sought my destruction." On July 29,1999 he entered the two Atlanta investment firms, systematically killed nine people and wounded many more. Cornered by police later that day, he shot himself. His murderous spree actually started two days earlier when he fatally beat his second wife, Leigh Ann Barton, twenty-seven, with a hammer in their house in Stockbridge, Georgia. The next day he took his two children, Matthew, twelve, and Michelle, eight, shopping and then murdered them that night as they slept in their beds. After their deaths, he submerged them in the bathtub to insure that they were dead and then tucked each in bed with their favorite toy. His suicide note read, "I killed Leigh Ann because she was one of the main reasons for my demise . . . I killed the children to keep them from suffering so much later. No mother, not father, no relatives." Police investigators also suspected that Barton had murdered his first wife and her mother six years earlier in Alabama, to collect insurance money and make it possible to marry Leigh Ann, his mistress at that time.

Case 161

Hatred of blacks, Jews and Asians fueled Richard Baumhammer's murderous crime spree on April 28, 2000 when he murdered five people and paralyzed a sixth in the Pittsburgh, Pennsylvania, area. Baumhammer, thirty-six, lived with his parents in Mount Lebanon, Pennsylvania. His victims included: Anita Gordon, his Jewish next door neighbor; Amil Thakur, an Indian computer engineer; Thao Pham, a Vietnamese delivery man; Ji-Ye Sun, the manager of a Chinese restaurant; Garry Lee, an African-American client at a karate school; and Sandip Patel, an Indian working in an Indian grocery store (whom he shot and wounded, paralyzing Patel from the neck down). In this killing rampage, Baumhammer traveled to different locations in the Mount Lebanon-Pittsburgh area seeking victims. Police finally apprehended him in Ambridge, Pennsylvania as he approached a nearby synagogue, presumably to add more victims to his total. Baumhammer's defense team argued that he suffered from paranoid schizophrenia and that voices ordered him to kill his victims. The Allegheny County jury that heard the case found him guilty on five counts of murder, and he received the death sentence on each of five killings. Because of the nature of his crimes and the underlying racism and ethnocentrism in them, Baumhammer is segregated from the other prisoners so as to protect him from them.

Serial Murder

More so than with any other type of homicide, serial murder commands the immediate attention of both law enforcement officers and the general public. Serial killers, such as Ted Bundy, John Wayne Gacy, David Berkowitz ("Son of Sam"), Wayne Williams ("The Atlanta Child Killer"), Jeffrey Dahmer, the most prolific of all, Gary Ridgeway ("The Green River Killer") are familiar to most of us. The true crime sections of our bookstores abound with accounts of dozens of other less familiar serial murderers. Fictitious serial killers command similar if not even greater familiarity; who among us is unfamiliar with Hannibal "the Cannibal" Lecter of *Silence of the Lambs* fame?

Serial killers mesmerize the public because their violence extends over time and differs substantively from the spontaneous violence of "ordinary" killers, and from the concentrated explosive mayhem of mass and spree murderers. They elude capture by their cunning, their carefully planned murder scenarios, and their disposal of their unwary victims. Were this not so, they would have been apprehended long before their body count exceeded the threshold of three victims, the generally accepted number necessary for the definition of serial homicide. One wonders how many more serial killers we might have encountered in the United States were it not for successful law enforcement efforts which nipped potential serial killers after their first or second murders.

Extrinsic and Intrinsic Motivators

Serial killers encompass a wide range of types. The lust killer, the mafia hit man, the adolescent "gangbanger," the killer intent on ridding the earth of certain types of undesirables, the "black widow" female who kills various companions for their fortunes, the drug lord assassin, the "killer angel" who murders nursing home and hospital patients—all are serial murderers who eliminate three or more victims over time, and all to varying degrees are anti-social personality types who sociopathic behavior fuels their lethal violence. Some may even be deranged and totally disorganized in their murders, though these acutely psychotic types tend to be apprehended quickly because of their failure to cover their tracks coherently and methodically.

What differentiates these diverse serial killers is their motivation. Why do they kill? In what way is the organized crime assassin different from the killer who chooses homosexuals, or prostitutes, or young children as victims? The compelling motivation can be either *extrinsic motivation* or *intrinsic motivation*; in the former, the reasons for killing relate to external factors in the killer's milieu, such as money, group esteem, personal status etc; in the latter, the reasons are internal, psychologically driven obsessive desires which propel the killer towards murder.

Extrinsic Type. The extrinsic type murders to attain some socially desired end—money, power, individual honor, group esprit de corps. This killer may even advertise his murders to his peers so as to enhance his own status within that group. Hence the "gangbanger" violence of a Los Angeles homeboy inflates his prestige and status within his set; through his violence he displays his devotion to his gang and its reputation, signaling to all that he is willing to kill for personal and gang honor. So also does the drug lord whose gangs may kill dozens of victims, oftentimes members of rival drug gangs, in an attempt to control a lucrative trade in heroin, crack or any similar substance that is highly desired by the public at large. These murders, often brutal and shocking, serve to intimidate police witnesses, eliminate rivals, and establish the ruthlessness of the gang and its leaders.

The organized crime hit man behaves in a similar fashion. His kills are business kills, accomplished because that's his job as he follows the orders of others. Money, professional competence, his group's respect and awe over his deeds—all can be motivating factors as he murders. His kills are quick, impersonal, and relatively efficient with littler or no regard or interest in his victim's persona. Sexual and violence fantasies, and elaborately planned torture/mutilation scenarios are not typically central to his killings either in their planning or execution. His actions are instrumental rather than expressive and emotional as he plies his trade. Thus a killer such as Sammy "The Bull" Gravano could murder nineteen victims with little regard for the havoc he has created. These murders constituted a major part of his "occupation" as he executed the orders of his "bosses," men like John Gotti and others in New York City's Gambino crime family. Similar motivations drive robber-murderers who kill those they have robbed so as to eliminate witnesses to their crimes. It's almost as if these killers announce to their victims, "nothing personal" as they dispatch them.

The drug lord who executes his rivals further exemplifies this extrinsic type of killer. Often the drug assassinations may involve elements of both mass murder, where numerous rivals are eliminated at one time, and spree murder, where a series of rivals are killed in a relatively short period. Also, these extrinsic types can include numerous killers collectively murdering multiple victims over time in order to establish the ascendancy of their gang in a given neighborhood or locale. Hence, a drug crew can include within it multiple serial killers who successively murder either multiple rivals, or members of their own gang who have angered them. Even a cursory glance of the newspapers in cities such as Los Angeles, Chicago, Miami, and New York City would reveal how extensive and violent these drug gangs, crews, and posses actually are, murdering each other in callous, grisly and heinous fashion whether in drive-by shootings, or planned executions, wreaking havoc on fellow criminals and innocent bystanders alike. A substantial proportion of all murders in America, particularly in our inner cities are either directly or indirectly related to drugs and their manufacture and distribution—tabooed substances which all too many live and die for.

A final example of the extrinsic type is the killer who murders a number of victims over time so as to obtain money from their insurance policies, benefit checks, and inheritances. Often, these killers are females who either poison or suffocate their victims.[9] Though they certainly know and interact often with their victims who more often than not are family members or spouses, their actions are primarily instrumental. They do not kill for vengeance, or out of anger; rather they kill for the instrumental end of obtaining money and the material comforts it can provide. "Black Widow" female killers thus may murder a succession of victims and "lonely hearts" male killers slay numerous women so as to obtain their fortunes. In all of these situations, it's "nothing personal."

Case 162

No one seems certain how Harry Strauss got his nicknames, "Pittsburgh Phil" and "Pep", but the first one became his "nom de plume" in the annals of the history of organized crime in America where many regard him as the most accomplished "hit man" or enforcer ever to work his trade. A minimum of twenty-five kills have been attributed to him, but knowledgeable observers believe the number closer to 100.

Pittsburgh Phil emerged as the chief enforcer for Murder, Inc., the Brooklyn-based crime organization which offered murder-for-hire to gangsters wishing to eliminate other criminals in the wide-open gangster wars of the late 1920s, 1930s, and 1940s. Some of the most famous criminals of that era worked with Murder, Inc.(Charles "Lucky" Luciano, Joey Adonis, Albert, "Lord High Executioner" Anastasia, Benjamin "Bugsy" Siegel etc.), enforcing the decrees of the syndicates and resolving the disputes they had with other underworld figures. But the core of Murder Inc. revolved around the gangsters in the Brownsville section of Brooklyn, centering on Pittsburgh Phil, "Kid Twist" Reles, "Happy" Maione and "Buggsy" Goldstein. They comprised the main corps of killers who hired themselves out to assassinate those who had displeased their syndicate patrons.

Pittsburgh Phil actually enjoyed killing others and did so without remorse, rarely inquiring about his victims or their backgrounds. His victims included the famous and not so famous of the underworld: Harry Millman of Detroit's Purple Gang whom he gunned down in a crowded restaurant; Walter "Harry" Sage, suspected of skimming pinball machine profits, whom he ice picked multiple times and whose body was discover in a Catskill Mountain lake, tethered to a pin-ball machine; Meyer Shapiro, a Brooklyn crime boss whom he allegedly buried alive; "Puggy" Feinstein whom he strangled, stabbed, and set on fire; and dozens of others whose identities are lost in the dustbin of organized crime history.

Always resourceful, Pittsburgh Phil cleverly dealt with the most bizarre circumstances. Carl Sifakis recounts the story of one of his Florida victims, a Mafia old-timer who knew no English. Pittsburgh Phil used sign language to communicate with him, leading him to believe he had been sent from Brooklyn to kill someone else, seeking the advice of the old-timer as to how best to do it. After he showed the unsuspecting victim his briefcase of possible weapons, the old-time chose a rope and led Pittsburgh Phil to a dark alley where he could murder in safety. Pittsburgh then strangled the naive victim and returned to Brooklyn, his task completed.

The work of Murder, Inc., quickly unraveled in 1940 after Pittsburgh Phil, along with Reles, Maione, and Goldstein were arrested for the murder of George Rudnick, a suspected police informant. In custody, Reles began to tell police everything about Murder, Inc. as well as the identities of victims assassinated by the crew eventually describing eighty-five separate murders. Pittsburgh Phil was indicted for one of these, the murder of "Puggy" Feinstein, and found guilty. His fate sealed, he was executed in the electric chair on June 12, 1941, along with Buggsy Goldstein (see Sifakis, 1982, pp. 571–573 for an interesting assessment of Pittsburgh Phil's life and "exploits").

CASE 163

A gang war between three factions seeking to control the drug trade in New York City's South Bronx's East 138th Street resulted in twenty-seven murders in a two-year period, from 1976–1978. The three gangs—the Teenager-Ramins, the Renegade-Colons, and the Julitos—abducted each other's members and systematically executed them, often in bizarre and brutal ways. The body parts of two such victims' (Gumersindo Torres and Oscar Ocasio) body parts were discovered in three separate cardboard cartons by local school children. Torres had been murdered by means of an electric saw that had been used to kill and dismember him. Ocasio died of fright as he awaited his turn to be cut up with the same saw by member of the Teenagers-Ramins on the makeshift execution platform, a ping-pong table set up in the basement of an area tenement building. Other victims in each faction were shot, stabbed, and beaten to death. Police finally rounded-up the main killers of each gang in 1978, ending the war on 138th Street. One killer, "Hollywood," told detectives that he had been a contract killer since age fifteen. He admitted to them, "I did 10, maybe 15 contracts, but never legitimate people. I wouldn't do anything like that. And I never used the same gun." Following the dismantling of all the gangs, police learned that a new gang had moved into the area, filling the vacuum left there. A new gang, and new victims—nothing really changed.

C ASE **164**

Dorothea Puente typifies the "Black Widow" killer. Similar to the black widow spider that disposes of her mate when he is no longer useful, Puente allegedly murdered at least seven elderly men and women to obtain their Social Security checks. Born in 1929 in Redlands, California, she was abused as a small child by both her parents, both of whom died before she was six years old. She married in 1946 but her husband died of natural causes in 1948. In need of money she began forging checks, was arrested, and served time in jail. She remarried but the second marriage ended in divorce. Eventually she began taking care of elderly, destitute people, and set up her own boarding house in Sacramento, California in 1968. She frequented many of the local bars seeking older men for company, particularly those receiving disability benefits or Social Security payments. Vivacious, friendly, and outgoing, she went out of her way to impress social workers who would refer elderly clients to her home.

One of her boarders, known only as Chief, became her handyman. His main job was to excavate the home's basement, and cover it with a cement floor. When Chief finished this task he disappeared, never to be seen again. The basement became the burial site for a number of her victims.

Her usual "modus operandi" involved befriending local elderly drunks, stealing, forging, and cashing their benefits checks. Many of her victims were so deranged they scarcely knew that Puente had scammed them. Eventually she was caught and sent to jail in 1982.

After her release in 1985, her tactics became lethal. From 1985 to 1988, a number of her boarders disappeared yet she continued to receive their pension and benefits checks and cash them. One such resident, Everson Gillmouth, seventy-seven, fell madly in love with Puente and opened a joint bank account with her. In November, 1985 he disappeared, the same time that she had hired a handyman to build a box six feet long, three feet wide and two feet deep. After he had built the box, she allegedly dumped Gillmouth's body in it and she and the handyman deposited it on a riverbank; she told him there was nothing in it but old household junk. Two months later, two fisherman found the box in the river with Gillmouth's remains inside. In August 1986 Betty Palmer, seventy-seven, disappeared as did Leona Carpenter, seventy-eight, in February 1987. James Gallop, sixty-two, Vera Martin, sixty-two, and Bert Montoya disappeared in the next few months, as did Dorothy Miller and Bert Fink. All had been residents at Puente's boarding house. A suspicious social worker alerted police who obtained a warrant to search the house and excavate the garden and basement. Eventually they unearthed seven bodies all of whom had lethal doses of the drug flurazepam in them. Puete had fled but was eventually captured when her new companion, Charles Willgues, lonely and ill, a recipient of disability benefits, recognized her picture on TV. With the help of a CBS news service editor, Gene Silver, police arrested Puente in Los Angeles in 1988. In 1990, her case was tried in Sacramento, charged with nine counts of murder. After many delays, the trial concluded in 1993. The jury found her guilty of three of the murders and Judge Michael Virga sentenced Puente to life in prison without the possibility of parole. Upon hearing the verdict, Puente said, "I didn't kill anyone."

Instrinsic Type. The intrinsic type murders because of internal psychological pressure to do so. Such killers derive enormous psychic satisfaction in fulfilling their obsessive and pathological desire to stalk, apprehend, and/or torture their victims before actually killing them. In their mind set and fantasies, they are continually on the hunt for potential prey. In those who eventually become serial murderers, the fantasy becomes reality, transformed from an illusion to actual murderous deeds.

When most people think of serial murderers, they visualize this intrinsic type, the killer whose *modus operandi* involves sexually sadistic fantasies, elaborately planned abductions, torture, mutilation, and bizarre corpse disposals. Most intrinsic types of serial murders involve some combination of these thoughts and behaviors as any analysis of some of the lives of the most notorious American serial killers will illustrate (e.g., Ted Bundy, Ken Bianchi "The Hillside Strangler," Richard Ramirez "The Night Stalker," etc.). The method employed in each murder may vary somewhat but his "signature" remains relatively constant, employing a sequence of obsessive actions in each killing that have a rational meaning only to the killer but to no one else. Thus the killer may select different types of victims, kill each by different means yet leave an unmistakable pattern, a signature in each killing which repeats itself in subsequent murders, confirming the pathological mind set of the killer.[10] Though far less com-

mon than their male counterparts, certain female intrinsically motivated serial murderers exist as, for example women classified as
Munchausen Syndrome by Proxy, described earlier; these women kill
their children, to fulfill their pathological desire to be the center of
attention and sympathy. Marybeth Tinning of Schenectady, New York,
whose nine children died "mysteriously" over a number of years would
exemplify this type.

Male or female, solo killer or team killers, these murderers are
motivated by their internal, psychological fears and pathological desires to act out their fantasies. They kill to satiate or silence the demons within, seeking to conceal their outrageous actions, hiding them
from the knowledge and the view of others. Team killers such as Ken
Bianchi and his cousin Angelo Buono jointly acted-out their bizarre
thoughts, elaborately seeking to actualize their fantasies as they
strangled and tortured more than a dozen women in the 1970s in
California and Washington. Yet even team killers are essentially lon-
ers, joining other similar sociopathic killers only for the purpose of
acting out their mutually bizarre scripts.

The intrinsically motivated serial murderer remains trapped in the
dungeon of his own mind, a loner and a social misfit who hides his
disturbed thoughts and fantasies lest others realize what evil lurks
within, which seeks to expend itself in the murders of others who fit
his predetermined pattern of the ideal scapegoat to be sacrificed.

R. Holmes and J. DeBurger present an interesting typology of four
types of serial murderers.[11] Though these researchers do not differentiate the extrinsic and intrinsic types, their classification schema encompasses the intrinsically-motivated serial killer. The four types they
identify are: the visionary killer (who sees visions or hears voices
from God or demons demanding that he kill); the mission killer (who
goes on a mission to eliminate certain categories of people deemed
undesirable by him); the hedonistic killer (who kills for the thrill of
killing, whether for sexual enjoyment or for the sheer excitement of
killing); the power/control killer (who gets satisfaction from the total
domination of his victim, bending the victims completely to his power).
All four types derive from the internal, intrinsically motivated psychological needs and desires of the killer even though the actual forms
and modus operandi of the killings may differ substantially from each
other. Whatever the motive, its origin lies within the disturbed thought
process of the killer.

Their victims typically come from certain groups within the general population—young children, runaways, prostitutes, and homosexuals. The common thread that unites these seemingly disparate groups is the willingness of the members of each group "to go with strangers," to trust in the initial relationship however fleeting or superficial it may appear. Thus prostitutes will enter cars with virtual stranger customers, and young children happily walk off with their murderers who promise them whatever it takes to get them under their control. These victims literally enter the traps set by their killers, unaware of the tragic and violent end that awaits them. The disturbed pathological frame of mind of the killer cunningly creates the rational scenario wherein the victim believes the killer and is eventually trapped in the horror of his fatal web.

CASE 165

In 1979 and 1980, William Bonin, the notorious "Freeway Killer" raped and murdered twenty-one young men in the Los Angeles area, dumping their bodies along the state's freeways. He confessed to all twenty-one slayings and was convicted of fourteen of them. On February 23, 1996, Bonin, forty-nine, was executed by lethal injection for his crimes; no relatives claimed his body which was cremated, his ashes scattered over the Pacific Ocean.

He rarely killed alone. Accompanied by different accomplices, he would cruise for boys, convince them to go with him, subdue them by handcuffing them, rape them, and then strangle them with the victim's own tee shirt. His victims ranged from ages twelve to nineteen. In 1980, police arrested Bonin as he was molesting a young boy in his van, ending the reign of the "Freeway Killer."

One accomplice, James Munro, indicated that Bonin often appeared to be in a frenzy as he murdered his victims. "It was like he was a monster," said Munro. He testified against his former partner, and received a reduced prison sentence of fifteen years for his cooperation.

Bonin's early life illustrates family dysfunction. Raised by an alcoholic and physically abusive father, and by a mother who extended little love or affection on Bonin and his two brothers, he lived in orphanages and detention centers. At age eight, he was molested in one such center where he agreed to homosexual contact with an older if the older molester would tie his own hands behind his back so

Bonin would feel safe in the encounter. Years later, when he murdered, Bonin tied up his victims before strangling them.

Psychiatrists and psychologists who examined Bonin before his trial found evidence of brain damage and manic-depressive psychosis, yet the prosecution successfully argued that he was sane, well-organized, and in control of himself and his victims at the time of the murders. Prosecutors reminded the jury that he had served honorably in the army in the Vietnam War and received several merit citations and medals. He was a killer in rational control of his actions as he pursued and murdered his victims.

His obsession and passion for killing eventually consumed him and Bonin even told reporters, "I'd still be killing. I couldn't stop killing. It got easier each time." The Deputy District Attorney Sterling Noris indicated in his prosecution of the case that, "Bonin loved killing. He delighted in talking about it."

CASE 166

In 1984, during an eight-month period the bodies of ten young females were found in various locations around Tampa Bay, Florida. All had been murdered; most had been bound and strangled, though one had been shot, and another had her throat cut. When discovered, each body yielded carpet fibers identical to those on the other bodies, except for two bodies which had been skeletonized, yielding virtually no forensic evidence. Most of the victims worked as either prostitutes or exotic dancers in the Nebraska Avenue-Kennedy Boulevard vicinity, an area known for prostitution. Police in the jurisdiction where the bodies were discovered knew they had a serial killer on the loose since the "signature" of the murdered—the ligatures used to bind and asphyxiate most of the victims and the dumping of the bodies—appeared identical in eight of the homicides. Furthermore, tire marks from the three locations where the bodies of Nageun Thi Long, twenty, Michelle Sims, twenty-two, and Kim Swann, twenty-one, had been discovered appeared to be identical. Police believed that the same vehicle transported these three victims, and probably the remaining bodies to the various locations where the killer discarded them.

The break in the case occurred when the killer abducted a teenager, Lisa McKey, seventeen, as she rode her bicycle from a local shop in Tampa. He raped her in an unknown apartment but did not kill her.

Instead, he blindfolded her and released her after driving to an ATM machine at 3AM on November 13, 1984. The victim managed to peer under her blindfold and saw that the car was a Dodge Magnum with a red interior. Police traced all transactions on Tampa ATMs at that time, as well as obtaining registrations on all cars fitting the description given by Lisa. Eventually the car and bank transactions led to an X-Ray technician and electrician Robert Joe Long as the chief suspect. Lisa identified Long as the rapist from a picture taken by Police who had photographed him on a traffic stop. After his arrest, police and forensic investigators from the FBI discovered that the carpet fibers found on most of the murdered women matched the carpet in Long's car. Long confessed to the murders and explained how he had abducted and murdered each of his victims. After his trial in which he pleaded guilty to all crimes, he received various life sentences for his crimes, and two death sentences for the murders of two of victims, Virginia Johns and Michelle Simms. Following numerous unsuccessful appeals and additional re-trials in the late 1980s and 1990s, Long awaits his execution in a Florida prison.

CASE 167

From August 1997 until his capture in July 1999, Angel Resendez, thirty-nine, murdered nine people in Texas, Kentucky and Illinois. Dubbed "The Railroad Killer" by police and the press, Resendez chose his victims close to railroad lines that he rode illegally and somewhat aimlessly throughout the South and Midwest.

In Lexington, Kentucky, in August 1997 he attacked Christopher Maier, twenty-one, and his girlfriend, twenty-three, as they walked along tracks near the University of Kentucky; she survived but Maier died after being bludgeoned by Resendez. In October, 1998, he beat to death Leafie Mason, eighty-seven, with a tire iron in her Hughes Springs, Texas home; In December 1998 he broke into the home of Dr. Claudia Benton, thirty-nine, and raped, stabbed, and bludgeoned her to death; his next victim was Reverend Norman Sirnic, forty-six, and his wife Karen, forty-seven, murdered in their parsonage in Weimer, Texas in May, 1999; a month later he bludgeoned Naomi Dominguez, twenty-six, in her Houston, Texas, apartment, killing her; on the same day in Weimar, Texas he murdered Josephine Konvicha, seventy-three, in her bed, using a garden tool as his weapon; his last victims, George

Morber, eighty, and his daughter Carolyn Frederick, fifty-two, were shot and clubbed to death by Resendez in June, 1999 in their home in Gorham, Illinois. All of the murders took place in close proximity to railroad tracks.

Policed identified Resendez as the chief suspect in the murders through fingerprints left on two vehicles he had taken from separate victims. However, he was difficult to apprehend since he had no known address and typically would ride freight trains with no fixed pattern nor particular destination. He was placed on the FBI's Top Ten Most Wanted list and his common-law wife Julietta Reyes offered to help him turn himself in to police. She turned over to police numerous pieces of jewelry from Resendez's victims that he had mailed to her home in Mexico.

On June 2,1999, the U.S. Border Patrol apprehended Resendez near El Paso, Texas as he tried to enter the United States illegally and deported him to Mexico, unaware that he was wanted for the various murders he allegedly committed. The mix-up proved fatal to his last few victims, all murdered after he again illegally reentered Texas.

Drew Carter, a Texas Ranger, enlisted the help of Resendez sister, Manuela, and indicated that if she could convince him to surrender to police, he would be treated fairly in jail, receive visiting rights from his family, and a psychological evaluation. Pursued by bounty hunters in Mexico, on July 13,1999 Resendez agreed and surrendered to Carter on the bridge joining Zaragosa Mexico, and El Paso, Texas. Eventually he was charged with seven of the murders, though he was tried and committed for only one of them, the murder of Dr. Claudia Benton, receiving the death penalty in May 2000.

Though Resendez was charged with only seven of the murders, investigators in both Mexico and the United States believe he committed many others, particularly since numerous bodies found along railroad lines in both countries match the modus operandi of "The Railroad Killer." A loner, a drifter, a part-time worker, Resendez certainly fits the description of a inadequate man prone to violent outbursts, which he vented on people whom he never knew or met before the fatal altercations. His family life, upbringing, and adolescence can only be described as chaotic and dysfunctional, foretelling the violent rage that manifested itself in the numerous killings of virtual strangers.

Notes

1. Dietz, 1986, p. 480.
2. Dietz, 1986, p. 482–483.
3. Holmes and Holmes, 2001, pp. 70, 76.
4. O'Reilly, 1996, p. 17.
5. Kelleher, 1997, pp. 31–39.
6. Shifrel and McQuillan, 2000.
7. Fessenden, 2000, p. 28.
8. Burney, 1999, p. 27.
9. Keeney and Heide, 1994.
10. Douglas, et al., 1992; Harbort and Mokros, 2001, p. 327.
11. Holmes and DeBurger, 1988, p. 55–59.

10

Methodology of Murder

Whether sane or insane, rational or irrational, the killer employs some rudimentary method in his deed, a method of which he may not even be fully conscious. With objective hindsight, one can note the presence of an orderly arrangement of sequential acts which culminate in the death of the victim, explicit in the highly planned, premeditated first-degree murder, implicit in the unintended, unwitting manslaughter. The professional planning of the contract killer, the bar room brawl homicide, the drunk driver killer—each illustrates an orderly progression of steps and actions which culminated in the death of a victim.

The already mentioned observable and measurable background demographic characteristics of killers and victims (e.g., gender, race, age, socioeconomic status, etc.) and the physical and temporal variables related to the killing (e.g., the locale of the murder, hour-day-month of the act) clearly reflect the arrangement of actors and events preceding the homicide. This methodology of murder—the ordered sequence of traits and behaviors before, during, and after the killing—suggest that murderous behavior is neither random nor inexplicable; there is method in the madness of murder.

The fateful progression of events preceding the actual murder illustrates this point. David Luckenbill provides a fascinating glimpse into this patterned pre-murder scenario, viewing murder as a collective transaction between a killer and a victim, each trying to "save face" at the other's expense. In this confrontation, not unlike a theatrical drama with its various acts and scenes, there are a series of stages that, if completed, inevitably result in the murder of the victim. He writes:

The transaction took a sequential form: the victim issued what the offender deemed an offensive move; the offender typically retaliated with a verbal or physical challenge; a 'working' agreement favoring the use of violence was forged with the victim's response; battle ensued leaving the victim deal or dying; the manner of the offender's exiting was shaped by his relationship to the victim and the movers of his audience.[1]

Ironically, the killer accomplishes his end by means of either a weapon or by psychological methods which result in the death of his victim: a gun, a knife, an automobile, a poison, a lead pipe, a rope, or an infinite number of items available at the moment of the fateful encounter, including parts of his own body, or nonmaterial means, such as so terrorizing a victim that he "dies of fright." Virtually anything can be, and has been, used as a weapon in slaying another. Older readers may recall the 1950s Alfred Hitchcock television episode in which a wife kills her husband with a frozen leg of lamb and days later serves the "weapon" to the unsuspecting homicide detectives in a dinner to which she invited them! Similar bizarre weapons are not uncommon in real life, as any conversation with veteran police officers will reveal.

Paradoxically, the research literature on homicide says little about the types of weapons used in killings other than statistically numbering the incidences of various types. Much of this literature relates to hand gun use and availability, along with the heated exchanges pertaining to the policy implications of gun control or its lack.

The main source of data of types of weapons used in homicide are the *Uniform Crime Reports* of the FBI. Each year the UCRs present a break down of the types of weapons used to murder victims within the year. Table 10.1 presents these data for 2003.

Guns

A cursory glance at this table will show the overwhelming preponderance of firearms in the commission of homicide in the United States. This pattern remains relatively constant year-to-year. In 2003, approximately 67 percent of murders resulted from the victim being shot, either with a handgun, rifle, or shotgun; in the same year, handguns accounted for 51 percent of all the murders where the circumstance and type of murder instruments were known to police. In essence, the handgun is the weapon of choice in the majority of all murders.

Table 10.1
Murder, Types of Weapons Used*
Percent Distribution by Region, 2003

Region	Total all weapons	Firearms	Knives or cutting instruments	Unknown or other dangerous weapons	Personal weapons (hands, fists, feet, etc.)
Total	100.0	66.9	12.6	13.9	6.6
Northeast	100.0	61.9	16.8	14.1	7.2
Midwest	100.0	68.1	10.9	14.9	6.2
South	100.0	67.7	12.3	13.7	6.4
West	100.0	67.8	12.0	13.5	6.7

*Source: *Crime in the United States—2003—Uniform Crime Reports*, Table 2.8, p. 19.

The lethal nature of contemporary handguns, with high velocity bullets used in automatic and semiautomatic weapons far surpasses the killing power of the guns used a few decades ago (e.g., zipguns, Saturday night specials, .22 and .38 caliber revolvers, etc.). Were it not for the equally phenomenal advances in medical care in the trauma units of major urban centers that help to contain this carnage, the murder rate in America would be astronomical. Anthony Harris and his associates found that from 1960–1999, advances in emergency medical care have consistently over time reduced the lethal nature of violent encounters. They argue that despite the proliferation of dangerous weapons and increases in serious assaults in the forty-year period, the actual lethality of such assaults has dropped dramatically, predominantly because of the parallel development in medical support services. Without such medical advances, the number of actual murders would be three times the current number—45,000 vs. 15,000.[2]

Guns are the great equalizers in the homicide confrontation. Unlike the physical inherent superiority of brute strength in other modes of assault (e.g., yielding a knife or a blunt instrument, beating another to death, physically overpowering, strangling a victim, etc.) shooting a firearm demands little physical strength or stamina; a mere child can shoot and kill a strong adult rapidly and almost effortlessly. And guns are far more lethal than other types of assault weapons. According to P.J. Cook, one out of every seven shooting victims dies of the assault[3]; in relation to robbery homicides, Cook found that the fatality of victims shot is three times greater than those accosted with knives, and ten times greater than those assaulted with other means of weapons.[4] Guns far surpass the killing power of other types of weapons, and their use in contemporary American society clearly sustains the high murder rates and human slaughter in the nation's killing zones.

CASE 168

On November 25, 1997 in Long Beach, California a jury convicted Richard Keech, seventy-seven, of first-degree murder in the shooting death of his son-in-law Nicholas Candy, forty-seven. The victim had recently broken up with Keech's daughter, Nancy, and the couple was engaged in bitter battle over the custody of their son. Keech told the court that his son-in-law mounted a "campaign of terror" against his family. In 1996, Keech confronted Candy and shot him once, then followed him down the street and shot him four more times. He said he killed Candy because he was suffering a flashback to his four-year incarceration in World War II in a Japanese prison camp in Corregidor in the Philippines where he was beaten daily by brutal Japanese guards. He claimed that he had fired the first shot in self-defense, fearing Candy's possible violence to him and his daughter. He testified that after the first shot, his next thought was, "I've just wounded a Jap guard. I realize that you never wound a Jap guard. You're a dead man. Since you're a dead man, you might as well kill him." He believed that he then went on "autopilot," and had no memory of pursuing Candy and shooting him four additional times. Neither the prosecutor nor the jury accepted the POW flashback defense. Richard Keech received a life sentence after being found guilty by a jury. After serving six years, his case was reversed on appeal and he was freed from prison.

CASE 169

Kenneth Payne, forty-two, a carpenter, and Curtis Cook, forty-four, a local hardware store worker, had been best friends for more than two decades in the upscale, posh Suffolk County, New York community of Shelter Island. In 1998, Cook had been arrested and charged with the sexual molestation of an eight-year-old girl. Because of his family connection to the Hershey candy family, Cook quickly raised the $100,000 bail and was released from custody. He indicated on a phone message to Payne that he would beat the sexual abuse charge. Enraged after drinking in a local bar, Payne sought out his friend and shot Cook in the chest with a 12-gauge shotgun in April 1998. Captured in his house trailer after the shooting, Payne confessed to th murder. It was reported to the police that he had telephoned the abused girl's mother indicating, "You don't have to worry about him any more." Authorities charged Payne with second-degree murder. At his trial, Payne unsuccessfully claimed self-defense and received the maximum, twenty-five years to life in prison. Cook's murder was the first and remains the only murder in Shelter Island's history.

CASE **170**

Philadelphia, Pennsylvania police believed the massacre was one of the worst shootings in decades. On December 28, 2000, seven victims died from gunshot wounds they received in a run-down crack house. On the fateful night, four masked men entered the house, lined ten people on the floor and shot them with automatic weapons; only three survived the attack. A month later, Jermel Lewis, twenty-three, and Sacon Youk, nineteen, Hezekiah Thomas, twenty-five, and Quiante Ferrin, twenty, were charged with the seven murders. Police indicated that the motive for the killing stemmed from a dispute over one group of drug dealers undercutting the drug prices of the other groups. They indicated that this was "nickel-and-dime drug deal" and did not involve large amounts of money; seven people murdered for a couple of bucks. Following the indictment of the suspects, the sister of one of the slaying victims told reporters that one of the suspects attended her brother's funeral and hugged her and comforted her. "All along one of the guys that did this to my brother was in our face" (Cappelo, 2001). Yet on July 11, 2002 the charges against the four men were dropped since the district attorney needed much more time to investigate further the crimes than the judge would permit. The shootings of the seven murdered people remained an open case until November 2002 when four new suspects were charged in the slayings: Bruce Veney, twenty-six; Dawud Faruqui, twenty-seven; Kalid Farugui, twenty-six; and Shihean Black, twenty. Police initially believed the massacre was drug related but then discovered that the killings stemmed from a simple dispute between the suspects and the murder victims over a broken clutch on a used car. The four incensed suspects allegedly stormed the row crack house occupied by the squatters with whom they argued, lined up ten victims and shot each, execution style, killing seven.

CASE 171

Baltimore, Maryland, police indicated that the February 2, 2001 murder of the popular co-owner of a well-known New Vernon area eatery, the City Cafe, resulted from a robbery-turned-bad. That morning, John Darda, forty-three, asked a young employee, Derrick Quarles, twenty, to accompany him for protection as he transported $3,000 in the cafe's receipts to the local bank. Unknown to Darda, his companion had telephoned his friends, Kion Eason, eighteen, and Jamaha Eason, twenty, and told them that "it was time to do the robbery." When confronted, Darda resisted the trio and was fatally shot in the head, apparently by Jamaha Eason. The Easons fled the scene without any money. Police became suspicious of Quarles since he could give no description of the two attackers; another witness to the killing saw a man with a fur-trimmed bomber jacket fleeing the scene. Eventually Quarles confessed to the crime and the circumstances leading to it. Jamaha Eason received a forty-year prison sentence; Derrick Quarles received a thirty-five-year sentence; Kion Eason was acquitted of murder charges but was found guilty of attempted robbery, conspiracy, and handgun crimes.

Knives or Cutting Instruments

The second most common type of weapon used in a homicide, accounting for about 13 percent of all murders, is a knife or some other type of cutting instrument. These can be just about any instrument capable of cutting or stabbing another individual (e.g., razor blades, swords, machetes, box openers, screwdrivers, scissors, pieces of glass, ice picks, etc.). The fatal wound can be brought about either by stabbing, thus creating a lethal puncture wound, or by cutting or slashing wherein the victim generally dies because of an excess loss of blood.

Single puncture wounds create very little external bleeding or obvious external damage to the victim who generally succumbs to death through internal bleeding if the piercing weapon has invaded a major organ or a blood vessel. Multiple stab wounds, and virtually all multiple slashing wounds, create a real mess since the blood on the weapon is dispersed through the room or area in which the assault occurred.

In many deaths of this type, overkill can be noted. A killer who stabs his victim twenty-thirty times indicates that far more violence ensued that would have been necessary to kill the victim, which could be accomplished by one or two stabs with the lethal instrument. Such overkill situations suggest an immense amount of anger toward the victim and is seen most typically in those situations where the parties in the fatal encounter know each other, generally very well. Typical examples include homosexual murders, estranged mate killings, and spurned lover / boyfriend-girlfriend slayings.[5]

The proportion of all homicides caused by knives and cutting instruments is relatively constant, averaging about 14 percent annually, or about one out of every seven killings where police can determine the type of weapon used. Table 10.2 gives the actual number of known cases in 2003.

Table 10.2
Murder Victims by Weapon 2003*

Weapons	
Total	14,408
Total Firearms:	9,638
Handguns	7,701
Rifles	390
Shotguns	452
Other guns	75
Firearms, type not stated	1,020
Knives or cutting instruments	1,816
Blunt objects (clubs, hammers, etc.)	651
Personal weapons (hands, fists feet, etc.)	946
Poison	9
Explosives	4
Fire	163
Narcotics	41
Drowning	17
Strangulation	184
Asphyxiation	128
Other weapons or weapons not stated	811

*Source: *Crime in the United States—2003—Uniform Crime Reports*, Table 2.9 p. 19.

In many cases, the knowledge of what type of knife was used, and in what circumstance, speaks volumes about who did the crime, and possibly why the killer murdered. A male found dead on a kitchen floor with a kitchen knife protruding from his chest suggests a domestic violence killing; more often than not the wife or the girlfriend killed him in a situation where alcohol or drugs were used, with the male abusing the woman, and she in turn retaliating to the abuse. Generally, she stays at the scene, calls police, and confesses immediately to the crime. Essentially, these are all open-and-shut cases, or what police describe as easy to solve "ground balls."

CASE 172

Kurt Imel, thirty-seven, a successful, well-paid, Wal-Mart executive in Phoenix, Arizona impressed everyone with whom he worked and socialized. Yet relations between him and his wife Theresa, thirty-five, had soured and she filed for a divorce in 1998. The Imels had three of their own children, ages five, seven, and nine, and an adopted daughter, Tiffany, nineteen. Police indicated that Theresa tried to turn the children against Kurt, indicating to others that he was physically and sexually abusive to her and them.

Theresa, Tiffany, and Tiffany's boyfriend, Troy Bertling, nineteen, concocted a plot to murder Kurt to obtain his life insurance money and his savings. Tiffany reportedly told a friend that Imel "was worth millions . . . I want him dead." The trio befriended Daniel Averett, twenty-five, who had suffered brain damage in an auto accident. Convinced that Imel was abusive and deserving of death and desperate to have Tiffany and Bertling like him, Avereet enthusiastically agreed to kill Imel for $500. On the night of July 28, 1999, Kurt and Theresa Imel met at the Imel's home; upon leaving the house, Kurt was confronted by Averett who jumped from the bushes, threw pool acid in Imel's face, and stabbed him eight times. Police quickly unraveled the plot and arrested Theresa and Tiffany Imel, Bertling, and Averett. Investigators found no evidence or indications of abuse on the murder victim's part and believed the motive for his death was his life insurance proceeds. Theresa Imel received a twenty-eight-year prison sentence for manslaughter and drug offences; her daughter received twenty-five years to life for conspiracy and a sixteen-year manslaughter sentence. Bertling received a twenty-two-year sentence for second-degree murder, and Averett received a twenty-five-year-to-life sentence for first-degree murder.

Case 173

Clara Schwartz, nineteen, Kyle Hulbert, eighteen, Michael Pfohl, twenty-one, and Katherine Inglis, nineteen, had a fascination with witch-craft, vampires, and the occult. All four conspired to murder Clara's father, Robert Schwartz, fifty-seven, a prominent DNA scientist in his Leesburg, Virginia, farmhouse on December 8, 2001.

Hulbert, a diagnosed schizophrenic, told police that the was an-gered at what Schwartz had done to Clara, abusing her, lacing her food with sulfuric acid, and poisoning her pork chops. She had told him that her father was planning a family trip and he wanted to make "sure she did not come back." Hubert claimed he would do anything to protect Clara.

On the fateful night, Hulbert, Pfohl, and Ingles drove to Schwartz's residence; only Hulbert entered the home. He claimed that the demons Nicodemus, Orga, and Sabba gave him permission to kill Schwartz which he did by stabbing him with a twenty-seven-inch sword. Fol-lowing the killing, he drank Schwartz's blood and went "into a frenzy." The murder was quickly solved when neighbors indicated that the saw the trio drive to the house and get stuck in the mud nearby. Clara Schwartz was not with them but was charged with plotting her father's murder. Mary Schwartz, the victim's wife, totally discounted as ab-surd that he was trying to poison Clara. It stunned her that her daugh-ter would have any role in the killing of her own father. Schwartz was sentenced to forty-eight years in prison; Hulbert received a life sen-tence and Pfohl eighteen years in prison. Ingles was indicted on mis-demeanor charges.

Case 174

Max Kolb, twenty, believed he could help Shaun Alexander, twenty-five, who confided to Kolb his problem with depression. The two men met as students at Hofstra University in Nassau County, New York. They agreed to meet at the Hicksville, New York Econo Lodge in April 2001 to discuss Alexander's problem. In his confession to po-lice, Alexander said he made sexual advances to Kolb who rejected them. He asked Kolb to "lay down and cuddle." Kolb reportedly said no, at which point Alexander told him, "if you don't give me what I want, someone's going to get hurt." Alexander than stabbed Kolb with a large butcher knife and eviscerated him; following the slaying he undressed the victim and performed a lewd act on the corpse. Alexander then stashed the body in a local storage facility, eventually burying it in his backyard behind a barbeque pit. At his pre-trial hearing, Alexander's defense attorney claimed that his client was insane at the time of the killing. Prosecutors argued that this was not true, as Alexander planned the crime by stocking his 2000 Land Rover with rope, duct tape, and plastic bags, as well as obtaining the butcher knife used in the homicide.

Case 175

Police indicated that the motive for the slaying entailed a business deed gone bad. Nathan Powell, thirty-nine, and Jawed Wassel, forty-two, had been partners in the making and producing of Wassel's autobiographical film "Firedancer." Wassel, an immigrant from Afghanistan, and Powell argued over the income from the film. On October 3, 2001, Wassel went to Powell's Queens, New York City, apartment to tell him he had to receive less of a share in the film's proceeds than they had agreed to previously. Angered, Powell hit Wassel in the throat with a pool cue and then stabbed him several times. Following the slaying, Powell used a hacksaw to dismember the body and placed the severed head in the apartment's freezer. A few hours later, he attended the opening of "Firedancer" in Manhattan. The next day, he loaded the body parts in his van, to bury them in a state park in Long Island. Officer Peter Ginn of NYPD spotted Powell's van driving erratically, with no lights and pulled him over. On inspecting the vehicle he saw one of the bloody boxes and eventually arrested Powell. Officer Ginn stated, "I knew it wasn't dealing with somebody going home from work." Powell confessed to the murder shortly thereafter.

Powell's defense attorney claimed that post-traumatic stress from the September 11 terrorist attack on the World Trade Center triggered the attack since Powell claimed Wassel was pro-Taliban, and told him the terrorist attacks were justified. Yet investigators found the opposite: Wassel clearly supported the United States, stating earlier that America is "the one place where everybody has a chance." Powell received a twenty-year sentence for his crime; after the judge learned that he had lied to a court representative, he added five additional years to his prison term.

Blunt Object Weapons

Blunt objects, which account for approximately 5 percent of homicides, can be just about anything material which can be used to bludgeon another. Clubs, hammers, pieces of lumber, rocks, chairs, lamps, shoes, telephones, shovels, oars, TVs, radios, wrenches, etc. all have been used to beat a victim to death. When the rage in the homicidal confrontation reaches its climax, the assailant will grab whatever is present to murder the victim. More often than not, these slayings are not classic first-degree murders; they are spontaneous and unplanned, hence the unusual assortment of weapons utilized in these kinds of homicides. Indeed it would be quite strange for a killer to plan and execute the murder with a bowling ball or a kitchen toaster. In this sense, if the item is not bolted down, it can be used as a weapon by an out-of-control assailant.

Interestingly one of the more common blunt objects used in American murders is the baseball bat. Why this instrument? Why are so many beaten to death with bats rather than with other items? Unlike the gun and knife which may be illegal to carry, conceal, and transport, the baseball bat is quite legal. It can be kept in one's car, carried in public, particularly by adolescents and young adults, and kept readily available without arousing without undue suspicion. The key item in "America's national pastime" can thus be utilized quickly if trouble arises. In the minds of many men who have no intention of killing another, "the bat is there if I need it; you never know when I might have to defend myself from some nut out there. And no one is going to arrest me for having a bat in my car."

Tragically, this is the common scenario in many road rage killings; two drivers confront each other in a rage; one lifts a bat from the back seat of his vehicle and pummels the other driver to death. No one planned it, no one wanted it, and no one wins in the confrontation. Pieces of lead pipes, and 2x4 pieces of lumber can also be there if "trouble arises."

Blunt object trauma homicides are neither "quick nor clean." Generally, the victim dies days later since the blunt force to the head produces, over time, unconsciousness, brain swelling, coma, pneumonia, infections, etc. eventually culminating in death. Unlike lethal gunshot and knife wounds which produce death rather quickly, the blunt object killings are long and drawn out.

CASE 176

The murder victim, David Crawford, seventeen, had been reported missing from a Michigan facility for adolescents with emotional problems in April 1996. A month later police arrested Frederico Cruz, sixteen, from Sparta, Michigan, and charged him with the grisly murder of the missing youth. Prosecutors indicated that Cruz bludgeoned Crawford to death, decapitated him, and then videotaped himself repeatedly slashing the severed head as well as removing the brain from the skull. Police discovered what happened when a father of one of Cruz's friends turned over the videotape to Michigan police. Police searched Cruz's home in Sparta and discovered the mutilated, unrecognizable head in a plastic bag outside the house. Cruz who had a number of prior arrests featured himself in the video recording dressed in black, with dark sunglasses, and a dark bandana concealing his face; inadvertently, he revealed his face briefly in the tape confirming that the was the killer. Neighbors of the killer were shocked by the incident and believed Cruz to be a normal, kind boy. Detective Charles Brown who helped solve the murder indicated that Cruz had a normal background and came from a family with loving and involved parents. Probably no one can say for certain what triggered Cruz's violence. A jury found him guilty of first-degree murder and sentenced him to life in prison.

CASE 177

In February 1998, Christopher Churchill killed five people with a hammer in Noble, Illinois. Drunk at the time of the massacre, Churchill bludgeoned his half-brother, his brother's girlfriend Debra Smith, and her three children, ages six, ten, and twelve. After attacking all five victims, the killer watched TV and proceeded to sexually abuse the twelve-year-old girl as she lay dying. Arrested almost a week later, Churchill claimed the victims had teased him, and he killed them to "relieve stress." Blood found on his shirt matched that of Debra Smith.

When arrested by police he cheerfully told them what happened and displayed no remorse over the murders. Sheriff Robert Foerster indicated that in his thirty-year career in law enforcement he had never encountered a killer as cold and remorseless as Churchill. Churchill received life sentences for the five murders.

CASE 178

Trouble started at a teenage party in Queens, New York in April, 1999, when a fight broke out and Boris Kunin, sixteen, was punched by another teen. Seeking to avenge his humiliation, Kunin and three other friends, Nick Prebeza, seventeen, Jason Figueroa, sixteen, and Thomas Hernandez, nineteen, roamed the local streets seeking his attacker when the encountered Tony Lee, seventeen, with a friend, Elisa Luu, fifteen. Both had been at the party but neither Lee nor Luu had anything to do with the fight. Prebeza pushed Lee into some bushes and started beating him with a baseball bat. Hernandez then struck Lee six times in the head with his aluminum bat fatally injuring him. Lee lingered in a coma and was finally removed from life support two days after the attack. Prebeza, Kunin, and Figueroa all pleaded guilty to manslaughter and agreed to testify against Hernandez who they claimed killed Lee. After the attack, Hernandez fled the area and eventually was arrested on an Amtrak train in Topeka, Kansas. Upon his conviction, the judge sentenced him to twenty-five years to life for second-degree murder. Friends of the victim took up a collection to help Lee's parents, immigrants from China, pay for the funeral expenses.

CASE 179

Adolph Hernandez was executed by lethal injection on February 8, 2001 in Huntsville, Texas at the Texas State Prison for the September 8, 1988 murder of Elizabeth Alvarado, sixty-nine. Hernandez denied fatally beating the victim with a baseball bat during a robbery of her home. Her skull had been struck eight times by the bat. As he ran from her home, carrying the bat and her purse containing $350, he encountered Alvarado's daughter and great-grandson with whom he briefly struggled. Both identified him as the assailant. Police soon found him hiding in bushes near the crime scene. After his conviction of first-degree murder, Hernandez claimed he had suffered an alcohol-induced blackout and had no memory of the murder; later he claimed a black man had murdered the victim. Before his execution, the killer told his family, "I'll see y'all one of these days. Just don't rush it."

Personal Weapons

Personal weapons refers to the use of parts of the body in killing a victim. These account for almost 7 percent of all killings and include hands, fists, and feet. Also included are pushing another to his or her death. Similar to blunt object murders, the use of personal parts of the body to kill another typically occurs in second-degree murders and manslaughter. The victim and the killer may engage in a furious struggle wherein the murder victim may be beaten or kicked to death, or pushed from a height, or pushed in front of a car, truck, or train.

Many of these types of killing result from domestic violence situations and encounters where the parties in the altercation are intoxicated. Intimate partner murder frequently involves a male killer fatally beating his female victim. Barroom brawls also evolve into beating deaths whereby one drunken patron beats and kicks his adversary to death either in the tavern or in the area immediately adjacent to it. Another, less typical, scenario involves adolescent/gang related brawls where one gang member will beat another to death. One of my early memories of murder in my Bedford-Stuyvesant Brooklyn neighborhood is of hearing about the war counselor of the El Quintos, "Napoleon," fatally stomping his rival from the Brevort Projects Chaplin's gang in a vicious street confrontation.

Beating deaths, similar to blunt object murders, do not generally occur instantaneously; the victim typically lies in a coma for a period of time before succumbing to the physiological ravages of the attack.

CASE 180

In March 2001, Robert Spangler, sixty-nine, of Grand Junction, Colorado pleaded guilty to first-degree murder in the death of his third wife, Donna Spangler, fifty-eight. He received a life in prison sentence in federal court in Phoenix, Arizona for his crime. He initially told police he had been backpacking with his wife in 1993 when she accidentally fell to her death in the Grand Canyon. Police suspected that he pushed her to death but could not prove it. In 2000, police learned that Spangler had been diagnosed with terminal cancer and decided to re-interview him to see if he wanted to confess before his death. During his visit with police investigators he readily admitted that he pushed her to her death! He also confessed to murdering her first wife, Nancy Spangler, and their two teenage children, Susan and David in Littleton, Colorado in 1978, making it look like Nancy murdered her children and then committed suicide. He divorced his second wife, and married Donna in 1990.

CASE 181

Betty and Emil Schell, both in their eighties and married for over fifty years, had been prominent community leaders in the affluent community of Mountain Lakes, New Jersey. Emil had been the president of the local school board and Betty was an active leader of the town's garden club. Their lives changed dramatically in 1992 when the husband suffered a number of paralyzing strokes that left him unable to speak or move his arms and legs. By 1995 his wife decided that they could no longer continue in this manner; on the night of September 15, 1995, she tied both herself and her husband to his wheelchair and maneuvered it into the deep end of the swimming pool on their property. County investigators ruled the deaths a murder suicide. Neighbors and close friends were shocked by the tragic crime. One close friend told a reporter investigating the incident that "this was just a way out to face eternity together."

CASE 182

Wendell White, twenty-two, from Griffin, Georgia broke into the home of this former girlfriend, Ayiesha Muddlebrooks, and abducted their six-month old son in November 1997. Distraught over her dating another man, White fled with his son leading Spalding County police on a two-hour chase that ended in the local elementary school. In the stand off between White and police, he repeatedly threatened to kill his son. Ignoring pleas from police and family members, White held his son by his feet and slammed his head several times onto the pavement, whereupon he was subdued by family members who beat him severely, and arrested by the police present. He was charged with kidnapping, burglary, and felony murder. A jury sentenced White to a life sentence, without parole in 1998.

CASE 183

Jin-Joo Byrne, eighteen, a member of Rev. Sun Myung Moon's Unification Church traveled from her home in Seattle, Washington, to Charlotte, North Carolina, to immerse herself in her faith and prepare herself for missionary work. On August 29, 2002, her body was found in a vacant apartment in Charlotte. She had been strangled, sexually assaulted, and robbed of her money as well as the costume jewelry that she had been selling door-to-door to raise money for the Unification Church. Hours later police arrested Eugene Evans, twenty-one, and charged him with her murder. He had been released on bond two days earlier on a break-and-entry charge. Neighbors in the housing complex where Byrne's body had been found told police that they had seen Byrne and Evans together before her murder. Evans claimed he had been high on crack at the time of the murder. A jury convicted him of second degree murder and first degree sexual assault, sentencing him to forty-nine years in prison.

Miscellaneous Weapons

In the approximate 10 percent of murders in any given year a variety of different miscellaneous weapons is used. Included here would be explosives, fires, poisons, drugs, strangulations, drownings, and asphyxiations. Of this list, strangulation is the most common type that can involve the assailant's hands (and thus overlap with personal weapons) or objects such as ligatures, telephone cords, articles of clothing, etc. Fires also are a common type in this overall category and frequently result from an assailant wishing to avenge some perceived wrong and using arson as a way "to get back" at another, frequently killing others who had nothing to do with the original disagreement. This miscellaneous category often includes unusual murders, sometimes even bizarre ones. They differ from the "typical" homicides that occur daily, not in their tragic outcome, but in the manner in which the victim was murdered. These types of killings tend to attract media attentions precisely because of their "atypical" nature. They are far from the ordinary, with weapons as diverse as bowling balls, curling irons, bows and arrows, boats, automobiles, and rocks. Also included are unusual means of killing others: starvation, physical neglect, frightening victims to death, and injections with unusual substances and poisons.

CASE 184

Donald "Pee Wee" Gaskins claimed to have murdered sixteen people in his career in crime in South Carolina and was serving nine life terms in that state's prison for those killings in 1980. On death row, another prisoner, Rudolph Tyner, awaited executions for the murder of Bill and Myrtle Moon but had successfully postponed his execution by various legal maneuvers. Members of the Moon victims' family fearing that Tyner would never die in the electric chair, contracted Gaskins to murder Tyner on death row. Gaskins agreed, enticed by the "fame" of murdering someone on death row. He fabricated a bomb constructed from explosives and materials smuggled into prison by Moon's relatives. Gaskins told Tyner that he had created a radio-intercom and asked him to help him test it. On September 12, 1982, Tyner placed a plastic cup loaded with explosives to his ear which then detonated, blowing off Tyner's head. Gaskins was charged with the murder and in 1991 was executed by the state of North Carolina.

• CASE 185

Solomon Riley, a deputy Los Angeles, California medical examiner, indicated that he could give no other reasonable reason why Bertha Kavanaugh, eighty-eight, died other than she died of fright as her home in El Monte was invaded by Sylvia Arizmendi and a companion. Kavanaugh and her niece, Marilyn Kavanaugh, sixty-six, kept sizable amounts of cash in the house and apparently neighbors and local vagrants knew this. In November 1994, Arizmendi and a male accomplice gained entry to the home; the unidentified accomplice beat and tried to strangle the niece, while Arizmendi began to tie the eighty-eight years old woman's hands when the victim suffered a fatal heart attack. Kavanaugh's death, caused by the stress-induced heart attack, turned the crime into a murder. Arizmendi started that his partner was Raymond Yanez, but Marilyn Kavanaugh could not positively identify him. Police recovered Kavanaugh's jewelry from Arizmendi's apartment, and cash from Yanez's apartment. Arizmendi received a life sentence in prison following his trial in July 1996.

Case 186

Genny Rojas, four, had been sent to live with her aunt, Veronica Gonzalez, twenty-nine, and uncle Ivan, thirty-one, in 1995. Her natural parents were both in prison at the time. At the Gonzalez home in San Diego, California, Genny receive horrific abuse; she was often starved, hanged by her hands from a hook, burned with a hair dryer, and forced to live in a box. On July 21, 1995 the Gonzalez couple submerged her in a bath tub with water so hot it scalded her to death. Both Veronica and Ivan Gonzalez were convicted and received a death sentence, making them the first married couple awaiting execution for the same crime.

Case 187

In March 2001, William Sybers, sixty-eight, a former medical examiner, was found guilty in Pensacola, Florida of the murder of his wife Kay Sybers, then fifty-two. Prosecutors successfully argued that he murdered his wife in May 1991 so as to marry his mistress and avoid losing half of the couple's six million dollars in assets in a pending divorce. They claimed he had injected his wife with a lethal dose of succinyl monocholine, a muscle relaxant, which killed her. Sybers, citing his dead wife's earlier wishes, rather than request an autopsy, had her body embalmed. An autopsy was later conducted. At the autopsy, needle marks were found on the victim's body; Sybers claimed they resulted from blood tests he had taker from her prior to her death because she had complained of chest pains. In 1999, new chemical tests confirmed that the lethal drug was present in her body at the autopsy, and that the process of embalming her had preserved the lethal drug. After ten years of legal maneuvering, the trial was conducted in 2001 and Sybers was convicted of first-degree murder and sentenced to life in prison (Kaczor, 2001). However in February 2003, an appeals court reversed Sybers' conviction, ordering a new trial stating that the poison evidence tests were too novel to be accepted as scientific fact. In place of a new trial Sybers pled guilty to manslaughter and received a sentence for the time he had already served—two years. In May 2003, the prosecutor notified the trial judge that the evidence in the case was not only novel, but wrong, though in 2001 he believed it to be reliable.

CASE 188

A New Jersey jury convicted Calvin Settle, nineteen, from Jersey City of manslaughter in the tragic death of Natalie Rivera, eight-months-old. Settle killed the infant by dropping a bowling ball from an overpass onto oncoming traffic approaching the Holland Tunnel on February 6, 1994. The ball hit an oncoming truck, which sent the projectile into the windshield of the Ramos car, killing the infant who was strapped to her car seat. Settle had testified earlier that he had rested the bowling ball on a railing of the overpass, and it slipped from his hands. Two young boys who were with Settle at the time of the crime testified that Settle actually threw the ball onto the highway.

CASE 189

Had Christina Black not confessed to the killing of her grandmother, Helen Gerstung, eighty-eight, in July 1995, she would literally have gotten away with murder. Black, with a history of mental illness, confessed to Orlando, Florida, police that she had suffocated her grandmother by stuffing a piece of kiwi fruit down her throat and placing a plastic bag over her face. The crime took place in Apache Junction, Arizona in April 1995 while she was visiting her grandmother. Initially, Orlando, Florida police did not believe her, and Arizona authorities thought that Gerstung had died of natural causes. After her body had been exhumed, an autopsy revealed kiwi seeds in the grandmother's mouth and piece of the fruit in her throat. Black also told police investigators of her vision years earlier of someone suffocating her grandmother with a piece of kiwi fruit. Black was found guilty of first-degree murder; she received a twenty-five-years-to life sentence to be served in the Arizona State Penitentiary.

CASE 190

Otisha Johnson, twenty-five, of Chicago, Illinois received a life in prison sentence for killing her six-month-old daughter, Dejah, burning her with a curling iron. On November 28, 1995, Johnson, after using marijuana and crack cocaine, placed the hot curling iron on her daughter's stomach, mouth, neck, face, back, and hands because she would not stop crying. Investigators told the court that Dejah died from internal dehydration and hypothermia, which led to heart failure. Johnson was spared the death penalty because of the severe abuse that she had received from her own mother.

Case 191

Salvatore Colavito, eighteen, claimed that the killing of his father, Leonard Colavito, forty-one, was an accident. In February 1999, the son was convicted of second-degree manslaughter for shooting his father with a bow and arrow and served thirty-two months in prison. In October 1996, the victim died inside his home in Middletown, Connecticut with a fifteen-inch arrow wound in his torso. His son claimed that the incident occurred when he stepped on the family cat while holding the bow and arrow. Prosecutors countered this defense by stating that Salvatore Colavito never called for medical assistance, lied to police in attempting a cover up, and had a stormy relationship with his father.

Case 192

A Florida court found Stanley Cameron, fifty-eight, guilty of manslaughter in the death of six people in November 1997 as a result of his actions in the Intercoastal Waterway in Fort Lauderdale. Cameron, drunk and speeding at the time, slammed his speedboat, the "Merry Maker," into a cabin cruiser which had been rented by attendees at a Florida sales conference. The boat's captain and five of the guests were killed in the mishap. The court in November 1999 sentenced Cameron to eighty-five years in prison.

Case 193

A Youngstown, Ohio woman set her boyfriend on fire following a beating she had received from him on February 5, 2000. Rita Ashford, thirty-seven, indicated to police that Kenneth Harris, forty-one, had beaten her earlier that evening and when he fell asleep, she poured alcohol on him and used a cigarette lighter to ignite it. In the ensuing fire that engulfed the house, Ashford's seven-year-old daughter Jamie Bennett died. Harris survived the assault, as did Ashford, and her two-year-old son, Mohammed Harris.

Case 194

Raul Conteras, nineteen, of Los Angeles, California received a thirty-two-years-to-life prison sentence in July 2000. Earlier, Conteras, angry at his former girlfriend, Rochelle Ramos, eighteen, had rammed his car into one in which Rochelle and four of her friends were traveling on a Los Angeles highway, causing it to go out of control, striking an on-coming van. One of Ramos' passengers, Ashlee Hernandez, twelve, was killed; her sister, Kathleen Hernandez, sixteen, was paralyzed from the waist down. Conteras fled the scene. At his trial, a friend told reporters that he did not mean to hurt anyone; he only wanted to talk to his former girlfriend.

Case 195

On May 7, 2000, Dallas Reinhardt, seven, drowned after her stepfather's boat capsized on Arkabutla Lake in northern Mississippi. Troy Carlisle, twenty-eight, was convicted of manslaughter in the child's death. Prosecutors argued that Carlisle stripped the child's life jacket from her, leaving her to drown. Her stepfather testified that the little girl had screamed "Quit, quit, you're drowning me" just after Carlisle swam toward her. His lawyers claimed that he had been trying to rescue the girl. A De Soto County jury found Carlisle guilty of manslaughter and he received a twenty-year sentence in the state penitentiary.

Case 196

Jacques Robidoux, twenty-nine, led a religious sect of approximately forty members from two extended families, living in communal homes in Attleboro and Seekank, near Boston, Massachusetts. He was convicted of the murder of his infant son, Samuel, who had been starved to death in 1999. The jury heard testimony that the only food the boy received for fifty-one days was his mother's breast milk. Robidoux said messages from God indicated that he and his wife should stop feeding Samuel solid foods. Samuel's deteriorating physical condition and misery were tests of the family's will to resist Satan, and that a miracle would save the boy—so argued Robidoux. Robidoux received a life sentence, without parole in June 2002.

CASE 197

Joey Virgo, twenty-one, from Webb City, Missouri claimed that he threw a rock at a car driven by Le Anne Hamm, seventeen, in August 1998 because she and her friends had annoyed him by speeding past his house yelling at him. Hamm's car ran off the road and hit a tree, injuring her and two companions. Hamm had been struck in the head with the twelve-inch rock thrown by Virgo, but recovered from the wound, succumbing months later to meningitis contracted from dirt on the rock. She died of the disease in October 1998. Virgo pleaded guilty of involuntary manslaughter and was sentenced to seven years in prison.

Notes

1. Luckenbill, 1977, p. 176.
2. Harris, et al., 2002.
3. Cook, 1985.
4. Cook, 1987.
5. Gebeth, 1998.

11

Epilogue

Day after day, month after month, year after year, murder in America continues on its inexorable path, leaving in its aftermath shattered lives, traumatized families, and broken communities. In a perverse sort of way, murder represents a highly predictable and expected phenomenon, somewhat unvaried and monotonous to those empowered by American society to deal with it. Police and homicide investigators; crime scene investigators; doctors, nurses and medical examiners; crime reporters; prosecutors and defense attorneys—all slowly become desensitized to the deadly dramas which unfold around them. Outsiders marvel at the nonchalant manner in which these professionals approach their grim task dealing with the debris of murder and its irreversible consequences. For those involved even indirectly with murder, its occurrence signals just "another day on the job," predictable as the day before, and the one to follow. Deaths caused by gang violence, domestic squabbles, drug transactions, barroom brawls, etc. no longer shock. Only child murders and murders of truly innocent victims amaze and anger these professionals. Even the general public evidences its boredom and casual acceptance of the daily, humdrum accounting of lives abruptly ended which they view on the nightly news and the countless cable shows sensationalizing actual murders.

We view the video representations of autopsies, murder scenes, police interrogations, and suspects' alibis with interest, even amazement but after a while, they all seem the same. Only the truly heinous and reprehensible killings awaken us to the horror of what one person can do to another.

Year after year, the patterns of homicide remain relatively stable.

The actual number of victims and rate of homicide do change from one time period to the next, but the pattern of who kills whom, why they kill, when and where they kill scarcely differ from decade to decade. Over the past forty years, homicide data show that the summer months have the highest incidence of murder, that Blacks are disproportionately represented as both victims and assailants, that most murders involved those who either are related to, or acquainted with each other, that males overwhelmingly are the killers and victims, that arguments are the main trigger in the act, that guns, particularly hand guns are the weapons of choice, that the vast majority of killings involve people of the same race, that the southern states are the predominant killing zone in the nation.

In this sense, very little ever changes, other than the persona of the actual victims and killers who presumably have no idea of the pattern in which they are unalterably fused. To them, the act of killing is personal and individualistic; to the criminologist, the homicide drama follows a distinctive pattern reasonably similar to the clear majority of previous homicides committed by others in different times and in different places. Yet its causes are to be found in the human heart, and social, psychological, and demographic factors can only go so far in explaining murder.

In this sense, homicide represents the ultimate act in what goes wrong in the human soul. The reasons and circumstances of murders at the dawn of the twenty-first century scarcely differ from those of classical times or those of the thirteenth century, or the nineteenth century. The wounded pride of the spurned lover of contemporary times triggers murderous aggression in modern-day Atlanta just as completely as it did centuries ago in classical Corinth, Medieval Milan, and Renaissance Rome. The body count changes but the reasons don't. It remains for the criminologist to connect these failures of the human condition to the sociological variables which helps explain why these moral and socio-psychological and demographic factors intersect in producing lethal violence, blending the moral with the sociological.

In its wake, murder leaves behind destroyed lives. The victim no longer remains in our midst; the killer either escapes punishment or languishes in prison, facing years of enforced solitude or possible execution; the victim's family members suffer the anger, revenge and sense of loss which, if not resolved through eventual forgiveness, condemns them also to the anger and resentment no different than that of the imprisoned. Yet forgiveness is not the initial response of families victimized.

Nor is remorse a viable emotion in the killer. After all, he believes that his deed to be justified, even noble. The victim deserved his or her fate. His rationalizations persuade him that his actions were more than suitable for the killing: "how dare he disrespect me in front of my friends"; "she doesn't deserve to live after what she did to me"; "those so-called innocent bystanders shouldn't have been on the corner when the shots flew"; "if she didn't resist my affectionate advances, she'd still be alive." These self-satisfying excuses convince the killer in the overwhelming number of murders that his actions were correct, even noble and honorable and that his subsequent time in prison is unfair, unjust, and incomprehensible. Yet, in time, many justly imprisoned for homicide do regret their actions. With the passage of years, with the solitude and loneliness of hard time in a jail where no one visits (except perhaps one's mother), where friends and acquaintances are distant memories, where one becomes a non-person to the outside world, many killers do begin to sense the wrongness of their actions, not merely because it has entrapped them in a state penitentiary, but because they can finally admit the evil act they have committed. What better reason can we offer for abolishing capital punishment which short circuits the healing process and reflection of time for some (who knows how many?) who have been imprisoned?

The society and the families of murder victims also need to move beyond the anger and desire for revenge so entwined with the murderous act. To fail to do so entraps those involved in an angry, resentful attitude that permeates their being, just as it does the killer they so loathe and hate. Without the remorse of the killer, and the forgiveness of families, there is no reasonable resolution, no constructive end to the enormous damage already committed by one human being upon another. Such is the nature of the human condition in which each of us lives and dies.

Appendix

Cases Cited

All of the cases cited in the book have been completely re-written from the media sources from which each had been selected. These adaptations include the main facts of each homicide, adapted from the original media or Internet source. For a full discussion of these sources, see *Case Sources* in the beginning of this book.

Case:	*Source:*
1.	Walker, 1976, 63–64
2.	Gerberth, 1990, 260–261
3.	Fisher, 1995, 194
4.	Barnhart and Mittleman, 1986, 30–31
5.	Sullivan, 1994, 26
6.	Leth and Vesleby, 1997, 65–71
7.	Frasier, 1996, 30–31
8.	Paulson, 1998
9.	Cardenas, 2002, B1
10.	Distraught Husband . . . , 1996, B2
11.	Gearty, 1999
12.	Man Acquitted in Killing 3 Men, 1997
13.	Butterfield, 1996; Maine Nun Killer . . . , 1996
14.	Death of Man, 85, Homicide, 1997
15.	Stingl, 2002
16.	P.G. Will Seek Death Penalty, 1996, 22
17.	Bank Robber Faces . . . , 1997
18.	Weigl, 2003

Case:	*Source:*
19.	Landlord Jailed . . . , 1996
20.	Man Receives 14 Years . . . , 1999, 23
21.	Grenz, 2001
22.	Nguyen, 1996, 20
23.	L.A. District Attorney's Office, 2000
24.	Ward, 2002
25.	Boy 14, Charged in Shooting . . . , 1996
26.	Trial to Open . . . , 1996
27.	Man Guilty of Accidental Slaying, 1999
28.	Hunt, 2001, 1–2
29.	Teen Held in Brother's Deather, 1995
30.	80-Year-Old Man Convicted, 1999
31.	Mesa Teen Pleads Guilty to Manslaughter, 1996, 82
32.	Fatal Accident Results . . . , 1996, B2
33.	Teens Kill Retiree . . . , 1996, A9
34.	Mother Charged in Kids Death, 1995
35.	Teen Guilty in Fatal Poisoning of Dad, 1996
36.	Walsh, 1996
37.	Daycare Worker Charged . . . , 1998
38.	Women Gets 35 Years . . . , 2003; Palmdale Man Convicted of Murdering Mother-in-Law, 2003
39.	Alleged Mobster Shot, 1998
40.	Pair Convicted in 2000 Stabbing Death, 2003, B2
41.	Man Pleads Not Guilty . . . , 2003
42.	Morrill, 1995
43.	Tailgaiting Leads to Slaying . . . , 1996
44.	Alleged Thrill-Killer . . . , 1997
45.	Miller, 1997
46.	Fernau, 1996, B1
47.	Ethiopian Runner . . . , 1997
48.	James, 1994, B3
49.	Man Killed Over Lost Quarter, 1994
50.	Gorman and Corwin, 1996, 1ff
51.	Zahniser, 1997, A3
52.	Giradot, 1996, A6
53.	Husband Hacks Wife . . . , 1998
54.	Wilson, 2001
55.	Henry, 1998

Case:	_Source:_
107.	Man Executed . . . , 1995
108.	Man Gets 28 Years . . . , 1998
109.	Police Continue Probe . . . , 1999
110.	Blair, 2000
111.	Fenner, Raftery, Marzulli, 2000
112.	Man Convicted of Killing Son, 1995
113.	Couple Sentenced in Starving Child to Death, 2000
114.	Mom's Debt . . . , 1998
115.	Wife Lets Husband Rot to Death, 1995
116.	Second Man Arrested . . . , 1998
117.	Jury: Death in Sledgehammer Slaying, 1999
118.	Man Tried . . . , 1998
119.	Kinney, 1999
120.	Sifakis, 1982, 73
121.	Sifakis, 1982, 281
122.	Asbury, 1968b, 340–344
123.	Teen Murder Suspect Charged, 1998
124.	Kids Charged in Fire Death, 1998
125.	Teens Found Dead, 1995
126.	Cook Allegedly Shoots Waitress, 1997
127.	Spilled Coffee . . . , 1997
128.	Hughes, 1998
129.	Wheeler and Callahan, 1998
130.	Two Killed . . . , 1998
131.	Georgia Man Accused . . . , 1998
132.	Husband Stabbed . . . , 1997
133.	Five Dead . . . , 2003
134.	Baden, 1989, chap. 9
135.	Cullen, 1990
136.	Pennsylvania Man Says . . . , 1997
137.	99-Year-Old Deacan Jailed, 1996
138.	Husband Pleads Guilty, 1997
139.	Toppo, 1999
140.	Police: Killer Planned Wedding, 1994
141.	Allison, 1997, B4
142.	Murder Suspect Says . . . , 1999
143.	Dead Groom Found . . . , 1999

Case:	_Source:_
144.	Roane, 1999, 32
145.	Police: Mom, Pals Beat Child to Death, 1998
146.	Report: No Money . . . , 1997
147.	Racher, 1998
148.	New Hampshire Teenager, 1997
149.	Boy, 11, Charged, 1999
150.	Teen Who Killed His Dad Sentenced, 2001
151.	Morrell, 2001
152.	Police Probe Md. Van Blast, 1995
153.	Report: Boy Killed His Family, 1996
154.	Martinez, 2000
155.	Hoffman, 1998
156.	Hoffman, 1999
157.	Geranios, 2001
158.	Lozano, 2001
159.	Stecker, 1998, B1
160.	Fox and Levin, 2001, 117–118
161.	McKinnon, 2001, A1
162.	Safakis, 1982, 572; Gribben, 2001
163.	Blum, 1978
164.	Bellamy, 2001
165.	Filkins, 1996, A32
166.	Terry and Malone, 1987
167.	Geringer, 2001
168.	Jury Rejects POW Flashback . . . , 1997
169.	Crowley and Starney, 1998; Gearty, 1998
170.	Caruso, 2002
171.	Hermann, 2001
172.	Miller, 2001
173.	Barakat, 2002
174.	Harmon, 2002
175.	Harmon, 2001
176.	Teen Ordered . . . , 1996
177.	Pearson, 1999
178.	Fenner, 2001
179.	Graczyk, 2001
180.	Man Sentenced . . . , 2001

Case:	_Source:_
181.	Swayze, 1995
182.	Man Charged with Baby's Standoff Death, 1997; Ellis, 1998, F01
183.	Police: Suspect Confessed to Murder, 2002
184.	Fischer, 1995, 112; Newton, 2002
185.	Saar, 1996
186.	Woman Sentenced . . . , 1998
187.	Liptak, 2003
188.	Man Convicted in Killing Tot . . . , 1995
189.	Walsh, 1996
190.	Mother Who Killed Baby . . . , 1998
191.	Teen Guilty in Slaying of Father, 1999
192.	Drunk Boater Jailed . . . , 1999
193.	Cops: Girl Killed . . . , 2000
194.	Car Ram Man . . . , 2000
195.	Man Guilty of Girls Death . . . , 2000
196.	Lavoie, 2002
197.	Man Pleads Guilty in Girls Death, 2001

Bibliography

Alaskan Village Teen Accused of Killing Young Boy. (1998, April 20). Reuters/ ClariNet. <*http://www.clari.local.alaska:165*>.

Alleged Mobster Shot Dead On His Way to US Trial. (1998, March 18). Reuters/ ClariNet. <*http://www.clari.local.pennsylvania:1288*>.

Alleged Thrill-Killer Arraigned on L.I. (1997, August 26). United Press International/ ClariNet. <*http://www.clari.net.news.murders.misc:9402*>.

Allison, W. (1997, April 3). Hayes Convicted in Death of Bride. *Richmond-Times Dispatch*, p. B4.

Anderson, D. (1997, February 9). Crime Stoppers. *New York Times*, pp. 47ff.

Arrillaga, P. (1998, July 27). Mom Sentenced in Death of Girl's Ex. The Associated Press/ClariNet. <*http://www.clari.local.texas:5166*>.

Asbury, H. (1929). *The Gangs of New York: An Informal History of the Underworld*. New York: Alfred A. Knopf.

Asbury, H. (1968A). *The Barbary Coast: An Informal History of the San Francisco Underworld*. New York: Capricorn Books.

Asbury, H. (1968B). *The French Quarter: An Informal History of the New Orleans Underworld*. New York: Capricorn Books.

Avakame, E. (1997). Urban Homicide: A Multilevel Analysis Across Chicago's Census Tracts. *Homicide Studies*, 1, (4), 338–358.

Baden, M. (with Hennessee, J). *Unnatural Death: Confessions of a Medical Examiner* (1929). New York: Ballentine Books.

Baller, R., Anselin, L., Messner, S., Deane, G., and Hawkins, D. (2001). Structural Covariates of U.S. County Homicide Rates: Incorporating Spatial Effects. *Criminology*, 39 (3), 561–590.

Bank Robber Faces Capital Murder Charge. (1997, February 16). United Press International/ClariNet. <*http://www.clari.news.issues.death_penalty:1292*>.

Barakat, M. (2002, October 6). Va. Teen on Trial for Dad's Murder. Associated Press / ClariNet. <*http://www.clari.local.virginia+dc.*>.

Barlow, H. (1986). *Introduction to Criminology. Third Edition*. Boston, MA: Little Brown and Company.

Barnhart, J.S., and Mittleman, R.E. (March, 1986). Unusual Deaths Associated with Polyphagia. *American Journal of Forensic Medical Pathology*, 7 (1), 30–34.

Bellamy, P. (2002). Dorothea Puente: Killing for Profit. *The Crime Library*. <*http://www.crimelibrary.com/serial7/puente/index.htm.to7.htm*>.

Bensing, R., and Schroeder, O. (1960). *Homicide in an Urban Community*. Springfield, IL: Charles Thomas.

Bizarre Dog Dispute Ends in Slaying. (1997, April 21). United Press International / ClariNet. <*http://www.clari.local.colorado:5509*>.

Black, H. (1968). *Black's Law Dictionary: Revised Fourth Edition*. St. Paul, MN: West Publishing Company.

Blair, J. Youth Held in Slaying at Deli. (2002, April 2). *New York Times*, Metro Section, p. 32.

Blau, J.R., and Blau, P.M. (1982). The Cost of Inequality: Metropolitan Structure and Violent Crime. *American Sociological Review*, 47, 114–129.

Block, C., Devitt, C., Donaghue, E., Dames, R., and Block, K. (2001). Are There Types of Intimate Partner Homicide? In P. Blackman, V. Legett, and J. Jarvis (eds.), *The Diversity of Homicide: Proceedings of the 2000 Homicide Research Working Group* (pp. 92–111). Washington, DC: Federal Bureau of Investigation.

Block, C., and Christakos, A. (1995). Intimate Parner Homicide in Chicago Over 29 Years. *Crime and Delinquency*, 41, (4), 496–526.

Blum, H. (1978, December 22). Scene of Battle Moves From Streets to the Courts. *New York Times*, pp. A1ff.

Blum, H. (1978, December 21). The War on 138th Street: Routine Killing Led Police to Gangs. *New York Times*, pp. A1ff.

Bohannan, P. (Ed.). (1960). *African Homicide and Suicide*. Princeton, NJ: Princeton University Press.

Book of Genesis. *Holy Bible: The Old Testament*. (1992). Douay Version (New Catholic Edition). New York: Catholic Book Publishing Company.

Bowes, M. (1997, February 25). Restaurant Shooting Recanted. *Richmond Times-Dispatch*, p.1.

Boy, 11, Charged in Sister's Death. (1999, January 27). Associated Press / ClariNet. <*http://clari.local.florida:14437*>.

Boy, 14 Charged in Shooting of Toddler Brother. (1996, March 22). Reuters / ClariNet. <*http://www.forest.clari.local.massachusetts:6285*>.

Boy Held in Shooting Death of Elderly Calif. Women. (1996, August 2). Reuters / ClariNet. <*http://www.local.california.southern:2375*>.

Braithwait, J., and Braithwaite, V. (1980). The Effects of Income Inequality and Social Democracy on Homicide. *British Journal of Criminology*, 20, 45–53.

Brown, A. (1997). Violence in Marriage: Until Death Do Us Part? In A. Cardarelli (Editor), *Violence Between Intimate Partners: Patterns, Causes and Effects* (pp. 48–69). Needham Heights, MA: Allyn and Bacon.

Browne, A., William, K., and Dutton, D. (1999). Homicide Between Intimate Partners. In M. Smith and M. Zahn (Eds.), *Homicide: A Sourcebook of Social Research* (pp. 149–164). Thousand Oaks, CA: Sage Publishers.

Bullock, H. (1955). Urban Homicide in Theory and Fact. *Journal of Criminal Law, Criminology, and Police Science* (January-February), pp. 565–575.

Burney, M. (1999, September 5). One of Nation's First Mass Killers Knows What Day This Is. *Sunday Star-Ledger*, Section One, p. 27.

Butterfield, F. (1996, January 29). Man Is Held in Deaths of 2 Maine Nuns. *New York Times*, p. A10.

Callahan, R. (1999, June 28). Cops: Man Fathered Baby to Kill to It. Associated Press / ClariNet. *<http://www.clari.local.indiana>*.

Campbell, T. (1997, April 23). He Only Wanted to Scare Girlfriend, Defendant Testifies. *Richmond Times Dispatch*, p. B3.

Capote, T. (1965). *In Cold Blood*. New York: New American Library.

Cappello, G. (2001, January 12). Crack House Slay Suspects Charged. Associated Press / ClariNet. *<http://www.clari.local.pennsylvania>*.

Car Ram Man Gets 30 Years. (2000, July 27). Associated Press / ClariNet. *<http://www.clari.local.california.los_angeles.>*

Cardenas, J. (2002, November 6). Businessman Found Not Guilty in Fatal Fall Off Balcony; Same Jurors Said the Lack of Signs of Struggle by Sandra Onellana Influenced the Verdict. *Los Angeles Times*, p. B1.

Caruso, D. (2002, November 29). Man Pleads Guilty in Crackhouse Massacre. Associated Press / ClariNet. *<http://www.clari.local.pennsylvania>*.

The Catholic Encyclopedia: An International Work of Reference on the Constitution, Doctrine, Discipline, and History of the Catholic Church. (1907). Edited by C. Herbermann, E. Pace, C. Pallen, T. Shanan, and J. Wynne. New York: Robert Appleton Company: Fifteen Volumes.

Census of Occupational Inquiries: Fatalities by Detailed Industry, 2002: U.S. Department of Labor Statistics. <http://www.data.bls.gov/servlet/surveyoutputservlet>.

Chilton, R. (2003). Regional Variations in Lethal and Non-Lethal Assaults. In M. Smith, P. Blackman, and J. Jarvis (eds.). *New Directions in Homicide Research: Proceedings of the 2001 Annual Meeting of the Homicide Research Working Group*. Washington, DC Federal Bureau of Investigation: 32–44.

Coates, C. (1998, February 6). DA: Serial Killer Admits Racial Slaying of Couple. *Philadelphia Inquirer On Line*. <http://www.phillynews.com.80/daily_news/98/Feb06/national/SNIP06.htm>.

Cohen, D. (1998). Culture, Social Organization and Patterns of Violence. *Journal of Personality and Social Psychology*, 75, 408–419.

Conviction in Crossbow Shooting. (1995, November 10). Associated Press / ClariNet. *<http://www.clari.net.crime.murders:13194>*.

Cook Allegedly Shoots Waitress Over Egg. (1997, July 25). United Press International / ClariNet. *<http://www.clari.local.california.sfbay.crime:8993>*.

Cook, P.J. (1985). The Case of the Missing Victim: Gunshot Woundings in the National Crime Survey. *Journal of Quantitative Criminology*, 1, 91–102.

Cook, P.J. (1987). Robbery Violence. *Journal of Criminal Law and Criminology*, 78, 357–376.

Cops: Girl Killed by Revenge Fire. (2000, February 5). Associated Press / ClariNet. *<http://www.clari.local.ohio>*.

Corzine, J., and Huff-Corzine, L. (1992). Racial Inequality and Black Homicide: An Analysis of Felony, Nonfelony, and Total Rates. *The Journal of Contemporary Criminal Justice*, vol. 8, 150–165.

Corzine, J., Huff-Corzine, L., and Whitt, H. (1999). Cultural and Subcultural Theories of Homicide. In M. D. Smith and M. Zahn (eds.), *Homicide: A Sourcebook of Social Research* (Chap. 4). Thousand Oaks, CA: Sage Publications.

Couple Die in Ohio Office Shooting. (1998, March 18). United International Press / ClariNet. *<http://www.clari.local.ohio:1846>*.

Couple Sentenced in Starving Child to Death (2000, January 14). Agence France—Presse / ClariNet. *<http://www.clari.news.crime.murders>*.

Crime in Maine 2003. Department of Public Safety–U.C. Reporting Division, Augusta, Maine.

Crime Watch. (1997, January 30). *Washington Post*, D.C.6.

Crime Watch. (1997, February 13). *Washington Post*, D.C.5.

Criminal Victimization in the United States. (1994), Washington, DC: Bureau of Justice Statistics, U.S. Department of Justice.

Crowley, K., and Stamey, M (1998, April 29). L.I. Vigilante—Stay Shocker. *New York Post.* *<http://www.nypostonline.com:80/042998/news/1372.htm>*.

Cullen, K. (1990, January 12). In Scheme, Carelessness Amid the Calculations $. *Boston Globe Archives.* <http://nl.newsbank.com/nlsearch/we/archives?p_action=&p_topdoc=17.

Curtis, L. (1975). *Violence, Race, and Culture.* Lexington, MA: D.C. Health.

Daly M., and Wilson, M. (1988). *Homicide*, New York: Aldine Publishers.

Daly, M., and Wilson, M. (1996). Violence Against Stepchildren. *Current Directions in Psychological Science*, 5, 77–81.

Daly, M., Wiseman, K., and Wilson, M. (1997). Women With Children Sired by Previous Partners Incur Excess Risk of Uxorcide. *Homicide Studies*, 1, 61–71.

Dawson, J. (1994). *Murder in Families: Bureau of Justice Statistics Special Report.* Washington, DC: Government Printing Office.

Daycare Worker Charged with Playground Killing. (1998, February 19). Reuters / ClariNet. *<http://www.clari.local.florida:2609>*.

Dead Groom Found in Storage Unit. (1999, September 24). Associated Press / ClariNet. *<http://www.clari.news.crime.murders.misc>*.

Death of Man, 85, Homicide; Wife Sought. (1997, February 6). ClariNet / United Press International. *<http://www.clari.news.crime.murders.misc:5284>*.

Defendant in Slaying To Be Released. (2001, January 9). Associated Press / ClariNet. *<http://www.clari.local.wisconsin>*.

Dietz, P. (1986). Mass Serial and Sensational Homicides. *Bulletin of the New York Academy of Medicine*, 62, (5), 477–491.

Dirty Look Gets Daughter Killed. (1999, April 18). Associated Press / ClariNet. *<http://www.clari.news.crime.murders.misc:11844>*.

Distraught Husband Is Shot Dead After Pointing Weapon at Police. (1996, March 14). *Arizona Republic*, p. B2.

Dixon, J., and Lizotte, A. (1997). Gun Ownership and the Southern Subculture of Violence. *American Journal of Sociology*, 93 (September), 383–405.

Doctor Held in Hospital Shooting. (1999, February 23). Associated Press / ClariNet. *<http://www.clari.news.crime.murders.misc:10372>*.

Douglas, J., Burgess, E., Burgess, A., and Ressler, R. (1992). *Crime Classification Manual.* New York: Lexington Books.

Drunk Boater Jailed for 85 Years for Killing Six. (1999, November 4). Reuters News (via Excite News). *<http://www.news.excite.com/news/n/991104/07odd-crime-bc>*.

80 Year-Old Man Convicted of Murdering Love Rival. (1999, August 30). Reuters News. *<http://www.news.excite.com/news/n/990830/09odd-crime-kansas>*.

El-Ghobashy, T. (2001, October 7). Gory Killing of Afghan Filmmaker. *New York Daily News Online*. <http://www.mostnewyork.com/2001_10–07/news_and_views/crimefile/a–127637>.

Elias, N., Goudsblom, J., Mennell, S., Dunning, E., and Jephcott, E. (translator). (2000). *Civilizing Process*, Revised Edition. Oxford: Blackwell Publishers, Chapter X.

Elias, R. (1998, October 17). Griffin Man Avoids Death Penalty: Convicted of Killing His Son, Wendell White Given Life Without Parole. *Atlanta Journal and Constitution*, p. F01.

Ethiopian Runner Gets Life for Murder. (1997, December 16). United Press International / ClariNet. *<http://www.clari.news.murders:1994>*.

Fatal Accident Results in 17-Year Sentence. (1996, January 28). *Arizona Republic*, p. B2.

Federal Bureau of Investigation. *Crime in the United States*. Uniform Crime Reports (various annual editions, 1970 to present). Washington, DC: Government Printing Office.

Fenner, A. (2001, February 16). Man Guilty of Beating Rego Pk. Teen to Death. *New York Daily News Online*. <http://www.mostnewyork.com/2001–02–16/newsandviews/crimefile/a–100016.asp>.

Fenner, A., Raftery, T., and Marzulli, J. (2000, September 7). *Daily News Online*. <http://www.mostnewyork.com/2009–09–07/news_and_views/crime_file/a–79151.asp>.

Fernau, K. (1996, February 29). 2 Get 17 Years in Foster Child's Death. *Arizona Republic*, pp. B1ff.

Fessenden, F. (2000, April 9). They Threaten, Seethe and Unhinge, Then Kill in Quantity. *New York Times*, p. 1ff.

Filkins, D. (1996, February 18). The Twisted Life That Led to Death Row. *Los Angeles Times*, pp. A3 and 32.

Fincher, D. (Producer). (1996). *Seven*. Hollywood, CA: New Line Cinema.

Fink, N. (1982). The Legal Defense of Homicide. In B. Danto, J. Bruhns, and A. Kutscher (Eds). *The Human Side of Homicide*. (pp. 251–261). New York: Columbia University Press.

Finkelhor, D., and Ormrod, R. (2001). Homicide of Children and Youth. *Juvenile Justice Bulletin*. Washington, DC: U.S. Department of Justice, Office of Justice Programs, 1–12.

Fischer, D. (1995). *Hard Evidence*. New York: Dell Publishing.

Five Dead in Apparent Murder-Suicide. (September 27, 2003). Clarinet/United Press International <http://www.clari.local.indiana>

Fox, J., and Levin, J. (2001). *The Will to Kill: Making Sense of Senseless Murder*. Needham Heights, MA: Allyn and Bacon.

Frasier, D. (1996). *Murder Cases of the Twentieth Century*. Jefferson, NC: McFarland and Company.

Fried, A. (1980). *The Rise and Fall of the Jewish Gangster in America*. New York: Halt, Rinehart and Winston.

Gearty, R. Cop Kills Man in Patchogue Parking Lot. (1999, October 5). *Daily News Online*. *<http://www.nydailynews.com.05/news_and_views/city_beat/a–4270>*.

Gearty, R. (1998, June 28). 1st Murderer on Shelter Is. Gets the Max. *New York Daily News*. *<http://www.nydailynews/doc/55611131>*.

Geberth, V. (1990). *Practical Homicide Investigation: Tactics, Procedures and Forensic Techniques Second Edition*. New York: Elsevier.

Geberth, V. (1998). Domestic Violence Homicides. *Law and Order Magazine*. vol. 46 no. 12. (November). pp. 51–54.

Georgia Man Accused of Murder With Baseball Bat. (1998, February 3). Reuters / ClariNet. *<http://www.clari.local.georgia:422>*.

Geranios, N. Wash. Teen: Chores Led to Slayings. (2001, January 5). Associated Press / ClariNet. *<http://www.clari.local.washington>*.

Geringer, J. (2001, November 7). Angel Maturino Resendez: The Railroad Killer. *The Crime Library*. *<http://www.crimelibrary.com/serial2/railroad>*.

Giradot, F. (1996, June 14). Suspect in Slaying Can't See Girlfriend, Child. *Pasadena Star News*. p. A1.

Gorman, T., and Corwin, M. (1996, January, 26). Stepfather Held in Deaths of 3 Youngsters. *Los Angeles Times*, pp. 1ff.

Graczyk, Michael. (2001, February 8). Texas Executes Convicted Killer. Associated Press / ClariNet. *<http://www.clari.local.texas>*.

Graham, H., and Gurr, T. (eds.). (1969). *The History of Violence in America*. New York: Bantam Books.

Grenz, C. (2001, June 9). Killer of Teen Gets 9 Years. *Topeka Capital Journal*. (CJ Online). <http://www.cjonline.com/webindepth/missilesilos/stories/060901_cordray.shtml>.

Gribben, M. Harry "Pittsburgh Phil" Strauss. (2001). *The Crime Library*. *<http://www.crimelibrary.com/gangsters/murdermain.htm>*.

Hackney, S. (1969). Southern Violence. In H. Graham and T. Gurr (eds.). *The History of Violence in America*. (pp. 505–527). New York: Bantam Books.

Hagan, J. and Peterson, R. (1995). Criminal Inequality in America: Patterns and Consequences. In J. Hagan and R. Peterson (eds.), *Crime and Inequality* (pp. 14–36). Stanford, CA: Stanford University Press.

Harbort, S. and Mokros, A. (2000). Serial Murderers in Germany From 1945–1995. *Homicide Studies*, 5, (4), 311–334.

Harmon, B. (2001, August 9). Court Told of Motel Kill Horror. *New York Daily News Online*. *<http://www.nydailynews/d . . . 4433634>*.

Harmon, B. (2002, February 13). 9/11 Stress Is Defense Offered in Grisly Crime. *New York Daily News Online*. *<http://www.mostnewyork.com/2002 . . . views/crime_filea–141206>*.

Harris, A., Thomas, S., Fisher, G., and Hirsch, D. (2002). Murder and Medicine: The Lethality of Criminal Assault 1960–1999. *Homicide Studies*, 6 (2), 128–166.

Heide, K. (1999). Youth Homicide: An Integration of Psychological, Sociological, and Biological Approaches. In M. D. Smith and M. Zahn (eds.), *Homicide: A Sourcebook of Social Research* (chapter 15). Thousand Oaks, CA: Sage Publications.

Henry, D. (1998, July 17). Suspect Surrenders in NM Shootings. Associated Press / ClariNet. <http://www.clari.news.crime.murders.misc:682>.

Hermann, P. (2001, February 7). Betrayal, Ambush Alleged in Killing of Café's Owner. *Baltimore Sun*. <http://www.sunspot.net/news . . . 07feb07.story?coll=bal0/02Dhome0/02Dheadlines>.

Hillbrand, M., Alexandre, J. and Young, J. (1997). Paracides: Characteristics of Offenders and Victims, Legal Factors, and Treatment Issues. *Aggression and Violent Behavior*, 4, 179–190.

Himes, K. (1989). Capital Sins. In R. McBrien (ed.), *The Harper Collins Encyclopedia of Catholicism*. San Francisco, CA: Harper Collins Publishers, 225.

Historical Statistics of the United States: Colonial Times to 1970, Part 1. (1975). Washington, DC: Government Printing Office.

Hoffman, K. Bail Denied in Infant Deaths Case. (1998, August 7). Associated Press / ClariNet. *<http://www.clari.local.pennsylvania:2884>*.

Hoffman, K. B. (1999, April 23). Colorado Attack Recalls 1927 Blast. Associated Press / ClariNet. *<http://www.clari.local.colorado:4597>*.

Hofstadter, R. and Wallace, M. (1971). *American Violence: A Documentary History*. New York: Vintage Books.

Holmes, R. and DeBurger, J. (1988). *Serial Murders*. Newbury Park, CA, Sage Publications.

Holmes, R. and Holmes, S. (2001). *Murder in America Second Edition*. Thousand Oaks, CA: Sage Publications.

Homicide in North Dakota—2002. (2003). Office of the Attorney General, State of North Dakota.

Horwitz, S. and Shields, T. (1997). 1 Shot Dead, 7 Injured in Club Attack. *Washington Post*, January 13, B1. and B5.

Hughes, J. (1998, February 3). Couple Confesses to Slaying. *Denver Post*, p. 1.

Hunt, S. (2001, February 14). Dad Refuses to Plead Guilty in Sons Death in Woods. *Salt Lake Tribune Online*, p. 1 and 2.

Husband Hacks Wife as Kids Watch. (1998, January 20). United Press International / ClariNet. *<http://www.clari.news.crime.murders:2825>*.

Husband Pleads Guilty in Car Bombing. (1997, February 6). United Press International / ClariNet. *<http://www.clari.news.crime.murders.misc:5284>*.

Husband Stabbed in New York Despite Court Order. (1997, January 30). Reuters / ClariNet. *<http://www.clari.news.crime.murders.misc:4952>*.

Inciardi, J. (1978). *Reflections on Crime*. New York: Holt, Rinehart and Winston.

Infant Found Dead in Microwave Oven. (1999, September 24). Agence France-Presse / ClariNet. *<http://www.clari.news.crime.murders>*.

James, G. (1994, October 31). Man, Struck by Stray Thrown in Egg Fight, Kills a Youth. *New York Times*, p. B3.

Jenkins, E., Castillo, L. and Castillo, D. (1993). NIOSH Occupational Homicide Data Questions and Answers in Lethal and Non-Lethal Violence. *Proceedings of the Second Annual Workshop of the Homicide Research Working Group*. Washington, D.C.: National Institute of Justice, 99–102.

Johnson, E. and Monkkoner, E. (eds.). (1996). *The Civilization of Crime: Violence in Town And Country Since the Middle Ages*. Urbana: University of Illinois Press.

Jury: Death in Sledgehammer Slaying. (1999, June 23). Associated Press / ClariNet. <*http://www.clari.news.crime.murder.misc:1,4226*>.

Jury Rejects POW Flashback Defense in Murder Case. (1997, November 25). Reuters News / ClariNet. <*http://www.clari.news.crime.murders.misc:1627*>.

Kaczor, B. (2001, March 23). Medical Examiner Guilty of Murder. Associated Press / ClariNet. <*http://www.clari.news.issues.death_penalty*>.

Katz, J. (1998). *Seductions of Crime*. New York: Basic Books.

Keeney, B. and Heide, K. (1994). Gender Differences in Serial Murderers: A Preliminary Analysis. *Journal of Interpersonal Violence*, 9: 37–56.

Keifer, M. (1996, March 14). Killing Time at Shadow Mountain High. *New Times*, pp. 15–20.

Kelleher, M. (1997). *Flash Point: The American Mass Murderer*. Westport, CT: Praeger Publishers.

Kids Charged in Fire Death of Father. (1998, February 17). United Press International / ClariNet. <*http://www.clari.local.arkansas:255*>.

Kinney, D. (1999, January 29). Teen Found Guilty in Lynching. Associated Press / ClariNet. <*http://www.clari.local.florida:14575*>.

Krikorian, G. (1997, September 6). Teenager Sentenced in Death of Watts Woman. *Los Angeles Times* (Record Edition), p. 3.

Lalli, M. and Turner, S. (1968). Suicide and Homicide: A Comparative Analysis By Race and Occupational Levels. *Journal of Law, Criminology, and Political Science*, 59, 191–200.

Landlord Jailed For Murder. (1996, March 6). Associated Press / ClariNet. <*http://www.clari.news.murders.misc:635*>.

Langford, L., and Isaac, N. and Adams, S. Criminal and Restraining Order Histories of Intimate Partner-Related Homicide Offenders in Massachusetts, 1991–1995, in *Varieties of Homicide and Its Research: Proceedings of the 1999 Meeting of the Homicide Research Working Group*. Quantico, Virginia: Behavioral Science Unit, FBI, pp. 57–66.

Lavoie, D. (2002, June 14). Man Gets Life Term in Son's Death. (2002, June 14). Associated Press / ClariNet. <*http://www.clari.news.crime.murders.misc*>.

Lester, D. (1991). *Questions and Answers About Murder*. Philadelphia: The Charles Press.

Leth, P. and Vesterby, A. (1997). Homicidal Hanging Masquerading As Suicide. *Forensic Science International* 85, 65–71.

Life Sentence in Student's Arson Murder. (1997, November 13). United Press International / ClariNet. <*http://www.clari.local.new_york.nyc:594*>.

LI Strangle Suspect Arrested in Vegas. (1998, February 2). United Press International / ClariNet. <*http://www.clari.local.new_york.nyc:1263*>.

Liptak, A. (September 21, 2003). Examiners Murder Case Becomes a Tangled Tale. *New York Times*, Nation Section, p. 24.

Liska, A. E., and Bellair, P. E. (1995). Violent-Crime Rates and Racial Composition: Convergence Over Time. *American Journal of Sociology*, 101, 578–610.

Loftin, C. and Hill R. (1974). Regional Subcultures and Homicide: An Examination of the Gaskil-Hackney Thesis. *American Sociological Review*, 39, 714–724.

Loftin, C. and McDowall, D. (2003). Regional Culture and Patterns of Homicide. *Homicide Studies*, 7, no. 4, 353–367.

Los Angeles County District Attorney's Office. (2000, April 25). Murder Conviction Nets 19-Year-Old Northridge Man 15 Years To Life. *<http://www.da.co.la.ca.us/ _text/mr/2000/042500a.htm>*.

Lozano, J. Police: Gunman Had Accused Victim. (2001, January 10). Associated Press / ClariNet. *<http://www.clari.local.texas>*.

Luckenbill, D. (1977). Criminal Homicide as a Situated Transaction. *Social Problems*, 25, 176–186.

Lyman, S. (1978). *The Seven Deadly Sins: Society and Evil*. New York: St. Martin's Press.

Maguire, K. and Pastore, A. (eds.). (1996). *Sourcebook of Criminal Justice Statistics 1995*. U.S. Department of Justice, Bureau of Justice Statistics. Washington, DC: Government Printing Office.

Maine Nun Killer Insane, Not Guilty of Murder. (1996, October 16). Reuters / ClariNet. *<http://www.clari.local.maine:869>*.

Man Acquitted in Killing 3 Men. (1997, December 16). United Press International / ClariNet. *<http://www.clari.local.maine:92>*.

Man Charged With Baby's Death. (1997, November 20). United Press International / ClariNet. *<http://www.clari.news.crime.murders.misc:1482>*.

Man Convicted in Killing Tot with a Bowling Ball. (1995, March 10). Reuters News / ClariNet. *<http://www.clari.local.new_jersey:2580>*.

Man Convicted of Murder; Body Never Found. (2000, February 8). United Press International / ClariNet. *<http://www.clari.local.indiana>*.

Man Executed for Meal Stabbing. (1995, June 20). Associated Press / ClariNet. *<http:/ /www.clari.news.crime.murders:10243>*.

Man Gets 28 Years For Killing Toddler. (1988, January 11). *New York Times*, p. 24.

Man Guilty of Girls Death After Taking Life Vest. (2000, October 12). Reuters News / Excite News. *<http://www.news.excite.com/news/r001012/11/odd-lifejacket-de>*.

Man Guilty of Accidental Slaying. (1999, March 27). The Associated Press / ClariNet. *<http://www.clari.local.virginia+dc:6870>*.

Man Killed Over Lost Quarter. (1994, December 12). Associated Press / ClariNet. *<http://www.ANPA:Wc:88/0;ID:V0400>*.

Man Kills Cousin, Himself, After Dole Nomination. (1996, August 15). Reuters / ClariNet. *<http://www.clari.news.crime.murders:16936>*.

Man Pleads Guilty in Girl's Death. (2001, January 4). Associated Press / ClariNet. *<http://www.clari.local.missouri>*.

Man Pleads Not Guilty in Slaying of Neighbor. (2003, July 3). *Chicago Tribune Online*. <http://www.chicagotribune.com/templates/m . . . g=chi–0307030281jul03 &section=/ printstory>.

Man Receives 14 Years in Deaths of Two Infants. (1999, March 28). *New York Times*, National Section, 23.

Man Sentenced to Life in Prison. (2001, March 12). Associated Press / ClariNet. *<http://www.clari.local.arizona>*.

Man Tried in Woman's Torture. (1998, December 2). Associated Press / ClariNet. <*http://www.clari.local.texas:7376*>.

Mann, C. R. (1988). Getting Even? Women Who Kill in Domestic Encounters. *Justice Quarterly*, 5 (1), 34–46.

Martinez, R. (2000, July 27). California Mom Convicted of Killing Kids. Associated Press / ClariNet. <*http://www.clari.local.california.los_angeles*>.

Martinez, R. (1997). Homicide Among Miami's Ethnic Groups. *Homicide Studies*, 1 (1), 17–34.

McDowall, D. (1986). Poverty and Homicide in Detroit, 1926–1978. *Violence and Victims*, 1, 23–34.

McKinnon, J. Death Times Five. (2001, September 7). *Pittsburgh Post-Gazette*, p. A–1 and A–6.

Md. Teen Says Demon Gave OK to Kill. (2002, February 9). Associated Press / ClariNet. <*http://www.clari.news.crime.murders.misc*>.

Memphis Police Question Suspect. (1998, January 3). Tennessee Local News Brief. ClariNet. <*http://www.clari.local.tennessee*>.

Mercy, J., Goodman, R., Rosenberg, M., Allen, N., Loya, F., Smith, J., and Vargas, V. Patterns of Homicide Victimization in the City of Los Angeles, 1970–79. *Bulletin of the New York Academy of Medicine*, 62, (5), 427–445.

Merisalo, L. (1997, December 18). In Milwaukee Post Office Shooting. Reuter / ClariNet. <*http://www.clari.news.crime.murders.misc:2198*>.

Mesa Teen Pleads Guilty to Manslaughter. (1996, February 3). *Arizona Republic*, p. B2.

Messner, S. (1985). Regional Differences in the Economic Correlates of the Urban Homicide Rate: Same Evidence the Importance of Cultural Context. *Criminology*, 21, 477–488.

Messner, S. (1983). Regional and Racial Effects of the Urban Homicide Rate: The Subculture of Violence Revisited. *American Journal of Sociology*, 88, 997–1007.

Messner, S. (1982). Poverty, Inequality, and Urban Homicide Rate: Some Unexpected Findings. *Criminology*, 20, 103–114.

Metzler, K. (2001, January 20). 38 Stabs Not 'On Purpose,' Killer Says. *Washington Times*, p. A9.

Miller, B. (1997, January 14). Wheaton Man Convicted of Murder in SE Barber's Death. *Washington Post*, Washington, DC, p. 1.

Miller, C. (2001, December 27). Scheme Claimed in Exec's Murder. *Arizona Republic*, pp. A1 and A8.

Mom Charged in Baby's Death. (1994, November, 10). Associated Press / ClariNet. <*http://www.ID:V0235;src:ap;sel:____Vi0193*>.

Man Convicted of Killing Son. (1995, March, 29). Associated Press / ClariNet. <*http://www.forest.clari.local.florida:8540*>.

Man Who Killed Baby With Curler Iron Gets Life. (1998, February 28). United Press International / ClariNet. <*http://www.clari.local.illinois.misc.:2897*.

Mom's Debt May Have Led To Son's Starvation. (1998, April 30). United Press International / ClariNet. <*http://www.clari.local.colorado:1534*>.

Monkkonen, E. (2001). *Murder in New York City*. Berkeley: University of California Press.

Morrell, A., Livadas, G., and Flanigan, P. (2001, May 31). Police Say Boy, 3, Killed by 6-Year-Old. *Rochester News Democrat and Chronicle*, Rochester, New York, p. 1

Morrill, S. (1995, January 18). Jilted Lover Shot Self, Rival With One Bullet. Reuters News. *<http://www.reut17:3401–18,BCRicochet01–180298>*.

Mother Charged in Kids Deaths. (1995, March 8). Associated Press / ClariNet. *<http://www.clari.news.crime.murders:8313>*.

Mother Who Killed Baby With Curler Gets Life. (1988, February 28). United Press International / ClariNet. *<http://www.clari.news.murders.misc:3459>*.

Murder Suspect Says It Was Accidental. (1999, March 7). United Press International / ClariNet. *<http://www.clari.news.crime.murders.misc:10707>*.

Nachtigal, J. (1999, June 17). Man Says He Accidentally Killed Wife. Associated Press / ClariNet. *<http://www.clari.local.arizona:2463>*.

Navy Rape-Murder Trial Continues. (1999, January 25). Associated Press / ClariNet. *<http://www.clari.local.virginia+dc:6042>*.

New Hampshire Teen-ager Guilty of Murder. (1997, May 28). Reuters / ClariNet. *<http://www.clari.news.crime.murders:20070>*.

Newton, M. (2002). Donald Henry Gaskins Jr. *The Crime Library*. <http://www.crimelibrary.com/serial_killers/predators/peewee_gaskins/>.

New York Police Department. (2002). *Statistical Report: Complaints and Arrests—2001*. New York: NYPD Crime Analysis Unit.

99-Year-Old Deacon Jailed. (1996, February 3). Associated Press / ClariNet. *<http://www.clari.news.crime.murders:14859>*.

Nguyen, L. (1996, February 2). Son Gets 8 _ Years in Father's Stabbing Death. *Washington Post*, p. 20.

Occupational Violence. (2003). National Institute for Occupational Safety and Health, Traumatic Injury. <http://www.cdc.gov/niosh/injury/trauma/violence.html>.

Ohio Traffic Stop Nets Grisly Find. (1998, March 17). United Press International / ClariNet. *<http://www.clari.news.crime.murders:3991>*.

O'Kane, J. (1992). *The Crooked Ladder: Gangsters, Ethnicity and the American Dream*. New Brunswick, NJ: Transaction Publishers.

O'Reilly-Fleming, T. (1996). The Evolution of Multiple Murder in Historical Perspectives. In O'Reilly-Fleming (ed.), *Serial and Mass Murder: Theory Research and Policy* (pp. 1–37). Toronto, Canada: Canadian Scholars Press.

Pair Convicted in 2000 Stabbing Death. (2003, June 24). *Boston Globe*, Metro/Region, p. B2

Pallone, N. and Hennessy, J. (1996). *Tinder Box Criminal Aggression: Neuropsychology, Demography and Phenomenology*. New Brunswick, NJ: Transaction Publishers.

Palmdale Man Convicted of Murdering Mother-in-Law. (July 7, 2003). Los Angeles County District Attorney's Office. <http://www.da.co.la.ca.us/mr/070707b.htm>.

Parker, R. (1989). Poverty, Subculture of Violence, and Type of Homicide. *Social Forces*, vol. 67: 983–1007.

Paulsen, D. (2003). Murder in Black and White. *Homicide Studies*, vol. 7, no. 3 (August): 289–317.

Paulson, S. (1998, June 1). Photo Made Kids Pursue Dad's Killer. Associated Press / ClariNet. *<http://www.clari.news.law_enforce:2892>*.

Pearson, M. (1999, March 2). Teen Convicted in Five Killings. Associated Press / ClariNet. <*http://www.clari.news.crime.murders.misc:10848*>.

Pennsylvania Man Says He Strangled Wife for Insurance. (1997, October 30). Reuters / ClariNet. <*http://www.clari.local.pennsylvania:234*>.

Peterson, E. (1999). Murder as Self-Help: Women and Intimate Partner Homicide. *Homicide Studies*, 3, (1), 30–46.

P. G. Will Seek Death Penalty For Suspect in Fatal Carjacking. (1996, March 5). *Washington Post*, Crime and Justice Section, p. 22.

Police Continue Probe of "Steak Murder." (1999, March 23). United Press International / ClariNet. <*http://www.clari.news.crime.murders:9604*>.

Police: Killer Planned Wedding. (1994, November 25). Associated Press / ClariNet. <*http://www.ANPA:wc:283/0;id:v0170*>.

Police: Man Killed Over $80 Loan. (1999, April 2). United Press International / ClariNet. <*http://www.clari.news.crime.murders:9897*>.

Police: Mom, Pals Beat Child to Death. (1998, April 2). United Press International / ClariNet. <*http://www.clari.news.crime.murders:4331*>.

Police Probe Md. Van Blast. (1995, September 12). Associated Press / ClariNet. <*http://www.clari.local.maryland:1318*>.

Police: Suspect Confessed to Murder. (2002, September 9). Associated Press / ClariNet. <*http://www.clari.local.north_carolina*>.

Polk, K. (1999, February). Males and Honor Contest Violence. *Homicide Studies*, vol. 3, no. 1:6–29.

Pollock, J. (1999). *Criminal Women*. Cincinnati, OH: Anderson Publishing Company.

Pokorny, A. (1965). Comparison of Homicides in Two Cities. *Journal of Criminal Law, Criminology and Police Science*, 56, 479–487.

Racher, D. (1998, February 18). Dad Held in Kids' Murders. *Philadelphia Inquirer Online*. <http://www.phillynews.com:80/daily_news/98/feb/18/local/dadd18.htm>.

Reeves, J. Woman Sentenced For Grisly Murder. (1998, December 15). Associated Press / ClariNet. <*http://www.clari.local.alabama:3109*>

Report: Boy Killed His Family. (1996, February 5). Associated Press / ClariNet. <*http://www.clari.local.california.southern.misc:49*>.

Report: No Money Led Mom to Her Death. (1997, May 4). United Press International / ClariNet. <*http://www.clari.news.trouble.misc:8781*>.

Resnick, P. (1970). Child Murder by Parents. *American Journal of Psychiatry*, 126, 1414–1420.

Roane, K. (1999, February 28). Woman Kills Former Boyfriend Who Beat Her, Authorities Say. *New York Times*, Metro Section, p. 32.

Saar, M. (1996, January 25). Death By Freight at Issue in Murder Trial. *Los Angeles Times*, 25, B1 and B3.

Sampson, R. (1987). Urban Black Violence: The Effect of Male Joblessness and Family Disruption. *American Journal of Sociology*, 93, (2), 348–382.

Schmitz, J. (1997, April 3). Accused Tells of Being Afraid of the Man He Shot. *Pittsburgh Post-Gazette*, p.2.

Second Man Arrested in Ore. Murders. (1998, July 22). Associated Press / ClariNet. <*http://www.clari.loca.oregon:415*>.

Shackelford, T. (2001). Partner-Killing by Women in Cohabitating Relationships and Marital Relationships. *Homicide Studies*, 5, (3), 253–266.

Sharpe, J. (1996). Crime in England: Long-Term Trends and the Problem of Modernization. In E. Johnson and E. Monkkonen (eds.), *The Civilization of Crime: Violence in Town and Country Since the Middle Ages* (pp. 18–34). Urbana, University of Illinois Press.

Shifrel, S., and McQuillan, A. (2000, May 29). Details of Slaughter: Two Charged in Bloodbath. *Daily News Online*. <*http://www.nydailynews.com/ . . . –29/news_and_ views/crime_file/ a68213.asp*>.

Sifakis, C. (1982). *The Encyclopedia of American Crime*. New York: Facts on File Inc.

Six Men Accused in Vat Death. (1995, April, 25). Associated Press / ClariNet. <*http://www.clari.local.wisconsin:2721*>.

'Skateboard Murder' Trial Set. (1996, January 30). Associated Press / ClariNet. <*http://www.clari.local.virginia+dc:3333*>.

Smith, M. and Zahn, M. Editors. (1998). *Homicide: A Sourcebook for Social Research*. Thousand Oaks, CA: Sage Publications.

Smith, M. and Zahn, M, Editors (1998). *Studying and Preventing Homicide: Issues and Challenges*. Thousand Oaks, CA: Sage Publications.

Spilled Coffee Triggers Road Rage. (1997, August 15). United Press International / ClariNet. <*http://www.clari.news.crime.murders.misc:9172*>.

Statistical Abstract of the United States, 2001: The National Data Book, 121st Edition. Washington, DC: U.S. Census Bureau.

Steckner, S. (1998, June 4). Killer of 17 is Executed in 2 Deaths. *Arizona Republic*, pp. B1 and B6.

Stingl, J. (2002, April 2). When a Mother Kills, Justice and Illness are Suddenly at Odds. *Milwaukee Journal Sentinel*. <*http://www.jsonline.com/news/metro/apr02/ 32211.asp*>.

Student Charged in Death of EIU Freshman He Dated. (1998, February 3). Champaign, IL: *News Gazette*, p. 1.

Super Bowl Tickets Lead to Shooting. (1999, February 2). United Press International / ClariNet. <*http://www.clari.local.florida:14763*>.

Sullivan, R. (1994, December 3). Meter Reader Discovers Human Skeleton in Queens Basement. *New York Times*, p. 26.

Swazey, B. (1995, September 17). Community Grapples with Death of Couple. *Star Ledger*. Sec. 1, p. 35.

Sykes, G. and Matza, D. (1957). Techniques of Neutralization: A Theory of Delinquency. *American Sociological Review*, 22, 664–670.

Tailgating Leads to Slaying in Orlando. (1996, October 15). Reuters / ClariNet. <*http://www.clari.local.florida:16588*>.

Tardiff, K. and Gross, E. (1985). Homicide in New York City. *Bulletin of the New York Academy of Medicine*, 62, (5), 413–426.

Teen Guilty in Fatal Poisoning of Dad. (1996, May 9). United Press International / ClariNet. <*http://www.forest.clari.local.texas:13784*>.

Teen Guilty in Slaying of Father. (1999, February 5). Associated Press / ClariNet. <*http://www.clari.news.crime.murders.misc:9910*>.

Teen Held in Brother's Death. (1995, March 20). Associated Press / ClariNet. <*http:// www.forest.clari.news.crime.juvenile:403*>.

Teen Indicted in Laundry Killing. (1998, February 13). United Press International / ClariNet. <*http://www.clari.news.crime.murders:3423*>.

Teen Kills Retiree in Apparent Identity Mistake. (1996, January 27). *Pasadena Star News*, p. A9.

Teen Murder Suspect Charged As Adult. (1998, February 17). United Press International / ClariNet. <*http://www.clari.news.crime.murders:3498*>.

Teen Ordered to Psychiatric Facility. (1996, August 16). United Press International / ClariNet. <*http://www.clari.local.michigan:9162*>.

Teen Who Killed His Dad Sentenced. (2001, May 22). Associated Press / ClariNet. <*http://www.clari.local.nevada*>.

Teens Found Dead in Drain Pipe. (1995, August, 14). Associated Press / ClariNet. <*http://www.forest.clari.local.michigan:4913*>.

Terry, G. and Malone, M. (1987, November and December). The Bobby Joe Long Serial Murder Case: A Study in Cooperation Parts 1 and 2. *FBI Law Enforcement Bulletin*: pp. 12–18 and pp. 7–13.

Thorne, C. Brothers Sentenced in Road-Rage. Associated Press / ClariNet. <*http:// www.clari.news.crime.murders*>.

Three Dead in California Chemical Plant Shooting. (1998, March 23). Reuters / ClariNet. <*http://www.clari.local.california.northern:947*>.

Toppo, G. (1999, January 16). Wife Convicted in 'Murder Mystery.' The Associated Press / ClariNet. <*http://www.clari.news.murders.misc:9423*>.

Trial To Open in Lake Erie Boat Death. (1996, April 21). United Press International / ClariNet. <*http://www.forest.clari.local.ohio:9526*>.

Turkus, B. and Feder, S. (1951). *Murder, Inc.: The Inside Story of the Syndicate*. New York: Farrar, Straus, and Young.

12-Year-Old Shot Over Quarter. (1995, July 19). Associated Press / ClariNet. <*http:// www.clari.news.crime.murders:10763*>.

2 Arrested in Pa. Deaths. (1995, February 17). Associated Press / ClariNet. <*http:// www.clari.news.crime.murders:7471*>.

Two Cops Killed Attempting Arrest. (2000, January 4). Associated Press / ClariNet. <*http://www.clari.local.georgia*>.

Two Killed in Shootings at Pizza Shop and at Store. (1998, January 30). *Philadelphia Inquirer Online*. <http://www.phillynews.com:80/inquirer/98/han30/city/cbcit30.htm>.

The Vera Institute Atlas of Crime and Justice in New York City. (1993). New York: The Vera Institute of Criminal Justice.

Victim Identified in Decapitation Murder. (1996, May 1). Reuters / ClariNet. <*http:// www.news.crime.murders:16095*>.

Violence in the Workplace. (1997). National Institute of Occupational Safety and Health, Centers for Disease Control. <http://www.cdc.gov/niosh/violfs.html>.

Von Hentig, H. (1948). *The Criminal and His Victim*. New Haven, CT: Yale University Press.

Walker, T. (1976). *Fort Apache*. Edited by T. R. Huehner. New York: Crowell Company.

Walsh, J. (1996, February 16). Apache Junction Death Takes Bizarre Twist. *Arizona Republic*, pp. A1 and A11.

Walsh, J. (1996, March 28). Gruesome Secret Kept for 5 Years. *Arizona Republic*, pp. A1 and A8.

Ward, P. (2002, November 28). Williams Gets Maximum for Manslaughter. *Savannah Morning News*. <http://www.savannahmorningnews.com/stories/112802/locwilliamssentencing. shtml>.

Weigl, A. (2003, June 13). Campbell Found Guilty of First-Degree Murder. *News and Observer Online*. <http://www.newsobserver.com/front/digest/v-print/story/2615613p–2426644c.html>.

Wheeler, S. and Callahan, P. (1998, January 25). Teen Held in Boulder Slaying. *Denver Post Online*, p. 1.

Wife Lets Husband Rot To Death. (1995, April 3). Associated Press / ClariNet. *<http://www.clari.news.crime.murders:8950>*.

Williams, K. (1984). Economic Sources of Homicide: Re-estimating the Effects of Poverty and Inequality. *American Sociological Review*, 49, 283–289.

Wilson, C. (2001, February 6). Tribe Objects to Murder Trial. Associated Press / ClariNet. *<http://www.clari.local.florida>*.

Wilson, J. and Kelling, G. (1982, March). Broken Windows. *Atlantic Monthly*, 29–38.

Wilson, M. and Daly, M. (1993). Spousal Homicide Risk and Estrangement. *Violence and Victims*, 8, 3–16.

Wilson, M, Johnson, H., and Daly, M. (1995). Lethal and Nonlethal Violence Against Wives. *Canadian Journal of Criminology*, 37, 331–361.

Wilson, M. and Daly, M. (1992). Who Kills Whom in Spouse Killings? On the Exceptional Sex Ration of Spousal Homicides in the United States. *Criminology*, 30, 2, 189–215.

Wilson, P. (1997, December 7). Six Unexplained Deaths Jolt Washington Community. Reuters / ClariNet. *<http://www.clari.news.murders.misc:1925>*.

Wolfgang, M. and Ferracuti, F. (1967). *The Subculture of Violence: Towards and Integrated Theory in Criminology*. Beverly Hills, CA: Sage Publications.

Wolfgang, M. (1996). Homicide in Other Industrialized Countries. *Bulletin of the New York Academy of Medicine*, 62, (5), 400–412.

Wolfgang, M. (1958). *Patterns in Criminal Homicide*. Philadelphia: University of Pennsylvania Press.

Woman Gets 35 Years To Life For Mother's Slaying. (August 13, 2003). *Los Angeles Times*, p. B3

Woman Held in Mate's Death. (1992, October 18). *Star Ledger*, p. 14.

Woman Sentenced in Niece's Death. (1998, July 21). Associated Press / ClariNet. *<http://www.clari.news.issues.death_penalty:1680>*.

Wright, K. (1991). The Violent and the Victimized in the Male Prison. *Journal of Offender Rehabilitation*, 16, 1–25.

Yates, N., Connell, R., and Merina, V. (1996, December 7). Accounts of Homicides. *Los Angeles Times*, p. A13.

Zahn, M. and McCall, P. (1999). Homicide in the 20th Century United States. In M. Smith and M. Zahn (eds.), *Studying and Preventing Homicide: Issues and Challenges* (pp. 10–29). Thousand Oaks, CA: Sage Publications.

Zahniser, D. (1997, May 28). Owner of AK–47 Testifies in San Marino Killings. *Pasadena Star News* p. A3.

Zimring, F. and Zeuhl, J. (1986). Victim Injury and Death in Urban Robbery: A Chicago Study. *Journal of Legal Studies*, 15 (1), 1–39.

Name Index

Subject Index